More praise for *Branded Entertainment*

"This book truly captures the essence of branded integration. The book is so well researched and the examples are very fresh and up-to-date. Jean-Marc has done a terrific job of documenting how entertainment marketing is evolving in Hollywood. Jean-Marc discusses the various approaches marketers are taking to follow the ever changing target audience. Written with knowledge of a true Hollywood insider, this is the most accurate, up-to-date book regarding branded entertainment that I have found"
Britt Johnson, Chief Executive Officer, Mediaplacement Entertainment inc, Los Angeles

"A veritable user's guide for any marketer with a touch of innovation."
Christian Polge, President, Coca-Cola France

"Some state that classic advertising is dead. This is probably not true, but consumers have certainly become mistrustful. To grow, brands now need to adopt a more subtle and seductive approach when conveying information to customers. Featuring in a movie is a powerful form of identification for the brand. Jean-Marc Lehu takes a scientific approach when exploring the success, the methodology and the limits of this new strategy of instilling the brand in the consumers mind."
Georges Lewi, General Manager, Brand Experts Center Institute, Paris

"Are you still wondering whether plugging your product or your brand in a movie, a TV show, a video game or even a novel is profitable? Then, take a look at Jean-Marc Lehu's delightful book. It contains everything you need to know about product placement and even shows you how to do it properly."
Alain d'Astous, PhD, Marketing Professor, HEC Montréal

"With a robust and thorough usage of examples of below and above-the-line (and everything in between) brand integrations, Jean-Marc has written the definitive textbook on the practice of product placement both from a historical perspective as well as a glimpse into the future of this form of branding. Lehu manages to deconstruct the various methodologies that are being used today in such a way that gives the layman insight to this very interesting marketing technique. It seems I have a lot to learn from his latest literary effort. Often where other accounts of product placement have gone wrong is in not looking forward and identifying that there are endless ways to place a product in an evolving media landscape. Branded Entertainment does this both effectively and clearly."
Matt Meyerson, Senior Vice-President, Product Placement, B|W|R PPI, Beverly Hills

"Jean-Marc Lehu expertly blends the perspectives of communication scholars, corporate marketers, creative professionals, and studio/network executives. The result is both instructive and entertaining for anyone who is interested in the growth and direction of brand placement and branded entertainment."
Jim Karrh, PhD, Chief Marketing Officer, Mountain Valley Spring Co,
Hot Springs National Park

"A masterpiece! An epic presentation of product placement practice and beyond. Lehu crafts a compelling and comprehensive account of the past, present and future of branded entertainment. He interweaves academic research and numerous case studies into a well-written 'story' that offers strategic insight into brand management. A marketing tour de force and must-read for anyone who studies or practices branded entertainment."
Michelle R Nelson, Associate Professor, University of Illinois at Urbana–Champaign

By the same author

Brand Rejuvenation, Kogan Page, London, 2006

L'Encyclopédie du Marketing, Éditions d'Organisation, Paris, 2004

Stratégie de fidélisation, Éditions d'Organisation, Paris, 2003

Lifting de marque, Éditions d'Organisation, Paris, 2002. Prix de la marque 2002 (Prodimarques)

Strategiesdemarque.com, Éditions d'Organisation, Paris, 2001

La fidélisation client, Éditions d'Organisation, Paris, 1999

Alerte Produit: quand le produit doit être retiré de la vente ou rappelé …, Éditions d'Organisation, Paris, 1998

Praximarket, Éditions Jean-Pierre de Monza, Paris, 1996. Adetem selection, Association Nationale du Marketing

Le marketing interactif, Éditions d'Organisation, Paris, 1996. Médaille de l'Académie des Sciences Commerciales 1997

Le marketing olfactif, in collaboration with Virginie Barbet, Pierre Breese, Nathalie Guichard, Caroline Lecoquière and Régine Van Heems, LPM, Paris, 1999

Contributions

MBA: L'essentiel du Management, marketing header and chapter on 'Customer relationship management', Éditions d'Organisation, Paris, 2005

Teaching and Learning with Virtual Teams, (ed) S Pixy Ferris and Susan Godar, chapter in collaboration with Kathryn Hashimoto, Information Science Publishing, Hershey, PA, United States, 2005

Persuasion: La théorie de l'irrationalité restreinte, with Pierre Grégory and Christian Derbaix, round table of professional experts, Economica, Paris, 2004

Branded
Entertainment

**Product placement & brand strategy
in the entertainment business**

Jean-Marc Lehu

**KOGAN
PAGE**

London and Philadelphia

Ouvrage publié avec l'aide du Ministère français chargé de la Culture –
Centre National du Livre

Publisher's note

Every possible effort has been made to ensure that the information contained in this book is accurate at the time of going to press, and the publishers and author cannot accept responsibility for any errors or omissions, however caused. No responsibility for loss or damage occasioned to any person acting, or refraining from action, as a result of the material in this publication can be accepted by the editor, the publisher or the author.

First published in Great Britain and the United States in 2007 by Kogan Page Limited
First published in paperback in 2009

Kogan Page Limited
120 Pentonville Road
London N1 9JN
United Kingdom
www.koganpage.com

Kogan Page US
525 South 4th Street, #241
Philadelphia PA 19147
USA

© Jean-marc Lehu, 2007, 2009

ISBN   978 0 7494 5337 4

British Library Cataloguing-in-Publication Data

A CIP record for this book is available from the British Library.

Library of Congress Cataloging-in-Publication Data

Lehu, Jean-Marc.
  Branded entertainment : product placement and brand strategy in the entertainment business / Jean-Marc Lehu. –– 1st paperback ed.
    p. cm.
  Originally published: 2007.
  Includes bibliographical references and index.
  ISBN: 978-0-7494-5337-4
  1. Product placement in mass media. 2. Product management. 3. Branding (Marketing) I. Title.
   HF6146.P78L43 2009
   658.8'27––dc22

                                        2008040877

Typeset by JS Typesetting Ltd, Porthcawl, Mid Glamorgan
Printed and bound in India by Replika Press Pvt Ltd

Contents

Integrating the limits of globalization 233; Designing targeted placements 236; Recreating an emotional link with the consumer 238

Note: in the interests of consistency, for all the film examples used, the date given is that of the film's opening in theatres in the country of origin and not the production date.

Foreword

Light!!!

In 1963, in Stanley Kubrick's *Dr Strangelove* Peter Sellers uses coins from a Coca-Cola machine to try to make a phone call in an attempt to halt the possibility of nuclear war.

In 1981, the legendary Coca-Cola bottle contour arrives to spice up ... the lives of the Bushmen in Jamie Uys's *The Gods Must be Crazy*.

In 1982, *E.T. the Extra-Terrestrial* discovers the unique refreshment of a can of Coca-Cola.

All of these examples remind us of the importance of the symbol that is Coca-Cola, the world's leading brand, and of product placement as the motor of cinematographic action.

What links Coca-Cola to the world of the cinema is a genuine love story, from comedy (from *When Harry Met Sally* to *Bridget Jones*) to sci-fi and fantasy (from *E.T.* to *Blade Runner*).

For Coca-Cola, what is at stake is not fame (it has already achieved this in great measure elsewhere); rather it is derived from a double logic:

- to establish the credibility of the action by featuring objects/brands that are emblems of reality;
- to contribute in a positive and evocative way to the progression of the plot.

The brand often contributes to bringing greater closeness. Beyond this direct contribution to driving the action, Coca-Cola strives to promote and encourage the emergence of new talents and new artistic expressions, from the organization of film-making awards in the United States, to the 'Talents Bruts' ('Raw Talents') and 'Réveille ton talent' ('Awaken your talent') operations in France.

For the other brands of the Coca-Cola group, those which didn't have the privilege of celebrating their 120th birthday this year, their presence on screen assumes a more important role in the construction of their image and popularity.

For this reason, Diet Coke chose to support Christian Volckman's ambitious project in his film *Renaissance*, set in Paris, 2054. For a brand to become involved in such a process is to refuse short-term aspirations, since this adventure took four years to complete; it is also to dare to support an artistic choice that is very modern in its graphics, very unlike the codes of traditional animated films; finally, it is to help the film to find its audience by opening means of communication for it.

This approach is justified for a brand that, only recently, was communicating the theme 'Enjoy Light', placing light (if not the heritage of the Lumière brothers) at the heart of its project.

In conclusion, product placements are based more on brand conviction than a reasoned media choice – even if it offers the opportunity for original communication – the success of a film being very uncertain in comparison with tried-and-tested gross ratings points (GRP) medias and traffic indexes. As long as this uncertainty remains, the choice of cinema will be 'light', because it is a synonym for the triumph of the irrational over the rational, of commitment over media planning, of magic over cards already dealt.

Product placement, however, is not limited solely to cinema films. New technologies, videogames, television series, mobile telephones, represent equally as many new opportunities for brands.

It is this diversity and richness that Jean-Marc Lehu brilliantly invites us to discover throughout this work, a veritable user's guide for any marketer with a touch of innovation.

The show must go on!!!

Christian Polge
President, Coca-Cola France

Introduction

There is no formula for success. You cannot play safe by mixing two parts of sex, two parts of violence, a few tears, and two dozen laughs. Even when the film is finished and acclaimed by critics it is impossible to predict its success at the box office. I follow my personal taste, my instinct.

(Otto Preminger, An Autobiography, Doubleday, New York, 1977)

The expression 'product placement', or 'brand placement', essentially describes the location or, more accurately, the integration of a product or a brand into a film or televised series. It is also possible, however, to find commercial insertions within other cultural vehicles, such as songs or novels. In the visual arts and entertainment world, these brand or product placements are grouped under the banner of 'branded entertainment'.

For some, seeing brands everywhere is a source of irritation. Other people derive amusement from spotting them. There are those who blank them out as little more than part of the consumer backdrop of life. Love them or hate them, product placements are nonetheless increasingly a part of our daily lives. In future, they will be the principal piece of a progressively more sophisticated communication strategy on the marketing chessboard that is 'branded entertainment' – or, quite literally, entertainment by or in conjunction with a brand. This is a world in which a brand is able to get closer to its target audience via a film, a television programme or series, a play, a novel, song, or show, indeed even a video game, using lines of communication quite different from those employed to date by the three main families of above the line, below the line and internet marketing. Hence the broader concept of 'entertainment marketing', sometimes used to describe the experiential consumption stemming from these many and varied brand and product placements.[1]

---

[1] Chris Hackley and Rungpaka Tiwsakul (2006) Entertainment marketing and experiential consumption, *Journal of Marketing Communications*, 12(1), March, pp 63–75.

Figure 0.1 Advertising poster used on the occasion of the opening of the film *Casino Royale* (2006), by Martin Campbell. Reproduced by kind permission of Bollinger Champagne.

Branded entertainment is an Anglo-Saxon term, but it does not follow that the method is the exclusive province of US marketers. It is certainly true that the United States was the cradle of its early development. For this reason, many examples from the United States will be used to illustrate the pages that follow, in order to fully understand the lead that this country has over others in this area, and the lessons that can be learnt from it. The sheer volume of examples will be necessary because, even if certain principles exist, we are far from achieving the rigorous model that will guarantee effective placement.

Concerning the power of fiction in films and series, for consumers' beliefs and attitudes see in particular Melanie C Green, Jennifer Garst and Timothy C Brock (2004) The power of fiction: determinants and boundaries, in L J Shrum (ed), *The Psychology of Entertainment Media: Blurring the lines between entertainment and persuasion*, Lawrence Erlbaum Associates, Mahwah, NJ, pp 161–76.

The hope is that this book will provide the reader with food for thought, with explanations and ideas, not only through the mostly US examples, but also through the professional expertise and academic research that we shall impart. Europe, for her part, is slow to wake up. While the old continent still talks about 'stealth advertising', for several years now on the other side of the Atlantic they have been discussing sophisticated communication strategies based on brand integration.

Brand management and communication are evolving at lightning speed. Product placement in the cinema is still often only associated with the adventures of James Bond. The directors of these films are even criticized for their apparent subservience to the despicable merchants of the Temple. And yet is it not logical to suppose that if this refined and distinguished character chose to drink champagne, it might as well be Bollinger? That if he chose to drive, he might as well drive an Aston Martin Vanquish? That if he wore shoes, they might as well be Church? That if he travelled, he might as well carry a Samsonite suitcase? That if he drank vodka, it might as well be called Smirnoff or Finlandia? That if he looked at his watch, it might as well be a Rolex, or perhaps an Omega? However unique he may be, perhaps even that remarkable character James Bond needs brands, to (re)create a link to reality. We shall, however, be analysing many other examples beyond the case of 007: despite being so often cited, the British secret agent is not always the most representative example.

All alert marketers are now on deck, trying to make out as best and as quickly as they can the contours of this new shoreline. *Variety* magazine recently compared product placement to cocaine for television networks, the infatuation is so strong.[2] But as soon as the demand to seize all available opportunities becomes urgent, prices rise rapidly and steeply.[3] Yes, the possible media become more numerous and diverse every day. Nonetheless, the 'good' platforms for the development of a pertinent and performing branded entertainment policy are not exactly legion. Despite the very high prices, in 2005, for the successful series *Desperate Housewives*, the three or four supplemental product placement opportunities available saw applications from 250 potential advertisers.[4] What yesterday was a simple agreement, even just an ordinary handshake, today appears increasingly as a complex communication process that must be established, if a precise goal is to be attained.

---

[2] John Dempsey (2005) Plugs spring a leak, *Variety*, 25 September.
[3] Jean Halliday and Marc Graser (2005), BMW pulls out of branded entertainment, *Advertising Age*, 3 October. See also Marc Graser and Claire Atkinson (2005) The escalating scramble for product placement fees, *Madison+Vine*, 4 June.
[4] Steve McClellan (2005) Product placement grows as nets worry about glut, *Adweek*, 22 August.

What are the carriers that can place brands and products to generate contact with the target? What are the potential assets, and above all the methods, of a competitive utilization? What are the risks that must be identified and sidestepped if possible? What are the elements of a win–win partnership contract? Beyond films, what are the complementary opportunities available to potential advertisers? What, therefore, are the new assets of modern brand management? These are the strategic questions that this book will attempt to answer, by giving the reader as many examples as possible of brands and products present in films, in series and other complementary supports, as branded entertainment requires.

The principle of product placement in films

Product placement in the cinema is an age-old technique, and at first glance a very simple one. It is a matter of 'placing' a product or a brand in one or more scenes of a film, in one form or another, in return for payment.[5] This communication technique, sometimes called a hybrid (given the fact that it can use many parallel media of communication), assumes an agreement, whether this is matched or not by a set of negotiations.[6] The placement principle rests on the fact that this unofficial 'advertising insertion' departs from the traditional screens that are generally reserved for it, and therefore speaks to an audience in a context different from that of classic advertising communication. In 1955, the director Henri Decoin opened his film *Razzia sur la Chnouf* (Drug bust) with the arrival of an Air France plane at Orly airport. The name of the airline is also mentioned by one of the characters later on, and written on a telegram shown on camera. During the film, the camera passes by advertisements for Saint-Raphaël, and the actor Jean Gabin orders a bottle of Bollinger champagne. In the first part of the film, however, another brand benefits from a rather original verbal placement. A discussion

[5] Steven L Snyder (1992) Movies and product placement: is Hollywood turning films into commercial speech? *University of Illinois Law Review*, 1, Winter, pp 301–37.

[6] Siva K Balasubramanian (1994) Beyond advertising and publicity: hybrid messages and public policy issues, *Journal of Advertising*, 23(4), pp 29–46. See also Winnie Won Yin Wong (2002) *Manufacturing Realisms: Product placement in the Hollywood film*, Master's thesis, Massachusetts Institute of Technology, Boston, MA; Maria Kniazeva (2004) Between the ads: effects of non-advertising television messages on consumption behavior, in L J Shrum (ed), *The Psychology of Entertainment Media: Blurring the lines between entertainment and persuasion*, Lawrence Erlbaum Associates, Mahwah, NJ, pp 213–32; and also Michael R Solomon and Basil G English (1994) Observations: the big picture: product complementary and integrated communications, *Journal of Advertising Research*, 34, January–February, pp 57–63.

during an identity check between two crooks centres on OCB cigarette paper, to the point of eulogizing it. The following exchange ensues:

> 'I can't roll a pipe with this paper!'
> 'Do you want some OCB?'
> 'I certainly do, OCB is perfect, especially when it's ...'
> '... gummed. Mine is.'
>
> (Extract from the dialogues of *Razzia sur la Chnouf*, 2005)

Placement may be visual or audible, or even a combination of the two, in order to maximize the impact.[7] Thus, Hertz and Europcar simply appear onscreen in Richard Curtis's film *Love Actually* (2003), and Princeton University is only mentioned in *Batman Begins* (directed by Christopher Nolan, 2005), whereas the Bellagio Hotel in Las Vegas is both seen and talked about in *Ocean's Eleven* and *Ocean's Twelve* (Steven Soderbergh, 2001 and 2004), and a BMW car is both seen and used in *Ultraviolet* (Kurt Wimmer, 2006). Placement may be a logo, a brand name, a product or its packaging.[8] The exact definition of a product placement is still uncertain today, however, and continues to evolve.[9] In its least elaborate form, it merely allows for the appearance of a brand or product onscreen. In its most effective form, it is so integrated into the storyline that its presence seems logical, even indispensable. Therefore, in both the original version of the film *The Italian Job* (Peter Collinson, 1969),

---

[7] See in particular Stephen J Gould, Pola B Gupta and Sonja Grabner-Kräuter (2000) Product placements in movies: a cross-cultural analysis of Austrian, French and American consumers' attitudes toward this emerging, international promotional medium, *Journal of Advertising*, 29(4), Winter, pp 41–58, and also Joseph Kouli and Gad Saad (2000) Le placement de produits dans les films: une comparaison interculturelle France-États-Unis, paper presented to the 16th Congress of the Association Française du Marketing, Montréal, Canada, 19–20 May; Jane Scott and Margaret Craig-Lees (2004) Optimising success: product placement quality and its effects on recall, Australian and New Zealand Marketing Academy Conference (ANZMAC), Victoria University, Wellington, New Zealand, 29 November–1 December.

[8] Eva Marie Steorz (1987) *The Cost Efficiency and Communication Effects Associated with Brand Name Exposure within Motion Pictures*, Master's thesis, West Virginia University, Morgantown, WV. In a reference paper on the subject, James Karrh proposes a distinction between product placement and brand placement. See James A Karrh (1998) Brand placement: a review, *Journal of Current Issues and Research in Advertising*, 20(2), Fall, pp 31–49.

[9] Isabelle Fontaine's PhD thesis (2002) *Étude des réponses mémorielles et attitudinales des spectateurs exposés aux placements de marques dans les films*, management thesis directed by Professor Joël Brée, Paris IX Dauphine University, is probably the most accomplished academic quality work about product placement in movies to date.

and the remake directed by F. Gary Gray in 2003, the use of Mini cars, for their compactness and mobility, seems perfectly natural, since they are chosen by the thieves for technical characteristics suitable for their plan.

Product placement is not designed as a matter of subliminal communication.[10] On the contrary: the objective of this approach is to ensure that the brand or product is seen, as much and overall as clearly as possible. In a study published by the US firm Simmons Market Research Bureau in August 2005, 46 per cent of the respondents claimed to pay no attention to product placement in films, a figure that rises to 51 per cent for products shown in television programmes. However, the study revealed two other pieces of information to be considered in parallel to the above: 33 per cent of these same respondents claimed to have noticed the brand of products used in films, and 43 per cent had noticed it in television programmes. Granted, only 20 per cent of respondents admitted to remembering the names of brands that had benefited from a placement in a film, and 24 per cent remembered a placement in a television programme.[11]

These facts do not really contradict each other; and they do so even less when we bear in mind the notion of implicit memory which does not engage

---

[10] An advertising technique which consists of inserting a visual and/or audio message that cannot be consciously perceived by the spectator, but is supposed to strike the subconscious. Even if its efficiency relies upon a fragile scientific basis, this technique is directly (or indirectly) forbidden in many countries, including France; or the producer of this type of advertising is required to inform the consumer (source: *L'Encyclopédie du Marketing*, Éditions d'Organisation Publishing, Paris, 2004, p 663). See also Philip Merikle (2000) Subliminal perception, in *Encyclopedia of Psychology*, vol 7, ed A E Kazdin, Oxford University Press, Oxford, pp 497–99; John R Vokey (2002) *Subliminal Messages, Psychological Sketches*, ed John R Vokey and Scott W Allen, 6th edn, Psyence Ink, Lethbridge, AL, pp 223–46; and also Thomas Zoëga Ramsoy and Morten Overgaard (2004) Introspection and subliminal perception, in *Phenomenology and the Cognitive Sciences*, vol 3, pp 1–23. Broadcasters, both European and American, remain vigilant about this technique for which critics complaining of manipulation of the masses arise quickly, even if scientific evidence is rare. In 2006, the ABC network stopped the airing of a KFC commercial because the ad invited the consumers to view it again in slow motion to discover the subliminal message that has been hidden: a secret code giving a reduced price on the new fast food chain's sandwich, the Buffalo Snacker. See in particular Kate McArthur (2006) KFC site visits Spike after ABC rejects spot, *Advertising Age*, 2 March. But the other networks NBC, Fox, CBS, TNT, USA, TBS, ESPN and MTV ran it.

[11] Bill Engel (2005) *Spring 2005 National Consumer Studies*, field study organized during January–May 2005 with more than 30,000 American consumers, Simmons Market Research, Ft Lauderdale, FL.

the same areas of the brain as conscious or explicit memory.[12] The temptation to place the full and entire responsibility for the impact of product placements on this implicit memory seems a dangerous shortcut, however, all the more so if the nature of the particular environment of the placement is not taken into account.[13] All placements, although perfectly visible or audible in most cases, are not necessarily consciously perceived by targets, particularly if they are very young;[14] they can nevertheless have an impact on their implicit memory,[15] and therefore we may perhaps speak of subliminal persuasion. We

---

[12] Olivier Droulers (2000) Perception subliminale: une expérimentation sur le processus d'activation sémantique des marques, *Recherche et Applications en Marketing*, 15(4), pp 43–59. See also Robert Heath and Agnes Hairn (2005) Measuring affective advertising: implications of low attention processing on recall, *Journal of Advertising Research*, 45(2), June, pp 269–81 about the way the implicit memory is working and above all, about the hidden emotional power of advertising. See also Angela Y Lee (2002) Effects of implicit memory on memory-based versus stimulus-based brand choice, *Journal of Marketing Research*, 39, pp 440–54; and linked to product placement, the interesting work of Susan Auty and Charlie Lewis (2004) The 'delicious paradox': preconscious processing of product placements by children, in L J Shrum (ed), *The Psychology of Entertainment Media: Blurring the lines between entertainment and persuasion*, Lawrence Erlbaum Associates, Mahwah, NJ, pp 117–33, for a specific application to children.

[13] Regarding understanding the different memories and how they work, see in particular Craig H Bailey, Eric R Kandel and Kausik Si (2004) The persistence of long-term memory: a molecular approach to self-sustaining changes in learning-induced synaptic growth, *Neuron*, 44(30) September, pp 49–57. Regarding the link with product placement in movies, see especially Larry Percy (2006) Are product placements effective? in Comments, ed John Ford, *Journal of International Advertising*, 25(1), pp 107–14; and also Sharmista Law and Kathryn A Braun-La Tour (2004) Product placements: how to measure their impact, in L J Shrum (ed), *The Psychology of Entertainment Media: Blurring the lines between entertainment and persuasion*, Lawrence Erlbaum Associates, Mahwah, NJ, pp 63–78.

[14] Susan Auty and Charlie Lewis (2004) Exploring children's choice: the reminder effect of product placement, *Psychology & Marketing*, 21(9), September, pp 699–716.

[15] This refers to the elements of memory used by the individual without becoming conscious of the previous storage phenomenon. The implicit memory represents the knowledge base accumulated by individuals during their life, which they constantly use, usually very quickly and without a real retrieving effort (source: *L'Encyclopédie du Marketing*, Éditions d'Organisation Publishing, Paris, 2004, pp 501–02). See in particular Peter Graf and Daniel Schacter (1985) Implicit and explicit memory for new associations, *Journal of Experimental Psychology: Memory, learning and cognition*, 11, pp 501–18; Stephen Holden and Marc Vanhuele (1999) Know the name, forget the exposure: brand familiarity versus memory of exposure, *Context, Psychology and Marketing*, 16(6), pp 479–86; Arnaud Pêtre (2005) Mémorisation non consciente des

should still do so with caution, however, and bearing this in mind: although a person has been exposed to and has possibly memorized the brand name, it is the individual alone who decides whether he/she likes the brand or not, and still further, whether he/she buys it. On this subject, Frank Zazza, CEP of the iTVX agency, explains:

> Today product placement has become a supplemental source for brand awareness. Alone it will not launch a brand, however as part of the brand advertising and marketing mix it can be a catalyst in generating enormous amounts of impressions.

The technique of product or brand placement brings together a cinema project (via its production studio, its director, or sometimes simply its props master) and an advertiser (whether an interested applicant, or one applied to for financial, technical or logistical help) for the placement of the latter's product or brand. The two may be brought together by a communications agency, or by an agent specializing in product placement,[16] that is, placement professionals whose experience and specialization can sometimes allow them to define the objective and the nature of the placement more clearly.[17] They may become involved for a single placement, or have an assignment contract, and in that case are paid on the basis of annual fees. In general, this type of contract is worth between €30,000–100,000. The price range is broad, but everything depends on the nature of the assignment (screenplay research, contacts, drawing-up of contracts, monitoring of the placement, definition and monitoring of tie-in communication operations and so on).

In the United States, the majority of these professionals are united as members of the ERMA (Entertainment Resources and Marketing Association).[18] This profession requires a double competence in cinema and mark-

---

publicités: apport d'une mesure implicite dans une application au netvertising, *Revue Française du Marketing*, 201(1/5), March, pp 23–47; Elizabeth Pridham and Margaret Craig-Lees (2004) Product placement: an implicit measure of effects, Australian and New Zealand Marketing Academy Conference, Victoria University, Wellington, New Zealand, 29 November–1 December.

[16] Joël Brée (1996) Le placement de produits dans les films: une communication originale, *Décisions Marketing*, 8, May–August, pp 65–74.

[17] In 1998, James A Karrh published a reference paper about this communication technique: Brand placement: a review, *Journal of Current Issues and Research in Advertising*, 20(2), Fall, pp 31–49.

[18] Jean-Marc Lehu (2005) Le placement de produits au cinéma: hiérarchie des critères d'utilisation ou hiérarchie des étapes? Une étude exploratoire qualitative auprès d'agents professionnels anglo-saxons, Fourth Congress of Marketing Tendencies, Paris, 21–22 January. ERMA is a Los Angeles-based trade group for product placement agencies: www.erma.org/web/

eting, as well as a certain ability to adapt, since not all product or brand placements are the same. The impact that a placement may have on its audience is affected by the manner of appearance. Four types of appearance are usually distinguished:[19] classic placement, institutional placement, evocative placement and stealth placement.

Classic placement

The classic placement has existed since the technique was first originated. It is much more tactical than strategic, since it is a matter of making a product or brand appear in the camera's view, during filming: a close-up on the back and front of a Pepsi-Cola sign in *The Interpreter* (Sydney Pollack, 2005); Compaq computers in *Alien vs. Predator* (Paul Anderson, 2004); the FedEx courier service in *Red Dragon* (Brett Ratner, 2002); the Converse trainers worn in *I, Robot* (Alex Proyas, 2004); the Louis Vuitton label glimpsed in *Monster-in-Law* (Robert Luketic, 2005); Amnesty International seen in *Collateral* (Michael Mann, 2004); the Rab and The North Face extreme-cold protection gear in *Eight Below* (Frank Marshall, 2006); the soft drink Orangina in *Le Boulet* (Alain Berberian, 2001); Ray-Ban sunglasses worn in *Sahara* (Breck Eisner, 2005); Motorola phones in *The Bourne Supremacy* (Paul Greengrass, 2004); the newspaper *USA Today* in *Coach Carter* (Thomas Carter, 2005); Jack Daniel's whisky in *Man on Fire* (Tony Scott, 2004); the Liz Claiborne cosmetics brand in *Vanilla Sky* (Cameron Crowe, 2001); the Apple computer brand in *Inside Man* (Spike Lee, 2006) .... Whatever the brand, whatever the product, whatever the industry, it seems that anything is possible for this form of placement, which makes few demands as to the form. It can nevertheless lead to a choice role for the brand or product. The supporting role alongside Steve McQueen in *Bullitt* (Peter Yates, 1968) is played by his Ford Mustang GT.[20]

---

[19] Jean-Marc Lehu (2005) Le placement de marques au cinéma, proposition de la localisation du placement à l'écran comme nouveau facteur d'efficacité potentielle, *Décisions Marketing*, 37, January–March, pp 17–31. About the multidimensional nature of the placement see also John A McCarty (2004) Product placement: the nature of practice and potential avenues of inquiry, in L J Shrum (ed), *The Psychology of Entertainment Media: Blurring the lines between entertainment and persuasion*, Lawrence Erlbaum Associates, Mahwah, NJ, pp 45–61.

[20] The association of Ford and McQueen was so relevant that the brand used the mythical actor (1930–1980) in its ads in 1997 (for Puma's launch in Europe), and in 2004 in a film for the new Mustang. The actor was digitally 'inserted' into the car. See also Eric Mayne (2004) Resurrecting McQueen, Ford hopes to do same for brand, *USA Today*, 14 October.

- Principal potential benefit: the classic placement is fairly simple and easy to put in place, at a relatively low cost (or no cost if, for example, the brand or product appears in the shot without the advertiser's express wish).
- Possible disadvantage: it may easily pass unnoticed, especially if there are a high number of placements in the same film.

Corporate placement

As its name suggests, corporate placement prioritizes the brand over the product. It is risky, in that if the audience does not know the brand before seeing the film, it may be absorbed by the décor and never noticed. This is often the fate that awaits service brands.[21] In contrast with the classic placement, which favours the product in most cases, the institutional placement does not enjoy the material support of a product, or any explicit activity of the brand. On the other hand, it is often easier to insert a brand name or logo into a shot than a particular product. In addition, an effective brand placement can bring benefits to all the products and services it sells. Finally, it offers the advantage of being more durable than a product. When films are reissued, some classic placements no longer serve the product since it is no longer on sale. Although a brand is not eternal either, its longer lifespan means that it can expect a longer onscreen career.

In Alfred Hitchcock's classic *North by Northwest* (1959) with Cary Grant, the Plaza hotel is cited and a scene takes place there. Ten years earlier, the Howard Hawks film *I Was a Male War Bride*, also with Cary Grant, made reference to the Ritz hotel, but as a corporate placement only: no scenes take place there and the hotel is never seen. In *Minority Report* (Steven Spielberg, 2002) advertising placards for Reebok, Pepsi and Aquafina among others may be spotted, but not the products of these brands. The car maker brands Ferrari and Jaguar are cited by the cat *Garfield* (2004) in the film of the same name directed by Peter Hewitt, but no car by these brands is used.

- Principal potential benefit: institutional placement is often easier to exploit onscreen, including after filming, and it ages less rapidly.
- Possible disadvantage: it may easily go unnoticed, since it assumes that viewers know the brand name before watching the film.

---

[21] Therefore, there are possibilities of using a service brand in a creative way, when the advertiser and the producer work upstream together on the movie. Verizon communications succeeded in doing so in Ridley Scott's *Hannibal* (2001). During one scene, the Hannibal Lecter character played by Anthony Hopkins rummages through papers and finds a telephone bill from Verizon.

Evocative placement

In the case of the evocative placement, the operation is more discreet, in the sense that the brand does not appear, nor is it clearly cited onscreen. Such placements generally require prior reflection in order to allow the most adequate integration possible into the storyline. Furthermore, not all brands and certainly not all products allow such an approach. Here, it is essential to have a product that is original and whose design is sufficiently distinctive to evoke its name or in any case its specificity in the mind of the target. Thus it is unnecessary to specify the name of the two-wheeled, individual mode of transport used in the film *Agent Cody Banks* (Harald Szwart, 2003), in *Win a Date with Tad Hamilton!* (Robert Luketic, 2004), in *Big Momma's House 2* (John Whitesell, 2006), or in *Grandma's Boy* (2006), by Nicholaus Goossen. The vehicle in question is a Segway, unique enough in its concept and design to be recognizable. The walking piano on which Tom Hanks and Robert Loggia play in the film *Big* (Penny Marshall, 1988) is an exclusive invention by Remo Saraceni. It was therefore unnecessary to emphasize the brand name.

Decades after its initial success, the Rubik's Cube played with in *Brick* (Rian Johnson, 2006) or in *The Pursuit of Happyness* (Gabriele Muccino, 2006) is automatically identified as soon as it appears onscreen. At the beginning of the remake of *The Italian Job* (2003), the principal actors, playing a group of thieves, celebrate their success by drinking champagne. No brand is seen or mentioned onscreen. Several bottles are passed from hand to hand, however. The champagne is Moët & Chandon, the Dom Perignon vintage: the shapes of the bottle and of the label are evocative enough for the target audience to identify the brand without hesitation. The same is true of the bottle of Tanqueray gin, whose label is barely visible in Dustin Hoffman's kitchen in *Meet the Fockers* (Jay Roach, 2004), but whose characteristic shape leaves no doubt as to its identity. Finally, such a placement may also be carried out in a humorous manner, in the form of a wink to the spectator, seeking their complicity, as in the case of the supposed 'fruit company' (Apple) cited in *Forrest Gump* (Robert Zemeckis, 1994) while only the company's logo is visible at the head of the letter held in the hands of actor Tom Hanks.

- Principal potential benefit: the evocative placement is subtler than the classic placement and *de facto* suggests a real differentiation between it and its competitors.
- Possible disadvantage: it might not be identified by an audience not familiar with the brand.

Stealth placement

How many viewers were able to identify the label of couturier Giorgio Armani in the impressive wardrobe of Julian Kaye (played by Richard Gere) in Paul Schrader's classic *American Gigolo* (1980)? As its name suggests, the stealth placement is highly discreet, almost undetectable. Often well integrated into the scene, its unobtrusive presence gives it a natural aspect, which may generate a more powerful impact and force of conviction when it is identified. However, it must first be identified! Stealth placements usually receive a mention in the credits. In the past, it was not uncommon for certain among them to appear in the opening credits, but nowadays they are generally found in the closing credits.[22] Few viewers read the credits in any detail, particularly on television where they are frequently truncated or accelerated to make space for – a commercial break. This is why it is preferable for a brand to profit *a posteriori* within the framework of the complementary communications operations (tie-ins).

Like the classic placement, a stealth placement can be visual. In *Great Expectations* (Alfonso Cuarón, 1998), Gwyneth Paltrow is dressed by Donna Karan. In *The Horse Whisperer* (Robert Redford, 1998), Kristin Scott Thomas is dressed by Calvin Klein. In the James L Brooks film *As Good as It Gets* (1997), many costumes were provided by the Cerruti 1881 label. Each time, the brand is neither placed nor mentioned during the film, and the characteristics of the garments are not specific enough for them to be identified spontaneously. The same is true of Tom Cruise's blow-dried hair by Lyndell Quiyou in *The Firm* (Sydney Pollack, 1993), of Julia Roberts's make-up applied by Richard Dean in *America's Sweethearts* (Joe Roth, 2001), or even the Westmore cosmetics that brightened the faces of Hollywood stars in innumerable films and series.[23]

Stealth placement may also be a purely audible phenomenon. In a quite original manner, in 2005, in an episode of *CSI: NY*, the ringtone of the mobile phone belonging to Danny Messer, played by the actor Carmine Giovinazzo, was the song 'Talk' by Coldplay. This was not accidental: it was the result of an agreement between CBS, the studio producing the series, and Capitol Records. Finally, one of the most 'original' cases, probably unnoticed by many viewers, was to be found in the Richard Quine film, *Paris When It Sizzles* (1964). Since 1953, the actress Audrey Hepburn had had a friendly relationship with the grand couturier Hubert de Givenchy, who had designed many of her

---

[22] Ruth La Ferla (1997) A star is worn: for fashion designers, the big screen becomes a celluloid runway, *New York Times*, 14 December.

[23] Frank Westmore and Muriel Davidson (1976) *The Westmores of Hollywood*, JB Lippincott, New York.

onscreen trousseaux since her role in *Sabrina* (Billy Wilder, 1954).[24] There is no classic placement of the Givenchy brand in *Paris When It Sizzles*. Instead, the opening credits mention that Miss Hepburn's wardrobe is signed Hubert de Givenchy. However, the mention passes into film legend when it also specifies that the perfume worn onscreen by the actress is also a Givenchy creation. It is hard to imagine anything stealthier!

- Principal potential benefit: the stealth placement is generally perfectly integrated into the story or the scene in which it appears, and thereby avoids criticisms of commercial overtones.
- Possible disadvantage: it can easily pass completely unnoticed!

---

[24] The very elegant Belgian actress became the first top model for the brand and its advertising before devoting her life to her role as an ambassador for UNICEF from 1988–92.

PART I

Origins of and reasons for product placement

1 History of product placement in the cinema

Believe me, if you jam advertising down their throats and pack their eyes and ears with it, you will build up a resentment that will in time damn your business.

(Carl Laemmle, president of Universal Studios – A message to other cinema producers regarding what he called 'prostitution of the screen' with brands, in the article 'Double barrage for advertising on screen by dailies and Laemmle', *Variety*, 4 March 1931)

When we study the origins of product placement, we generally think of the pioneering, often hesitant applications that were to be found in cinema more than a hundred years ago. Yet a more meticulous study of the history of communication quickly makes plain that well before the cinema, cabaret and actors of all genres used product placement for brands that also used them occasionally as advertising spokespersons. To cite only one famous example, before ever a camera had been cranked into action, Sarah Bernhardt appeared on stage wearing La Diaphane powder.[1]

In addition, any reader who is a lover of Impressionism will perhaps recall a famous tableau by Édouard Manet, titled *Un bar aux Folies-Bergère* (Bar at the

---

[1] In addition, Jules Chéret painted the comedian's portrait for a brand's billboard in the 1890s.

Figure 1.1   Jules Chéret, Advertising poster for La Diaphane, 1890s

Folies-Bergère) (1881–82). Passing over the placement of the brand name of the establishment in the title of the work, many people will undoubtedly have noticed the presence of numerous bottles on either side of the bar. On each side of the picture is a beer bottle, which, although shown in profile, bears a label whose shape and characteristic red triangle allow it to be identified as Bass beer! It is useless for us to wonder whether the painter had found an extra source of income, or whether he simply aspired to a consummate realism, for which he is still credited today. In order to exist, a brand must be known: not necessarily by everyone, but in every event by those who are likely to buy its products. For this to occur, it must be placed in all the strategic locations that will enable it to connect with this potential audience. Owing to the mania that it soon stirred up, the cinema was quickly perceived as a vector of huge potential, and one to be prioritized.[2]

---

[2] Patrick Rössler and Julia Bacher (2002) Transcultural effects of product placement in movies: a comparison of placement impact in Germany and in the USA, *Zeitschrift*

Figure 1.2 Édouard Manet, *Un bar aux Folies-Bergère* (1881–82). Oil on canvas 96 × 130 cm. P.1934.SC.234 – The Samuel Courtauld Trust, Courtauld Institute of Art Gallery, London, UK

Jay Newell's research has led him to conclude that certain films made by Auguste and Louis Lumière in 1896, at the request of François-Henri Lavanchy-Clarke, representative of Lever Brothers in France, represent the first cases of product placement on record.[3] Others see these films as merely the first steps into advertising films, in this precise case for Sunlight soap.

Cinema's first steps

The studios understood very early the advantages that could be gained from associating with brands. From the beginning of the 1910s, the famous Model

für Medienpsychologie, 14, NF 2(3) pp 98–108; Bonnie Brennen and Margaret Duffy (2004) *Product placements and the construction of consumers*, paper presented to the Association for Education in Journalism and Mass Communication Conference, 4–7 August, Toronto, Canada.

T Fords were frequently found in the credits of Mack Sennett comedies. At the beginning, it was not necessarily a matter of placement of the brand's name, but of its products. This was for the simple and very good reason that it was not about making the advertisers pay, but above all benefiting from accessories, vehicles, services for free, the quid pro quo being that they are allowed to appear onscreen. In his autobiography, the director Robert Parrish[4] tells of the 'choice' of automobile brands dictated by the producer because of a contract with a car maker.

The historian Kerry Segrave[5] recounts how at the same time, these brands made short ads, generally only one reel long, dedicated to their products, in order to offer them to cinema operators under advantageous conditions. In 1931, *Variety* observed that more than 50 per cent of cinemas showed advertising programmes. At the dawn of the 'talkies', towards the end of the 1920s, the phenomenon was so remarkable that the cinema had become *the* place of entertainment. The brands even organized factual communications operations in cinema lobbies. However, advertising films, as well as the commercial direction of cinemas, eventually succumbed to their opponents. Carl Laemmle, the great head of Universal, even talked of 'prostitution of the screen'.[6] In contrast, placement ·in films resisted opposition and evolved. Cinema is a captive medium for its audience and therefore particularly interesting to advertisers.[7]

---

[3] Stuart Elliott (2005) Greatest hits of product placement, *New York Times*, 28 February. Jay Newell is assistant professor of journalism at the Iowa State University. See in particular Jay Newell and Charles Salmon (2003) Product placement from Lumière to E.T.: the development of advertising in motion pictures, paper presented to the Association for Education in Journalism and Mass Communication Conference, Ad Division: Special Topics, 29 July–2 August, Kansas City, MO.

[4] 'We chose a black Chevrolet two-door sedan because we had seen a lot of Warner Brothers gangster movies and that's what Humphrey Bogart, Edward G Robinson and James Cagney always drove. I didn't find out until years later that they drove Chevies because Jack Warner had made a deal with General Motors. They furbished all the cars Warner needed and he showed them in his movies.' Robert Parrish, *Growing Up in Hollywood*, Harcourt Brace Jovanovich, New York (1976). Always a partner of the seventh art, nearly a century later, in 2006, for the 48th Oscars, the same General Motors supplied a special edition vehicles fleet to drive stars to the Los Angeles Staples Centre where the ceremony took place.

[5] Kerry Segrave (2004) *Product Placement in Hollywood Films: A history*, McFarland, Jefferson, NC. See also the rich analysis by Mark Crispin Miller, Ads on 50% of US screens, *Variety*, 13 May 1931.

[6] Double barrage for advertising on screen by dailies and Laemmle, *Variety*, 4 March 1931.

[7] Joël Brée (1996) Le placement de produits dans les films: une communication originale, *Décisions Marketing*, 8, May–August, pp 65–74.

The whole history of cinema is marked by representative examples. In 1916, the LKO/Universal studio produced a silent film with the explicit title, *She Wanted a Ford*. In 1929, Alfred Hitchcock subtly used a luminous sign for Gordon's gin, in order to dramatize the dark thoughts of the murderess Alice White, played by Anny Ondra in *Blackmail*. In 1930, RCA-Victor used the last film by George B Seitz, *Danger Lights*, to highlight his last ever photograph. A scene from *Manhattan Melodrama* (W S Van Dyke, 1934), showed Times Square, in the heart of Manhattan, in wide shot, where signs for Squibb, Coca-Cola and Chevrolet are clearly identifiable. In *Week-End in Havana* (Walter Lang, 1941), it was specified that Nan Spencer, played by Alice Faye, worked at Macy's. In *The Big Sleep* (Howard Hawks, 1946), the car brands Packard and Plymouth are not only seen, but also find their way into the script. In *The Quiet Man* (John Ford, 1952), when John Wayne orders a dark beer, in Ireland, it could only be a Guinness. In 1964, in *Dr. Strangelove, or How I Learned to Stop Worrying and Love the Bomb*, Stanley Kubrick uses the words of the Russian ambassador to present the newspaper the *New York Times* as the utterly trustworthy bastion of the press. In 1977, in Steven Spielberg's film *Close Encounters of the Third Kind*, a placement was visible in the form of a television advertising spot for Budweiser. The scene simply showed a television set during an advertising break.[8]

The interpretative and evocative power of the cinema also allows it to take a great many creative liberties. Although she had never smoked a cigarette in her entire life as a comic character, in *Superman II* (Richard Lester, 1980) the character of Lois Lane conspicuously smokes Marlboros.[9] The brand admitted to having paid the sum of US$42,000 for 22 placements throughout the film.[10] In one of the film's fight scenes, Superman was even thrown into

---

[8] The trick is common considering the number of advertising screens on television; it doesn't seem strange to see some commercials on a television screen, even in a movie. In *Analyze This* (Harold Ramis, 1999), a scene shows a television screen in which Merrill Lynch Investments can be seen. In *Bubble Boy* (Blair Hayes, 2001), one scene offers a close shot on a television screen just when 'accidentally' a commercial for Bubblicious sweets is running.

[9] William Benjamin Lackey (1993) Can Lois Lane smoke Marlboros?: an example of the constitutionality of regulating product placement in movies, *University of Chicago Legal Annual Forum Proceedings*, pp 275–92. The problem is that a young audience may not necessarily be aware that the brand or product's appearance is not at all fortuitous, but is paid for by the advertiser concerned. See in particular Stanton Glantz's study (2001) Smoking in teenagers and watching films showing smoking, *British Medical Journal*, 323, December, pp 1378–79, and research from Janet Hoek, Philip Gendall and Aimee Patton (2002) Tobacco product placement and young people, paper for Australian and New Zealand Marketing Academy Conference (ANZMAC), Melbourne, Australia, 2–4 December.

[10] Joanne Lipman (1989) Outcry over product placement worries movie ad executives, *Wall Street Journal*, 7 April.

the side of a truck in the brand's colours, situated in mid-screen. Bearing in mind the target audience for this film, the association with the heroic world of Superman was very important for the advertiser in order to re-legitimate the consumption of its product.[11]

A placement can therefore take on multiple forms to achieve multiple aims.[12] In 1982, in Sydney Pollack's *Tootsie*, Dorothy Michaels (the character played by Dustin Hoffman) ordered a Dubonnet in a restaurant in the heart of New York in highly original style. In the same year, Steve Martin preferred Jack Daniel's whisky in Carl Reiner's *Dead Men Don't Wear Plaid*, and offered it to actor Fred McMurray, thanks to the subtle insertion of a scene from another film. In 1985, in Richard Donner's film *The Goonies*, several close-ups of the Nike shoes worn by actor Jonathan Ke Quan made it the must-have choice for adolescents, a target particularly sensitive to placements.[13]

Numerous placements of the Coca-Cola brand are present in *Independence Day* (Roland Emmerich, 1996), but not all of them have the same reach. The film contains classic placements, such as a can glimpsed in a refrigerator, or the appearance of a vending machine bearing the brand's icon, in the background of the décor of the television station offices where actor Jeff Goldblum works (in which may also be seen a Minute Maid vending machine, another brand of the Coca-Cola group). More interestingly, however, at the beginning of the film, Goldblum sets an example by insisting on the role of recycling, with the help of a Coca-Cola can that he places in the appropriate bin. The action itself is very positive and may also, by transference, benefit the brand image.[14]

Another interesting placement takes place in the second half of the film, when Goldblum explains the workings of a spacecraft's protective shield by using and talking about a Coca-Cola can. The brand is no longer 'placed'; it is completely integrated into the screenplay. In *Runaway Bride* (Garry Marshall, 1999) Richard Gere is a journalist for *USA Today*, proving a pretext for many different forms of placement for the newspaper, its logo, its offices and so

---

[11] Curtis Mekemson and Stanton A Glantz (2002) How the tobacco industry built its relationship with Hollywood, *Tobacco Control*, 11 (Suppl 1), pp 181–91.

[12] Samuel A. Turcotte (1995) *Gimme a Bud! The feature film product placement industry*, Master's thesis, University of Texas, Austin, Texas.

[13] Michelle R Nelson and Laurie Ellis McLeod (2005) Adolescent brand consciousness and product placements: awareness, liking and perceived effects on self and others, *International Journal of Consumer Studies*, 29(6), pp 525–28. If children and adolescents are often mentioned to illustrate vulnerable targets, the image of vulnerable women should not be ignored. See Barbara B Stern, Cristel Antonia Russell and Dale W Russell (2005) Vulnerable women on screen and at home: soap opera consumption, *Journal of Macromarketing*, 25(2), December, pp 222–25.

[14] Manfred Auer, Udo Kalweit and Peter Nüssler (1991) *Product placement: Die neue Kunst der geheimen Verführung*, ECON Taschenbuch, Düsseldorf.

on. In *America's Sweethearts* (Joe Roth, 2001), much of the film is set in a Hyatt hotel, but the Evian, Sacco, Prozac, Pepsi and Corona brands, in particular, are also present onscreen. In 2006, the opening scenes even of the trailer of the Paul Weitz film *American Dreamz* begin with a lengthy placement for the daily newspaper *The Guardian*.

All of these examples illustrate how placements have always been present in films, but for reasons that are sometimes very different, as we will examine. They confirm, in fact, that there is no one placement, but multiple possibilities for stage direction, satisfying different objectives.

Sponsored shows

Marketing and entertainment have always been allies, particularly in the United States. From the beginnings of radio, then television, until today, many programmes have been produced or simply financed by major brands. In 1929, more than 55 per cent of radio programmes were financed or directly produced by advertisers or their agencies.[15] Among the famous examples we may note, over the decades, *Little Orphan Annie,* sponsored on the radio by Ovaltine, but also *The Kraft Musical Show, The Lux Radio Theater, The Texaco Star Theater, The Philco Television Playhouse, The Colgate Comedy Hour, The Alcoa Hour, Coke Time, Mutual of Omaha's Wild Kingdom, The Dinah Shore Chevy Show, General Electric Theater, The GM All-Car Showdown, Nike Training Camp* and *The Victoria's Secret Fashion Show*[16]. For each of these sponsored programmes, the boundary between the entertainment itself and the advertising content was (and still is) fragile, even nonexistent. Televised shows of this type still exist in certain countries, of which the United States is one, since the explosion in available media has generated such competition that profitability dictates that products and brands cannot always be prevented from appearing in the programmes themselves.[17]

These shows have one considerable advantage: their length, which the 'infomercial' sought to re-establish in the late 1980s. In the case of a sponsored show, it is possible to escape the straitjacket of the 30-second advertising spot. Not only are these few seconds of screen time expensive, but also it is sometimes difficult to make the consumer understand how a product is

---

[15] J Fred MacDonald (1979) *Don't Touch That Dial: Radio programming in American life, 1920–1960,* Burnham Inc/Nelson-Hall, Chicago, IL.

[16] Nat Ives (2003) Television shows like *Nike Training Camp* widen the scope of product placements, *New York Times,* 27 October.

[17] Jeanne McDowell (2004) The sponsors move in, *Time Magazine,* 23 August. See also Kathleen J Turner (2004) Insinuating the product into the message: an historical context for product placement, *Journal of Promotion Management,* 10(1/2), pp 9–14.

used, or what its benefits are, in such a short space of time. For technological goods, product placement offers the following advantage: during a film or a television series, it is possible to place a product in the hands of a character and show explicitly how it is used.[18] For both a series and a film, it is also advantageous to be able to use the latest fashionable gadget or to benefit from the latest technological advances, sometimes even before the product has gone on sale, as was the case with the very latest Nokia mobile phone used in David R Ellis's film *Cellular* (2004); or with the telephonic video security systems designed and built by Cisco and visible in the television series *24*.

In historical terms, three elements contributed to the evolution of the system of shows where the sponsor was the only advertiser. First were the manipulations of which various sponsored game shows were accused during the 1950s.[19] Second, there was the increasing independence of the major television networks, which allowed them to group the majority of advertising discourse together in specialized commercial breaks. Third came the fact that these same networks realized that it could be much more profitable to sell spaces of 30 seconds to several advertisers in commercial breaks, rather than one or two hours exclusively to a single advertiser. The all-powerful 30-second television spot quickly became the reference of modern advertising communication, and, above all, the principal source of finance for free-to-air television channels.

---

[18] Michael Grebb (2005) Gadget promos creep into television shows, *Wired*, 3 June.
[19] Bill Carter (2003) Skipping ads? TV gets ready to fight back, *New York Times*, 10 January.

2 Films under a necessary advertising influence

According to Al Ries and Laura Ries, traditional advertising has lost its credibility.[1] Sergio Zyman claims that marketing and advertising as practised in the past have been irrevocably changed.[2] Florence Amalou offers a grim analysis of advertising, believing that it has now gone too far.[3] Joseph Jaffe explains why the traditional 30-second spot is dead and gone, and why we must now look to all the other potential solutions.[4] Georges Chetochine hazards a guess

---

[1] Al Ries and Laura Ries (2002) *The Fall of Advertising and the Rise of PR*, HarperCollins, New York.

[2] Sergio Zyman (2002) *The End of Advertising as We Know It*, Wiley, Hoboken, NJ.

[3] Florence Amalou (2001) *Le livre noir de la Pub: Quand la communication va trop loin*, Stock, Paris.

[4] Joseph Jaffe (2005) *Life After the 30-Second Spot: Energize your brand with a bold mix of alternatives to traditional advertising*, Wiley, Hoboken, NJ. See also A Kishore (2003) The death of the 30-second commercial, media & entertainment strategies, August, *The Yankee Group Report*, Boston, MA; and Deloitte (2005) *TMT Trends: Predictions, 2005: A focus on the media sector*, ed Paul Lee, Deloitte and Touche Tohmatsu Consulting Group, USA, Netherlands, Hong Kong; Lynn Smith (2006) When the plot pushes the product, *Los Angeles Times*, 12 February.

that of 3,000 brands in existence today, only 20 per cent, or 600, will remain in five years![5] As for Seth Godin, he chooses not to beat about the bush, claiming that all marketers are liars.[6] At first glance, the situation appears to be extremely – worrying! But each of us knows that in the clamour all around us, only the doom-mongers can make themselves heard. For, if we look closely, things are not quite so desperate.

The congested communications environment

There are hundreds of radio stations and television channels accessible through terrestrial means or by satellite, or by computer, thousands of daily newspaper or magazine media, tens of millions of internet sites producing billions of pages, so that an entire lifetime on this earth would not be long enough to read them all, even if one dedicated oneself exclusively to the task, not to mention the new books, new songs, new shows and new films that arrive each day to enlarge the communications environment and the cultural world of this small planet, or the à la carte digital sampling offered by podcasting.[7] Nonetheless, the speed of the planet's rotation has not changed to any marked degree in the meantime, and there are still only 24 hours in a day and 7 days in a week. We are therefore powerless spectators of a complete saturation of the communications environment.[8] This malady is not confined to so-called developed countries. The same congestion of the classical media poses the same problem of an escaping audience in the Middle East or in India, for example.[9] In 2006, *The Financial Express* stated that more than 13,000 brands had communicated via television (of which the number of

---

[5] Interview with Georges Chetochine, *Le Figaro Économie*, 6 January 2006.

[6] Seth Godin (2005) *All Marketers Are Liars: The power of telling authentic stories in a low-trust world*, Penguin, New York.

[7] A combined word associating iPod and broadcasting. It designates audio, video or data downloaded on a portable player via an internet connection. The process may or may not use RSS (rich site summary or really simple syndication) technology, for an automatic updated download according to a subscription. The term was coined in 2004 following the launch of the Apple iPod portable player, but it applies to all digital portable players. Many individuals are now using the process to broadcast their own programmes. In 2005, the *New Oxford American Dictionary* admitted the term as a generic descriptor. See also Alice Z Cuneo (2006) Device & content ready – mobile TV set to take off, *Advertising Age*, 6 February.

[8] Mary Hilton (2003) *AAF Survey of Industry Leaders on Advertising Trends*, American Advertising Federation/Atlantic Media Company, September, Washington, DC.

[9] The successful Saudi series *Tash Ma Tash* is a relevant example of placement opportunities. They are carefully studied by local advertisers. Local spin-offs of foreign shows like *Star Academy* are also concerned. See in particular Faisal Abbas (2006)

channels has increased from 50 10 years ago to over 200 today), compared with 2,154 a decade previously.[10]

There is worse in store for the television and its sacrosanct 30-second spot, however: the increasing sales of pre-recorded programmes, via download or video on demand. Essentially limited to films or series, these programmes are nevertheless going to monopolize the small screen (whichever one it is), and consequently, the attention of viewers, who cannot be exposed to advertising during this time. An even more disastrous picture for the marketer in this gloomy panorama is the extraordinary boom in videogames. Nielsen United States revealed in 2004 that more than three-quarters of all homes on its panel housing a male between the ages of 8–34 years had a games console.[11] *Fortune* magazine even showed, in 2005, a US couple who had spent 1,248 hours the previous year playing *World of Warcraft*.[12] The study also showed that the average player spent at least 30 minutes playing each time the console was switched on, and that this happened on a fairly regular basis during television programmes that are 'key' from an advertising perspective.[13] Not only are the players often loyal to their videogames, but they are also concentrated on their screens, a combination much sought-after by advertisers.

A Harris Interactive study noted that since 2003, in the United States, millennials[14] (the internet generation), or in other words young people aged

---

Arab media: finding a place for 'product placement', *Asharq Al-Awsat*, 28 March. The worldwide interest for integrating products in alternative media also concerns videogames. See in particular Puru Gupta (2006) Emerging role of advergaming: a global and Indian perspective, *Advertising Express*, IFCAI Press, June, pp 23–28.

[10] Naveen Surapaneni (2006) Adding to the content, *Financial Express*, 12 February. See also Neelika Arova (2005) In-film advertising, in V Partha Sarathy (ed), *The Changing Face of Advertising*, ICFAI University Press, Hyderabad, pp 24–29. It would also be an error to believe that because it takes place in India, product placement uses 'softer' processes. In fact advertisers have the same concerns about efficiency and the measurement of voids. See in particular Ajita Shashidhar (2006) A service of value, *Indu Business Line*, 2 March.

[11] *Video Game Habits: A comprehensive examination of gamer demographics and behavior in US television households*, a survey by Activision/Nielsen Entertainment 10–19 February 2004. See also James Newman (2002) In search of the videogame player, *New Media & Society*, 4(3), pp 405–22.

[12] Roger Parloff (2005) From megs to riches, *Fortune*, 28 November. *World of Warcraft* (WoW) is an online game, more precisely a MMORPG (massively multiplayer online role-playing game). The theme is a quest in a fantasy universe. For more details about this very popular game, visit www.worldofwarcraft.com or www.wow-europe.com from Europe.

[13] Michael Dowling (2004) You got game? How in-game product integration can reach elusive 18- to 34-year-old males, *Insights*, November.

[14] The 'millennials' expression comes from Neil Howe and William Strauss's *Millennials Rising*, Vintage Books/Random House, New York (2000).

13–24, spent more time on the internet than in front of the television set,[15] or 16.7 hours per week on average in front of the computer screen (excluding e-mail) as opposed to 13.6 hours in front of the television screen. The problem facing advertisers is not so much that the use of these games monopolizes the home television set – in most cases, the home contains more than one television set – but that while these consumers, principally of generations X and Y, are playing on their consoles they cannot be exposed to television advertising. Even the baby-boomers are deserting television programmes to go and play, persuaded by their own children.[16] This is a 'sad' state of affairs that leads to a single conclusion, that of the profound metamorphosis of the communications environment. This conclusion invites more attentive contemplation of the content – in order to attempt to retain the attention of a few consumers – and of the possibilities of placing the brand in a good position there.[17]

Fragmentation and dispersal of the audience

The linearity and stability of the model are no more! In 2006, the director Steven Soderbergh organized the opening of his film *Bubble* simultaneously, over a few days, in cinema theatres, on a cable channel and on DVD.[18] A few weeks prior to this, linked to Intel through his production company Revelations Entertainment, the actor Morgan Freeman declared himself to be in favour of simultaneous video on demand and the must-have technologies of the new media landscape. The explosion of the media on offer has been progressively and naturally accompanied by a fragmentation and dispersal of the audience, disrupting the traditional segmentation and targeting processes.[19]

---

[15] Tobi Elkin (2003) Teens now spend more time online than watching TV, *Advertising Age*, 28 July. See also Lynn Smith (2006) When the plot pushes the product, *Los Angeles Times*, 12 February.

[16] Andy Swanson, Wendy Wallner and Christopher Daniels (2004) The target is moving: videogames as a marketing medium, *Know by Knowledge Networks*, Fall/Winter, pp 17–22. See also Nicole M Schmoll, John Hafer, Michael Hilt and Hug Reilly (2006) Baby Boomers' attitudes towards product placements, *Journal of Current Issues and Research in Advertising*, 28(2), Fall, pp 33–53.

[17] Kirk Cheyfitz (2004) Goodbye media commercial, hello commercial content, *Admap*, World Advertising Research Center, April, pp 30–31. See also T L Stanley (2002) Brand X: Ready, on the set! *Brandweek*, 43(19), 13 May, pp 34–40.

[18] Such an engagement kept the Oscar-winning movie director away from theatre networks, as his behaviour disturbed the established order. Gary Gentille (2006) Entertainment industry braces for *Bubble* to burst onto screen, *San Diego Union-Tribune*, 18 January.

[19] Chris Hackley (2005) Communicating with the fragmented consumer, *Admap*, 459, pp 41–43. Regarding the audience's evolution, see also Mike Bloxham (1998) Brand

For television alone, the first instrument of this 'tragedy' for the advertisers sprang from the Zenith research laboratories, when in the mid-1950s, Robert Adler developed the first remote control. From the remote control, zapping was born, allowing the viewer to change channels without effort, and in particular when the programme being shown became uninteresting or too *commercial*.[20] Today, the range of television on offer comprises several hundred channels, and therefore contributes to dispersing the television-watching population, according to their interests or moods.[21] To reach the same target, certain advertisers must be present in more places and of course at higher corollary cost. Add to this a society whose structures are undergoing full metamorphosis (the family unit put together, broken up, put back together again; different times and methods of working; asynchronous evolution of lifestyles; selfishness and identity claims; communitarism and collective claims; loss of reference points and an anxiety-inducing environment, and so on), and it is not difficult to see that the principle of the single stereotypical consumer requires a certain amount of moderation.

From a communication point of view, this assumes the necessity for a corollary metamorphosis. This is a particularly difficult metamorphosis, since it does not assume merely a change of tools, but the creation of new tools and the profound evolution of those used to date.[22] Not only does the sacrosanct 30-second spot today seem too expensive in terms of audience volumes reached, but the doubt cast on its actual effectiveness seems increasingly justified. Taking into account the lower audience figures, in absolute terms, more spots are needed to achieve a desired gross ratings points score (GRP),[23] but even this does not guarantee the desired result.

---

affinity and television programme sponsorship, *International Journal of Advertising*, 17(1), pp 89–98. See also Abbey Klaassen (2006) McKinsey study predicts continuing decline in TV selling power, *Advertising Age*, 6 August.

[20] Alan Ching Biu Tse and Ruby PPW Lee (2001) Zapping behaviour during commercial breaks, *Journal of Advertising Research*, 41, May–June, pp 25–29. In a very disturbing book for advertisers and agencies, in 2006, Rex Briggs and Greg Stuart revealed that 37.3 per cent of advertising budgets were wasted. Of course, some might see the positive side of it, remembering John Wanamaker (1838–1922), the famous New York and Philadelphia retailer, saying 'Half my advertising is wasted, I just don't know which half.' Also see Rex Briggs and Greg Stuart (2006) *What Sticks: Why most advertising fails and how to guarantee yours succeeds*, Kaplan Business, New York.

[21] Josh Bernoff and George F Colony (2004) Peter Chernin's 10 rules for media survival, *Quick Take Report*, Forrester Research, Cambridge, MA, 28 September.

[22] See in particular David Croteau and William Hoynes (2005) *The Business of Media: Corporate media and the public interest*, 2nd edn, Pine Forge Press/Sage, Thousand Oaks, CA, ch 6, pp 191–221.

[23] GRP (gross rating point) is the index for measuring communications effectiveness. This US-born measure allows assessment of the power of a media plan. It is essentially

Marketers' growing interest in the internet and its multiple possible forms of communication is therefore increasingly justified. This medium represents a growing population of internet users, increasingly better and better identified, with communication costs much more accessible than those of the traditional media. Without a doubt, the classic advertising model is not dead, but it has not been working correctly for several years now.[24] Most disturbing for marketers is that it is extremely difficult to reinvent it, since the change is not to another model, but to other models. New and increasingly sophisticated combinations between above the line, below the line and the internet are appearing. It is a process that is no longer searching systematically for the broadest possible audience, but one that consists of identifying those whose 'connectivity' with the programme will arouse a greater involvement with the programme and its content.[25] Among the most promising avenues, branded entertainment has the look of a highly relevant proposition, even though it is even more difficult to precisely identify its impact on sales than it is for a 30-second spot.[26]

The advantage of film production is that it is completely 'compatible' with this fragmented audience. In fact, the spectrum of genres and types of films is particularly broad. Admittedly, it is one of the more difficult genres to 'sell' to potential advertisers. This being so, it is not always a question of audience volume, but of the foreseeable quality of the audience. When BMW participated in the Geoffrey Sax film *Stormbreaker* (2006), the German car maker knew that its cars would be presented to an adolescent audience of potential future buyers. In contrast, the somewhat controversial film by Frank Miller and Robert Rodriguez, *Sin City* (2005), sought an entirely different audience. The box-office receipts of this feature film were US$74.103 million in the United States and US$84.630 million internationally.[27] This total of

---

used for radio and television. It can be calculated by multiplying the reach of the media schedule by the average frequency. Its CPGRP (cost per gross rating point) differs from one medium to another. Source: *L'Encyclopédie du Marketing*, Éditions d'Organisation Publishing, Paris, 2004, p 376.

[24] Scott Donaton (2003) Reinventing the marketing communications business, *Advertising Age*, 10 February. See also Brian Steinberg and Suzanne Vranica (2004) Five key issues could alter the ad industry, *Wall Street Journal*, 5 January.

[25] On this particular subject, see the very interesting study by Cristel A Russell, Andrew T Norman and Susan E Heckler (2004) People and their television shows: an overview of television connectedness, in L J Schrum (ed), *The Psychology of Entertainment Media: Blurring the lines between entertainment and persuasion*, Lawrence Erlbaum Associates, Mahwah, NJ, pp 275–90.

[26] Lorne Manly (2005) The future of the 30-second spot, *New York Times*, 27 March. See also Erwin Ephron (2003) The paradox of product placement, *MediaWeek*, 2 June.

[27] Source: Box Office Mojo LLC, November 2006.

US$158.733 million is respectable, but not exceptional. However, due to its strong positioning, its markedly noir style and its original direction, it was clear from the beginning that this film was aimed at a highly characteristic adult target. As a result, it succeeded in seducing numerous advertisers. This explains why the brands AAA, American Express, Beretta, Cadillac, Chevrolet, Chrysler, Converse, Discover, Ferrari, Ford, Jaguar, Lincoln, MasterCard, Mercedes, Motorola, Pez, Porsche, Springfield Armory, Steyr, UZI and Zippo, in particular, might be seen on screen.

Globally, consumers in developed countries have never watched so much television. At the same time, they have never shunned advertising so much. A paradox? No, just a mathematical problem. Advertising pays for the content. No advertising equals no creation and no broadcasting of content. But if the public shuns advertising, advertisers no longer have any interest in investing in it. The content is therefore no longer financed. In 2005, in the United States, certain networks such as ABC even demanded that producers of prime-time series factored in not four, but six commercial breaks, so that, once hooked during the first, advertisement-free 10 or 11 minutes, the audience would tolerate the proposed interruptions. The audience's protests fell on deaf ears, as did its growing interest in digital recorders that made it possible to avoid advertisements.[28] Product placement could therefore appear to be one of the possible solutions to this equation, not only for the advertiser seeking to reach a particular audience, but also for the television channels. Very good placements for big advertisers are somewhat thin on the ground. It is therefore hardly surprising if, in order to obtain them, they must 'also' buy classic 30-second spots, still indispensable to the channels' finances.

DVR and TiVo, the enemies of advertising

In 2005 according to a Neilsen study, the good news for US television networks was that the public was watching much more television.[29] The bad news was that more and more people were using all kinds of electronic methods to avoid the advertising content of the programmes, in particular through the use of DVRs (digital video recorders). These recorders make it easy to suppress the commercial breaks (skipping) or to pass over them very rapidly (zipping), which amounts to zapping without the inconvenience of waiting for the programme to restart. In a parallel phenomenon equally worrying for advertisers, 2005 saw a dangerous rise in peer-to-peer video exchanges, according to a study by Magna Global. Another complementary study issued

---

[28] Gary Levin (2005) Ad glut turns off viewers, *USA Today*, 11 October.
[29] Claire Atkinson (2005) Americans watch more TV than ever, *Advertising Age*, 30 September.

by the Interpublic group revealed that series such as *24*, *The Simpsons* or *Stargate Atlantis* headed the list of programmes copied and exchanged. The combination of the information contained in these two reports is of great interest, since it indicates that the programmes exchanged had been cleaned of all their advertising content, not only to create smaller files, but also for the convenience of the viewer. The Magna Global survey suggests that this provides an added incentive to the practice of product placement and brands within the series since, not being 'deleted', their capacity to communicate would endure.[30]

In the film *War of the Worlds* (Steven Spielberg, 2005), the young actress Dakota Fanning strongly recommended that her father (played by the actor Tom Cruise) should buy a TiVo. It was not the first time that the brand has been placed in a film. It could also be seen for example in *Mr & Mrs Smith* (Doug Liman, 2005), and in *Scary Movie 3* (David Zucker, 2003). However, Dakota Fanning's plea was not only well integrated into the screenplay, it was also very convincing. Millions of viewers saw the film in the cinema alone.[31]

The TiVo is a device, or more accurately a technology, that allows the viewer to watch a television programme pre-recorded and/or cleaned of its advertising content. One of the main motivations for buyers is clearly the possibility of avoiding commercial breaks.[32] Pointing the finger at TiVo alone, or at one of its competitors, such as ReplayTV, would however be naïve, even foolhardy. The rapid development of the market for digital recorders constitutes an even bigger threat for traditional television advertising, which many consumers increasingly avoid. As early as 2004, a study carried out by the Forrester agency showed that almost 60 per cent of TiVo owners watched pre-recorded or recorded television, and 92 per cent of advertisements were avoided. Only 46 per cent of the commercials had the possibility of being seen by the audience. The rates measured among TiVo owners were higher than those found among owners of other DVRs.[33]

---

[30] Claire Atkinson (2005) Internet piracy of US TV shows on the rise, *Advertising Age*, 21 April.

[31] *War of the Worlds* collected US$234.280 million on its domestic market, to which US$357.465 million must be added from the international market. It was one of the biggest successes of the year 2005. Source: Box Office Mojo LLC, November 2006.

[32] Eileen O'Neill and Marianne Barrett (2004) TiVo: The next big thing: DVRs and television advertising models, paper presented to the 6th World Media Economics Conference, HEC Montréal, Montréal, Canada, 12–15 May. See also Ronald Grover and Jon Fine (2006) The sound of many hands zapping, *BusinessWeek*, 22 May; D Gayatri (2005) DVRs in advertising, in V Partha Sarathy (ed), *The Changing Face of Advertising*, ICFAI University Press, Hyderabad, pp 105–21; Kate Maddox (2006) Assessing DVR's impact on TV ads, *BtoB Magazine*, 3 April; and Matt Carlson (2006) Tapping into TiVo, *New Media & Society*, 8(1), pp 97–115.

[33] *The Mind of the DVR User: Media and advertising* (September 2004), a study by Josh Bernoff, Forrester Research, Cambridge, MA.

The advantage of product placement is that, to date, it cannot be avoided. Admittedly, it is possible to imagine that in future, an electronic system working in parallel with the broadcasting of programmes might mask a placement or simply delete it from the image. But even if a professional broadcaster can blur or hide an alcohol brand or a packet of cigarettes during a television report, or digitally insert one product in place of another in a sporting encounter, we have not yet reached that stage for the public at large.

Consequently, product and brand placements offer the opportunity to by-pass this viewer censorship,[34] even in pirated programmes exchanged on the internet.[35] The assessment remains, however, that the target audience of an advertiser present on these screens diminishes day by day. In 2005, the US advertising space-buying agency Initiative signed a placement contract with the programme *World Series of Poker*, on ESPN, explaining that it was looking for an 'anti-TiVo' method for its client Levitra, which it wanted to present to a male audience aged 18–49 years.[36]

TiVo itself quickly opted for an original form of branded entertainment. In 2001, in a special operation, subscribers could gain access via their terminal, if desired, to documentary mini-films paid for by advertisers such as Lexus, to present their product. A type of advertising on demand, accessible 24 hours a day for the length of the contract's duration, these films of a few minutes only presented the product and generally offered interactive content. The interactive functions could be used to gain more information about the product.

The corollary: growth in investment

At its 2005 annual conference, the ANA (US Association of National Advertisers) presented the results of a study among its members, indicating that 63 per cent of its members were already integrating branded entertainment activities into their communications plan.[37] Even more revealing, 52 per cent explained that the finance came from their television advertising budget. Very large advertisers such as General Motors and Procter & Gamble confirmed that from 2005, their investments in classic television advertising would

[34] June Deery (2004) Reality TV as advertainment, *Popular Communication*, 2(1), pp 1–20.

[35] Claire Atkinson (2005) Internet privacy of US TV show on the rise, *Advertising Age*, 21 April.

[36] T L Stanley (2005) Levitra gets center stage in World Series of Poker, *Madison+Vine*, 9 November.

[37] John Consoli (2005) ANA Survey: 63 pct. use branded entertainment, *Brandweek*, 23 March.

shrink rapidly in favour of non-traditional communication. Several academic studies confirm this trend, and the corollary of a growth in investments in this direction.[38] In the United States alone, the number of product placements on television increased by 30 per cent in 2005, to reach 108,261, according to Nielsen Media Research.[39]

On the basis of various studies,[40] the PQ Media agency calculated that for the United States, investments in product placement in the media had risen from US$190 million in 1974, to US$512 million in 1985 and US$1.130 billion in 1994 to reach US$3.458 billion in 2004. According to the terms of the study, the sectors still bringing together the biggest investors were agricultural produce, drinks, household equipment, and health and beauty products. These sectors accounted for more than half of total expenditure. Taking all media together, the annual rate of growth between 1999 and 2004 was 16.3 per cent. However, more than 90 per cent of expenditure on product placement was aimed at television and cinema. Although cinema's share has decreased due to the explosion of placement opportunities on

---

[38] Rare are those studies that lead to the conclusion of a relative slow down in the number of placements (especially in movies), such as the one by Nicolas Rubbo and Corinne Berneman (2004) La pratique du placement de produits dans le cinéma américain: une analyse de contenu de films entre 1985 et 2001, paper presented to the 9th Journées de Recherche en Marketing CERMAB-LEG, Bourgogne University, Dijon, 4–5 November. Confirming the tendency of a growing number of cases, see in particular Mary-Lou Galician (ed) (2004) *Handbook of Product Placement in the Mass Media*, Haworth Press, Binghamton, NY; Kathy Brittain McKee (1998) Conceptualizing brand placement as a viable media strategy: perspectives and prescriptives, *American Academy of Advertising Conference Proceedings* ed Darrel D Muehling, AAA, Lexington, KY, pp 305–07; Rosemary J Avery and Rosellina Ferraro (2000) Verisimilitude or advertising? Brand appearances on prime time television, *Journal of Consumer Affairs*, 34(2), pp 217–44; Cristel Antonia Russell (2002) Investigating the effectiveness of product placements in television shows: the role of modality and plot connection congruence on brand memory and attitude, *Journal of Consumer Research*, 29, December, pp 306–18; Ian Brennan and Laurie A Babin (2004) Brand placement recognition: the influence of presentation mode and brand familiarity, *Journal of Promotion Management*, 10(1/2), pp 185–202; Abram Sauer (2006) Brandchannel's 2005 product placement awards, *BusinessWeek*, 2 March.

[39] Lynn Smith (2006) When the plot pushes the product, *Los Angeles Times*, 12 February.

[40] See especially the reports: First-ever report to size and structure product placement market says value of television placements rocketed 46.4 % to $1.87 billion in 2004 (29 March 2005), and Product placements in videogames, internet and recorded music will drive growth in the 'other media' sector in 2005 and over the next five years (27 July 2005), from PQ Media LLC, Two Stamford Landing, Suite 100, Stamford, CT.

television with reality TV shows, the value of placements in feature films has continued to grow, with more than US$1 billion injected into the big US television networks alone in 2006.[41]

For the most part, these expenses come from budgetary reallocations and not from new budgets. The various studies conducted by PQ Media also indicate, however, that placements paid for by advertisers were not the most numerous, although this area has seen an acceleration in growth over recent years as competition increases. Paid placements therefore represented 18 per cent in 1974 and reached 29.3 per cent in 2004, while at the same time the number of free placements fell dramatically: they represented 24.3 per cent in 1974 and accounted for only 6.6 per cent in 2004. As a result, in 2004, 64 per cent of expenditure was on product placements carried out on the basis of an exchange of goods.

Expenditure on product placements for media other than films and television was estimated at US$384.9 million in 2005 (or an increase of 18.1 per cent over 2004). Based on an annual growth rate fixed at 14.9 per cent, the projections of the experts at PQ Media foresaw that expenditure on product placement in all media in 2009 would be US$6.94 billion. Among the leading sectors, analysts believe that transport and accessories, clothing and accessories, agricultural produce and drinks, and tourism and leisure will continue to lead the market; but categories such as electronic or techno-logical products, toys and products linked to the world of sport, as well as media and the entertainment sector in general, should see a marked growth in investment.

---

[41] John Dempsey (2005) Plugs spring a leak, *Variety*, 25 September.

3 The useful association of cinema and advertising

On 18 March 1993, episode 417 of the successful television series *Seinfeld* was titled 'The Junior Mints', inspired by the confectionery of the same name.[1] The writers had come up with a storyline with a Junior Mint as a central element. At the time, the placements company AIM Productions had to obtain permission from the brand to use the name, but there was no request made by the brand, and there were no payments related to the operation.[2] The comedy of the script was reinforced by the use of a 'prop' that every viewer could recognize. This was a placement desired by the scriptwriters. Such cases still exist today, but they are rare. It is, however, certain that the role of the props master has evolved considerably over the past few years, the

---

[1] *Seinfeld* was a very popular series, suitable for product placements. See in particular Dana T Weaver and Mary Beth Oliver (2000) Television programs and advertising: measuring the effectiveness of product placement within Seinfeld, 50th International Communication Association Conference, Mass Communication division, Acapulco, Mexico, June. See also Shane Gunster (2005) All about nothing: difference, affect and *Seinfeld*, *Television & New Media*, 6(2), May, pp 200–23.

[2] Lorne Manly (2005) When the ad turns into the story line, *New York Times*, 2 October.

goal being to reflect as far in advance as possible on the relevant placement possibilities.[3]

Nowadays, the props master is provided early on in proceedings with a wish list, less and less general and increasingly specific, which lists the places, services, products and brands that the film needs. Established in concert between the director and the producer, sometimes with the help of the scriptwriter, a wish list can also benefit from the early advice of the props master. It will sometimes contain 'generic' items (a beer, an office lamp, a bus service, a restaurant), which will be left to the discretion of the props master. It is his/her job to find the cheapest and most coherent 'arrangements' from the point of view of the script. The distribution varies from country to country, even from studio to studio, but as a general rule, excluding general costs and unforeseen expenses, three main families of costs must be considered in the production of a film (to which it is appropriate to add, possibly, a marketing budget):

- *Above the line cost*: the total costs of the rights (story, music, and others), the actors (principal casting), producers and director.
- *Below the line cost*: the total costs of running the film crew (excluding above the line cost) including personnel costs (including extras), technical equipment, logistical services, financial and insurance fees and so on.
- *Postproduction cost*: the total costs after filming (special effects, editing, soundtrack, credits, digital development or editing, and so on).

Although the below the line cost is often unknown to the public at large, it may quickly come to represent the main item on the budget, according to the requirements of the screenplay and the demands of the director, in particular. Originally, after the manner of Honoré de Balzac, who would appease his creditors by placing their names in his novels, placement contracts were designed to shrink this budget item.[4]

In benefiting from the loan of a Beechcraft private aeroplane for the filming of *Executive Decision* (1996), director Stuart Baird managed to save several thousand dollars. A contract that allows the cost of the marketing budget to be 'diverted' on to partners can quickly come to represent tens of millions of dollars.

---

[3] Janet Wasko (2003) *How Hollywood Works*, Sage, London.
[4] In 2006, for its international print advertising campaign, Breguet watches even used an excerpt of Balzac's *Eugenie Grandet* (1833) quoting the brand. The campaign also used other authors like Alexander Pushkin, who mentioned the Swiss brand in *Eugene Onegin* (1829).

A significant source of finance

The professional association the Motion Picture Association of America has calculated that the average cost of producing a feature film for the major studios had climbed to US$98 million in 2004. Admittedly, the standard deviation either side of such an average value is naturally high. On the other hand, the average value is still symptomatic of an overall increase in production costs, as well as of distribution and marketing costs in particular.[5] *Die Another Day* (Lee Tamahori, 2002) is often presented as the all-time record-holder: between US$120 and US$160 million was obtained from the associated brands for the 20 or so placements surrounding Her Majesty's favourite spy, in both placement fees and in advertising support on the film's release.[6] Funding can also come from not having to pay for the products or services used. Many Hummer, Pontiac and Chevrolet cars (all from General Motors) for instance, are used in *Transformers* (Michael Bay, 2007). If the production had had to buy (or rent) all those cars, it would have increased the production budget. In France, too, the cost of a feature film is mounting,[7] and *Michel Vaillant* (Louis-Pascal Couvelaire, 2005) for example, relied in part on the financial support of Total, Peugeot and Michelin.[8]

On average, a film costs more year on year: in fact, as competition becomes more fierce, the initial investment required is more important in order to ensure a quality team, actors and a director who can generate box-office interest, and post-production with all the necessary special effects. Even when filming is relocated to Eastern countries, to New Zealand, to South Africa or to a North African country, productions costing tens of millions of dollars are not uncommon. A film's budget has never been a guarantee of success, but paradoxically, its breadth reassures potential investors. Hence the fundamental (sometimes indispensable) role of placement contracts, which

---

[5] Kenneth E Clow and Donald E Baack (2003) *Integrated Advertising, Promotion, and Marketing Communications*, 2nd edn, Prentice Hall, Upper Saddle River, NJ. See in particular Daniel Read (1999) *Product Placement: Cases in consumer behaviour*, ed Gerrit Antonides and W Fred Van Raajj, Wiley, Chichester, pp 67–72. See also the detailed paper by Laura M Holson (2005) Can Hollywood evade the death eaters? *New York Times*, 6 November.

[6] Even if those millions are not strictly 'paid for' by the placement, but mostly represent associated advertising promoting the movie when it is released. See Denman Maroney (2003) Top topic: product placement, *Informed*, 6(4), August, ARF, pp 4–6; Lara Magzan (2002) The business of Bond ... James Bond, *Money*, 25 November.

[7] Nathalie Silbert (2005) Cinéma: des films de plus en plus chers à produire, *Les Echos*, 11–12 March.

[8] Léna Lutaud (2005) Les marques entrent en force dans le cinéma français, *Le Figaro*, 5 November.

can thus contribute to the financing of the project, directly or indirectly, even in countries such as India that might wrongly be assumed to have escaped this inflation.[9]

At this point, we must also bear in mind that not all product or brand placement contracts give rise to a payment.[10] The majority are based on a partnership contract detailing the products and services that the advertiser commits to providing in return for the placement. In a film where a number of sets are used, some of which require numerous props and several electronic and computer devices, such agreements can quickly come to represent several million dollars.[11] It may also be a question of supplying the studio, or supplying the production directly, with free products (or freebies) which contribute to reducing the production costs, or the provision of services.

Clos du Val is a small producer of high-quality Cabernet Sauvignon in California's Napa Valley. Its brown label is easily identifiable. (See Figure 3.1.) Not enjoying the same resources as the major Californian vineyards, it sends, on average, 240 cases of the 65,000 produced each year to props masters. During the filming of *The Terminal* (2004), the director Steven Spielberg, always attentive to detail, decided that the bottle of champagne called for in the script for the dinner between Tom Hanks and Catherine Zeta Jones was somewhat too expensive. The props master David Harlocker, who had in his possession a bottle of Clos du Val, suggested it, and it was immediately put to use. The previous year, Clos du Val was also used in Alejandro Gonzalez Iñárritu's *21 Grams*. It could likewise be seen in episodes of the series *Las Vegas* (NBC), *The O.C.* (Warner), *The Sopranos* (HBO) and *Two and a Half Men* (Warner). Clos du Val pays monthly fees of US$5,000 to its agent Aaron Gordon to enable these placements. The *Los Angeles Times* revealed in 2004

[9] See in particular Michelle R Nelson and Narayan Devathan (2006) Brand placements Bollywood style, *Journal of Consumer Behaviour*, 5, May–June, pp 211–21, and Sukhbinder Barn (2005) Product placement and Bollywood movies: an exploration of the industry structure, film themes and placement opportunities with indigenous and Indian Diaspora audiences, paper presented to the 5th Conjoint American Marketing Association/Academy of Marketing Conference, Dublin Institute of Technology, Dublin, Ireland, 5–7 July. About the rise of placements in Indian television shows and especially in the Deeya Singh and Tony Singh *Jassi Jassi Koi Nahin* series, see in particular Somashukla Sinha Walunjkar (2006) It's a marketer's delight, *Financial Express*, 12 February.

[10] See in particular Michael J Baker and Hazel A Crawford (1995) *Product Placement*, research paper 95/2, Marketing Department, Strathclyde University, Glasgow, and Cristel Antonia Russell and Michael Belch (2005) A managerial investigation into the product placement industry, *Journal of Advertising Research*, 45(1), pp 73–92.

[11] Harriet Marsh (1995) Bond product deals add a licence to sell, *Marketing*, 16 November.

Figure 3.1   Clos Du Val bottle, 2001

that the total number of bottles distributed gratis had a resale value of approximately US$36,000.[12]

As early as 1951, for the Charles Walters film *Three Guys Named Mike*, MGM signed a partnership agreement with American Airlines, which stipulated that in exchange for a highly visible placement (the story centres on an air hostess working for the company), American Airlines would provide aeroplanes and logistics, as well as advertising support when the film opened. The exchange of goods is also often the case in car placements. The financial advantages are identical, indeed much more favourable than if the production had had to pay for the acquisition of the necessary vehicles. In 2002, David Wilson, Ford's vice-president of global business strategy, acknowledged that for the filming of the 20th James Bond film, *Die Another Day* (Lee Tamahori, 2002), the value of the vehicles obtained from the partner car makers was above and beyond what a classic placement contract would have allowed for.[13] As a reminder: the

---

[12] Jerry Hirsch (2004) Winery wins the game of product placement, *Los Angeles Times*, 7 June.

[13] Jeff Chu and Reema Ameer (2002) For your wallet only, *Time*, 18 November. As the contract between MGM and BMW was estimated to be worth US$25 million, Ford agreed to invest US$35 million to see an Aston Martin coming back on screen, alongside some other models of the Ford Group. See in particular Ron Grover (2001) James Bond's new $35 million wheels, *BusinessWeek*, 31 August, and Braden

famous secret agent returned to the Aston Martin of his origins (in this case, a V12 Vanquish),[14] the character of Jinx used a Thunderbird, the character of Zao drove a Jaguar XKR, and various Range Rovers, Ford Kas, GT40s, and Volvos S60s and S80s were also used. In short, some see the success of placement products and its financial resources as a means to compensate for the loss of income because of piracy and peer-to-peer exchanges of cultural works. Neil Netanel, professor of law at UCLA, believes that a tax of 4 per cent on new computers and other copying materials would enable the collection of almost US$2 billion in the United States alone,[15] a figure considerably less than the promises of product placements, considering all media together.

The natural evocative power of the brand

In 1923, when Alfred Hitchcock designed the set of *Woman to Woman*, directed by Graham Cutts, he reproduced there the façade of the Moulin Rouge and instantly evoked Paris. In 1941, in the Clarence Brown film *They Met in*

Phillips (2006) Luxury; the Aston Martin aura, shaken not stirred, *New York Times*, 25 October. This last article is well documented on the brand, and the journalist ironically reminds the unlikely novice reader that Aston Martin is to James Bond as maple syrup is to Vermont.

[14] In Terence Young's *Dr No* (1962), the James Bond character drives a Sunbeam Alpine. From the same director, in *From Russia With Love*, a Bentley 3.5 litre. In Guy Hamilton's *Goldfinger* (1964) and in Terence Young's *Thunderball* (1965), an Aston Martin DB5; in Val Guest's (*et al.*) *Casino Royale* (1967) a Bentley Special 4.5 litre; in Lewis Gilbert's *You Only Live Twice* (1967) a Toyota 2000GT; in Peter Hunt's *On Her Majesty's Secret Service* (1969) an Aston Martin DBS and a Mercury Cougar; in Guy Hamilton's *Diamonds are Forever* (1971) an Aston Martin DB5 once again, and he rents a Mustang Mach; from the same director, in *Live and Let Die* (1973) no car, except a double-decker bus in one scene; still from Guy Hamilton, in *The Man with the Golden Gun* (1974) an AMC; in Lewis Gilbert's *The Spy Who Loved Me* (1977) a Lotus Esprit; from the same director, in *Moonraker* (1979) no 'terrestrial' car but a lunar vehicle; in John Glen's *For Your Eyes Only* (1981) a Lotus Esprit and a 2CV Citroën; in Irvin Kershner's *Never Say Never Again* (1983) a Bentley and a Yamaha XJ 650 motorcycle; in John Glen's *Octopussy* (1983) an Alfa Romeo GTV and a Volkswagen Love Bug; from the same director, in *A View to a Kill* (1985) a Renault 11; also from John Glen, in *The Living Daylights* (1987) an Aston Martin V8 Vantage and an Aston Martin V8 Volante; again from John Glen, in *Licence to Kill* (1989) a Kenworth truck; in Martin Campbell's *GoldenEye* (1995) a BMW Z3 fights against an Aston Martin DB5 for the screen; in Roger Spottiswoode's *Tomorrow Never Dies* (1997) a BMW 750iL; in Michael Apted's *The World is Not Enough* (1999) a BMW Z8; in Lee Tamahori's *Die Another Day* (2002) an Aston Martin Vanquish. In Martin Campbell's *Casino Royale* (2006), he drives an Aston Martin DBS and an Aston Martin DB5.

[15] Chris Taylor (2004) Invasion of the movie snatchers, *Time*, 11 October.

Bombay, Clark Gable had to pass as an inspector for an insurance company. The choice of the most famous of all insurers, Lloyd's of London, dating back to the seventeenth century, was not an innocent one. Upon mention of its name, all the mental imagery associated with the insurer is immediately projected on to the character, who also gains in credibility. In 1989, for *In Country*, director Norman Jewison has Bruce Willis lay before the Vietnam Veterans Memorial Wall his war decoration and a packet of Camel cigarettes, both heavy with symbolism, and the silent camera pauses on a close-up.

In Billy Wilder's classic 1954 film *Sabrina*, Humphrey Bogart plays a busy New York businessman. At the beginning of the film, while he is introduced by a voice off-camera while he takes part in a family photograph, the photographer asks him to remove a newspaper from his pocket so that it will not appear in the photograph. Any newspaper would have done, in principle. Its identification was not a matter of course while it was folded in the actor's jacket pocket. However, the specific folding of the newspaper, the transfer from one pocket to another and an *ad hoc* camera movement mean that it is easily identified as the *Wall Street Journal*. A coherent association with the world of business, a logical evocation, a relevant placement.

In 1992 another press title, *The Hollywood Reporter*, is used in Mick Jackson's *The Bodyguard*. As a reference, it instantly lends credibility to the world of show business in which the story takes place. In 1998, in a scene from *Stepmom*, by Chris Columbus, Julia Roberts plays a photographer conducting a photo shoot. Her character has not yet been described when we see her taking photographs of people who appear to be models. When the Valentino label appears, the character played by Julia Roberts is naturally identified as a fashion photographer. These cases, although very different, nevertheless rely on the same machinery of evocation.

There are other examples of resorting to product placement for which this evocation is pushed to the limit by an advertiser, in order to launch a new product or a new brand. In 2005, in the film *Ocean's Twelve* by Steven Soderbergh, the Ambilight flat screens provided by Philips had not yet gone on sale at the time of filming. In 2003, the Mercedes E-class driven by Will Smith and Tommy Lee Jones in *Men in Black II* (Barry Sonnenfeld, 2002) had not yet arrived in showrooms when the film opened in the United States.[16]

Such placements remain difficult to orchestrate, however, for the simple reason that they require an ideal coordination between the film's opening in cinemas and the product's arrival on the shelves. This is rarely possible,

---

[16] Greg Hernandez (2002) Carmakers see screen time for flashy models, *Los Angeles Times*, 7 July. Make actor Russell Crowe read the *Financial Times* and involve him in some stock exchange operations in Ridley Scott's *A Good Year* (2006), so that one could believe him to be a top finance achiever. Then sit him in a tiny Smart car, not at all the kind of car his character has been using to drive, and it becomes quite plausible that he has much trouble in controlling it.

unless the brand planning is sufficiently flexible to fit in with that of the film. Hence the advantage of a television series, whereby the frequent broadcasts offer greater flexibility.[17] Thus, in 2000, a doll modelled on the singer Cher was central to the plot of the 16 November episode of the series *Will & Grace* shown on NBC. Created by Mattel, it was due to be launched several months later.[18] In 2004, Procter & Gamble successfully used the programme *The Apprentice* to launch its new toothpaste Refreshing Vanilla Mint, by the Crest brand. The Crest internet site registered more than 4.7 million hits. Of these 800,000 were counted in less than two hours, generating more than 40,000 requests for samples. There was a competition visitors were invited to take part in, requiring them to submit ideas, and this received more than 100 idea suggestions per minute immediately after the end of the programme.[19]

The use of product placements in a film for launching a product should nevertheless be undertaken only with precautions, and while bearing in mind that the placement may be seen again (on DVD, television, video on demand (VOD) and so on) long after the launch. Taking into account this product specificity, it is important to think about the placement modalities so that they do not contravene the product or brand communication.

In the vast majority of other cases, products and brands exist before the creation of the film. This means that they possess a specific identity and positioning before appearing in the scene of a film. When Jennifer Garner moves house in *Catch and Release* (Susannah Grant, 2007), it is 'naturally' with the help of a U-Haul removal van. Beyond the functionality of the product or brand name, the placement's objective may be to profit from this positioning and identity. Watching Sky News on television in Great Britain in *Basic Instinct 2* (Michael Caton-Jones, 2006) is logical since it is the most-watched news channel. The presence of Hermès or Prada in *Hitch* (Andy Tennant, 2005), or Louis Vuitton in *Monster-in-Law* (Robert Luketic, 2005), does not follow

---

[17] Russell and Stern's researches (2005) tend to prove that the spectator knows how to differentiate a temporary character from a recurrent one in a television show, and that associations with placed products happen more often with recurrent characters. See in particular Cristel Antonia Russell and Barbara B Stern (2005) Product placement effects: product–character associations (PCAs) in sitcoms, *Advances in Consumer Research*, 32, ed Gita Menon and Akshay Rao, pp 233–35, Association for Consumer Research, Provo, Utah.

[18] When the episode was about to be shot, the series production was given a prototype costing US$60,000. At this time, choosing *Will & Grace* raised questions: did Mattel target the gay and lesbian community, as the two main characters of the series were homosexual? See in particular the paper from Stuart Elliott (2001) A Mattel doll modelled after a certain singer does turn on Will & Grace: is it product placement? *New York Times*, 16 November.

[19] Source: official press release from Procter & Gamble, Cincinnati, 28 September 2004.

the same positioning objective as that of Phat Farm in *Coach Carter* (Thomas Carter, 2005) or of Schott in *Four Brothers* (John Singleton, 2005). In the same way, the placement of *People* magazine in *Fantastic 4* (Tim Story, 2005) or *Cosmopolitan* in *Charlie's Angels: Full Throttle* (McG, 2003) do not follow the same objective as that of *Fortune* in *Collateral* (Michael Mann, 2004) or *Forbes* in *Along Came Polly* (John Hamburg, 2004). This observation intends no disrespect to either brand. Nonetheless, their identities, their positioning, their statuses, their images and quite naturally their preferred targets, are not the same.

Car placements are especially revealing in terms of what a brand or a product may spontaneously evoke in the viewer's mind. Directors therefore often make great demands on their props master in this regard. The choice to entrust the disoriented character of Travis, played by Harry Dean Stanton, with a Chevrolet El Camino (a partial pick-up), in the desert of *Paris, Texas* (Wim Wenders, 1984), was not random. Neither was the choice of a Mustang to express the independence of the detective Nick Curran, played by Michael Douglas in *Basic Instinct* (Paul Verhoeven, 1992). The foreign DS Citroën of a radio entertainer used, in the very heart of the United States, in *Betrayed* (Costa-Gavras, 1988), has an entirely different meaning from the Jeep® Rubicon (see Figure 3.2) of the adventuress Lara Croft, played by Angelina Jolie in *Tomb Raider: The Cradle of Life* (Jan de Bont, 2003), or the Porsche of the highly ostentatious Joel Goodsen, played by Tom Cruise in *Risky Business* (Paul Brickman, 1983).

The aggressive power of the Audi A8 W12 driven by the private agent Frank Martin, played by Jason Statham in *Transporter 2* (2005), directed by Louis Leterrier, is at the opposite end of the spectrum from the evocations of the Ferrari 250 GT California 1961, a rare model borrowed by the debonair Ferris Bueller (Matthew Broderick), in *Ferris Bueller's Day Off* (John Hughes, 1986); and both play a completely different role from that of the very reassuring Volvo 850 estate driven by the housewife – played by Sally Field – to transport her children in *Mrs Doubtfire* (Chris Columbus, 1993). This is not to mention the charismatic 1959 Peugeot 403 Cabriolet driven by Peter Falk, who plays Lieutenant Columbo in the series *Columbo*. In each of these cases, the car is a powerful evoker of the character's status and role, of the environment and of the intended use.[20] Different models, and most certainly different brands, will be used to distinguish the 'good guys' from the 'bad guys', the 'rich' from the

---

[20] Phil Patton (1996) Now it's the cars that make the characters go, *New York Times*, 21 April. See also Phil Rosenthal (2006) *Sopranos* song: can't pay us to show products, *Chicago Tribune*, 15 March, about the specific case concerning the social status of a Porsche Cayenne Turbo and its buyer, in an episode of *The Sopranos* series. It was a supposedly unpaid placement (HBO network specified that it ran against its politics) but wanted by its screenwriters.

Figure 3.2 Jeep® Rubicon advertisement on the release of the film *Tomb Raider: The Cradle of Life* (2003). Reproduced by kind permission of Daimler Chrysler.

'less rich' or from the 'poor', single from married, city-dwellers from country cousins, and so on. The same is true for motorcycles. How could we imagine Peter Fonda and Dennis Hopper on anything other than Harley-Davidsons in *Easy Rider* (Dennis Hopper, 1969)?

A placement can say a great deal about the intended target on the part of the advertisers,[21] or on the director's part, the coherence of what he or she wishes to invoke. Hence the advantage for the brand of being involved in the project as early as possible, in order to ensure that the placement is indeed compatible with its intrinsic characteristics; hence the advantage for the film makers of knowing the brand, apart from its financial support, in order to ensure that it does indeed correspond to the impression they hope to evoke. When Domino's was the pizza eaten by the Ninja Turtles in *Teenage Mutant Ninja Turtles* (Steve Barron, 1990), the brand aimed at achieving a well-known effect on children, who dictate their own food choices and those

---

[21] See in particular the very interesting study about placements in shows more specifically targeted to Afro-Americans, conducted by Claudine Cleophat (2005) A content analysis of product placement of African-American-oriented programming on United Paramount Network, Florida State University, Register 123, Dept Communications, Tallahassee, FL.

of the household.[22] In *The Firm* (Sydney Pollack, 1993), a Mercedes is offered to the young lawyer played by Tom Cruise, in order to convince him to come and work for the firm of Bendini Lambert & Locke,[23] because the brand's positioning is symbolic of career success. A similar procedure took place with *In Good Company* (Paul Weitz, 2004), when Carter Duryea, played by Topher Grace, is promoted to the position of sales manager: his first purchase is a Porsche 911 Carrera, to symbolize his success.

At the other end of the scale, the target of a beer such as Budweiser corresponds to a large, little-segmented audience, which is consistent with its placement in large-audience films such as *The Dukes of Hazzard* (Jay Chandrasekhar, 2005) or *Wedding Crashers* (David Dobkin, 2005). The place-ment of a Jeep® in *Chasing Papi* (Linda Mendoza, 2003), a comedy aimed at young Hispano-Americans, was clearly intended to sensitize the community to the brand's vehicles. *Wired* magazine is considered to be at the cutting edge of the most futuristic technology, so that its appearance in *Fantastic 4* (2005) is meaningful within the world of the film. *Batman Begins* (Christopher Nolan, 2005) tackles the subject of the homeless: the mention of the Salvation Army reinforces the idea and locates the milieu in which the title character, played by Christian Bale, is developed. The appearance of the Chicco brand in *Meet the Fockers* (Jay Roach, 2004), where part of the story centres on a birth and another part centres on a baby, is perfectly consistent. So is the appearance of Trojan condoms in *The 40 Year Old Virgin* (Judd Apatow, 2005).

The Dalloz *codes rouges* (red codes) are to French law what the famous little red book of Mao Zedong is to Chinese communism: the ultimate reference. Dalloz is a renowned brand. In French television series or films, not a scene goes by in a lawyer's office without the red-bound books. By themselves, these legal codes express, represent and justify the law. There is no 'product placement' department at Dalloz, although the French publishing house receives more than a hundred requests from production companies each year. Some of these requests are even recurrent, as with the French television

---

[22] Stacy M Vollmers (1995) The impact on children of brand and product placements in films, Dissertation Abstracts International, Florida State University, Tallahassee, FL. About the television show's power, see also researches from Patti Valkenburg and Tom H A Van der Voort (1994) Influence of TV on daydreaming and creative imagination: a review of research, *Psychological Bulletin*, 116, pp 316–39, and for a specific study about television commercials, see Nathalie Guichard (2000) *Publicité télévisée et comportement de l'enfant*, Economica, Paris.

[23] On the other hand, there is no need to specify that Bendini Lambert & Locke, the name of the law firm which orders the murder of some of its own partners to protect its intimate links with the mob, is fictional. It is understandable that, in this case of a story inspired by John Grisham's novel *The Firm*, it was slightly difficult to impossible to get a law firm interested in such a placement.

series *Avocats & Associes* (Lawyers and Associates), on the France 2 channel. Whether for the *codes rouges* or the firm's encyclopaedias (bound in black), the loan request is freely granted, subject only to a deposit cheque to ensure that they are returned at the end of filming. Requests are rarely made according to speciality, but rather by the linear metre, according to the length of the shelves that the props master has to 'fill'! Most of the time these are naturally at the farthest edges of the screen, but if a scene requires a close-up or handling by an actor, the latest edition is made available.

Finally, certain brands – notably US brands – possess in addition such an evocative power that, like those brands that have entered the lexicon, they are often used not only in films but also in the press or in novels, as both verbs and common nouns. We should name here the classics Kleenex, Dictaphone, FedEx, Google, Frigidaire and Scotch. Does the audience really see a Frigidaire refrigerator in Ridley Scott's *Hannibal* (2001), or simply 'a refrigerator'? Do we really identify the Kleenex brand in *The Forgotten* (Joseph Ruben, 2004), or the generic name for a simple tissue? As for Google, the omnipresent and indispensable internet search engine, is it really what the audience sees in *The Fog* (Rupert Wainwright, 2005) or in *Hitch* (2005), or do they simply see the now-standard tool for online searches? Do you Yahoo?

The reality of a brand-consumerist world

We live in a brand-consumerist world. How could we imagine Rocky Balboa stepping into the ring again in 2007, in the film directed by and starring Sylvester Stallone, without sponsors around him, when the world of boxing is to a large extent financed by these partnership contracts? And how could it appear without Everlast, NEC, Pepsi, Boyd's Coffee, HBO PPV, Fuji Film and Miller, in particular, appearing around the ring? The US brewer Budweiser pays to place its beer in eight to 10 films per year on average, but all in all it appears in 40 to 50 feature films each year, because the producer or the props master judges it advantageous or even useful to have the brand appear in the shot.[24] This brand consumer realism, in accordance with the modern consumer society,[25] can even be 'helped' in some cases by the brand.[26] In

[24] Gail Schiller (2005) This Bud's for 'crashers', *Wired*, 15 July.

[25] Winnie Won Yin Wong (2002) *Manufacturing Realisms: Product placement in the Hollywood film*, Master's thesis, Massachusetts Institute of Technology, Boston, MA. For a specific case study about Steven Spielberg's *The Terminal* (2004), see also Michael McCarthy (2004) And co-staring United, *USA Today*, 21 June.

[26] Denise E DeLorme and Leonard N Reid (1999) Moviegoers' experiences and interpretations of brands in films revisited, *Journal of Advertising*, 28 (2), Summer, pp 72–95.

the Mike Figgis film *One Night Stand* (1997), the advertiser played by Wesley Snipes is dressed by Giorgio Armani. What could have remained a simple stealth placement, however, becomes particularly explicit when, during the film, the advertiser himself makes an advertising film for – Armani. Films set in an advertising agency are naturally auspicious for the citing of brands.

On 17 September 1964, when ABC showed the first episode of the television series *Bewitched*, created by Sol Saks, one of the principal characters – played by Dick York and later by Dick Sargent – was an advertiser working at the McMann & Tate advertising agency (a fictional name).[27] Very few real brands benefited from a placement, however. On television, the custom of the time was to mask any that might appear, or to use false names or dummy products. Those rare brand names cited were, moreover, outside the agency's business sector. Different eras, different approaches. Nothing was more natural, in Nancy Meyers's film *What Women Want* (2000), itself also set against the background of an advertising agency, than to find countless placements for FedEx, Johnnie Walker, Advil, Visa, Sears, Mustang, Wonderbra, Kleenex, Ameritech, Apple, Saks, G-Shock, US Air, CNN and Adage, in particular. The Nike brand even plays a part in the screenplay as the subject of a bid in which the agency participates. A world littered with brands is here completely logical.

An advertising agency is, of course, an extreme case. However, the world of consumption in which we live day to day is itself full of brands. A scene in a supermarket where all the products were turned back to front or masked so that none of the brands could be identified would appear very strange, simply because the brands form part of our everyday life and because they have, in fact, become necessary to the realism of certain scenes.[28] When the brands Mattel, Coleco, Fisher Price and the FAO Schwartz shop are cited or seen in *Big* (Penny Marshall, 1988), nothing about it seems strange since they are all linked to the world of toys: the film is set in the context of a toy-making company. In 2005 alone, Coca-Cola was present notably in *Are We*

---

[27] In 1947, the Kimberly advertising agency's name and Beauty Soap products were fanciful names specifically created for Jack Conway's *The Hucksters*. It is not Pepsodent but Dazzledent (on purpose) that is mentioned in Billy Wilder's *The Seven Year Itch* (1955). In Preston Sturges' *Christmas in July* (1940) the Maxwell House coffee brand fades behind the 'Maxford House' one. See also Stuart Elliott (2006), Fake product and the movies that loved them, *New York Times*, 9 January, and for a critic praising the use of fictional names, see Sean Macaulay (2004) Bucks are the stars, *The Times*, 25 May. But if the airline used in David Ellis's *Snakes on a Plane* (2006) is called South Pacific Airlines, maybe it is just because it would have been difficult to convince a real airline to welcome snakes on board and let them frighten and kill its passengers.

[28] Pola B Gupta, Siva K Balasubramanian and Michael L Klassen (2000) Viewer's evaluations of product placements in movies: public policy issues and managerial implications, *Journal of Current Issues and Research in Advertising*, 22(2), pp 41–52.

There Yet? (Brian Levant), *Boogeyman* (Stephen T Kay), *Diary of a Mad Black Woman* (Darren Grant), *Four Brothers* (John Singleton), *Guess Who* (Kevin Rodney Sullivan), *Hitch* (Andy Tennant), *Just Like Heaven* (Mark Waters), *King Kong* (Peter Jackson), *Madagascar* (Eric Darnell and Tom McGrath), *Sahara* (Breck Eisner), *The 40 Year Old Virgin* (Judd Apatow), *The Dukes of Hazzard* (Jay Chandrasekhar), *The Hitchhiker's Guide to the Galaxy* (Garth Jennings), *The Interpreter* (Sydney Pollack) and *War of the Worlds* (Steven Spielberg). Since Coca-Cola, the world leader in its class, is also present everywhere, it is a logical element of the world of consumption.

We might also cite here the particular case of animated films. If once the appearance of brands, particularly in large numbers, would have seemed strange, even incongruous, in the great Walt Disney classics, the times have changed. The subtle insertion of the popular magazine *Life* in *The Incredibles* (Brad Bird, 2004), drew the viewer into this world, even though it was populated by superheroes. In 2006, *Curious George,* the cartoon by Matthew O'Callaghan, showed placements for Dole fruits,[29] US Postal services, and Volkswagen cars. Dole also participated in the advertising for the film's opening, by placing *Curious George* stickers on 100 million bananas. The fruit producer also distributed a board to be coloured in, on which the collected stickers could be placed (see Figure 3.3).

In 2007, when Lionsgate studios set the Lawrence Kasanoff film *Foodfight!* in a grocer's shop, it seemed almost imperative to consider the 'real' products that 'should' be placed there. Dreamworks studios based the animal story *Madagascar* (Eric Darnell and Tom McGrath, 2005) in real zoos. Even if the behaviour of the animals there diverged somewhat from the ordinary, and even if they talked without any great difficulty, the presence of familiar brands contributed to the process of identification transference. Familiarity with the brand, as well as the frequency of consumption, are important points for the memorization of the brand that appears onscreen.[30] Thus, the brands Animal Planet, Central Park Zoo, Circuit City, Coca-Cola, Denny's, Essex House, HP, Hugo Boss, Lincoln Center, MetroNorth, New York Giants, New York Knicks, San Diego Zoo, Spalding, Swatch, TK Maxx and Ziploc appear in the film.[31]

---

[29] See in particular T L Stanley (2006) Product placement in animated *Curious George* movie, *Madison+Vine*, 8 February.

[30] Isabelle Fontaine (2002) *Étude des réponses mémorielles et attitudinales des spectateurs exposés aux placements de marques dans les films*, PhD management thesis, Paris IX Dauphine University.

[31] Source: Interbrand, Brandchannel, 2005. In John Lasseter and Joe Ranft's animated movie *Cars* (2006), in which the characters are automobiles, as the title suggests, it would have been possible and easy to draw non-branded cars. But those cars are alive, so giving them a name *and* a real brand automatically reinforced realism. So Beetle, BMW, Cadillac, Chevrolet, Corvette, Dodge, Ferrari, Fiat, Hudson, Hummer, Jaguar, Jeep, Lincoln, Mack, Maserati, Mercury, Peterbilt, Plymouth, Porsche and

Figure 3.3 Sticker collector used for the release of the film *Curious George* (Matthew O'Callaghan, 2006). Dole, Westlake Village, CA, United States © 2006 Dole Food Company Inc. CG Movie: ™ & © Universal Studios and/ or HMCo. Reproduced by kind permission of Dole Food Company and Universal Studios.

Dreamworks adopted this strategy in 2001 and 2004, for the animated films *Shrek* (Andrew Adamson and Vicky Jenson) and *Shrek 2* (Andrew Adamson and Kelly Asbury), by adapting the brand placements in the context of the Middle Ages. Baskin Robbins became Baskin Robinhood, Versace changed into Versarchery, Old Navy was transformed into Olde Knavery, Starbucks appeared as Farbucks, and so on. This humorous note facilitated placements that would otherwise not have been 'natural' here. In *Shark Tale* (Bibo

Volkswagen got out of the garage. See also Linda Hales's analysis (2006) Forget product placement: movies should sell artistry, *Washington Post*, 11 February, about brand logos inserts in *Curious George* (2006), among others.

Bergeron and Vicky Jenson, 2004), since the story was set underwater in the middle of the sea, the 'characters' were in fact fish. Even here, however, realism was supported by brand placements, adapted once again to the circumstances. The use of real brands, in their usual form, would have had a completely opposite effect. However, an attentive viewer would have seen an underwater representation of Times Square, where the brands Gup (Gap), Coral-Cola (Coca-Cola) and even Fish King (Burger King) were present; not to mention the references, during the film, of the magazines Newsreef (*Newsweek*), FQ (*GQ*), FIN (*SPIN*) and Pisces (*People*). Each time, in these different examples, the name was modified, but not enough to prevent the identification, the more so because the graphics of the logo were retained. This kind of placement is almost a complicit game of hide-and-seek between the film and the viewer; moreover, the brands appear more sympathetic for having lent themselves to the game. Interviewed by the magazine *Marketing News*, J Walker Smith, president of the Chapel Hill, NC-based marketing consultancy Yankelovich Partners Inc, pertinently analysed this process:

> More and more brands are looking for fresh ways in which to connect with consumers .... It's exactly the kind of anti-marketing that people think is interesting and more engaging these days. Consumers are looking for brands to do things that show that they take themselves less seriously. Brands that take themselves too seriously and exercise iron-lifted control over the ways consumers encounter them are kind of swimming against the tide.[32]

The credibility of a particular environment

In 2006, for his film *Click*, Frank Coraci uses the name of the specialist distribution brand Bed Bath & Beyond to enable Michael Newman, the character played by Adam Sandler, to find the remote control that goes 'beyond' his expectations. Although it goes beyond the world of the bathroom or bedroom, the scene, played in the key of comedy, gains natural credibility. Except for historical films taking place in a distant past like *300* (Zack Snyder, 2007) or *Apocalypto* (Mel Gibson, 2006) or those where the action takes place in an imaginary world like *The Lord of the Rings* trilogy (Peter Jackson, 2001–03), all screenplays can nowadays be subject to placement. These placements are even used by directors to lend credibility to the surroundings or the story itself. The director Steven Spielberg has clearly explained why he inserted brands such as Bulgari, Gap, Lexus, Century 21, Fox, *USA Today*, US News, Guinness, Revo, Burger King, Ben & Jerry's, Aquafina, American Express,

---

[32] Michael Fielding (2005) Consumer products ripe for film parody: marketers capitalize on trend to grow brand, *Marketing News*, 39(3), pp 12–14.

Iomega, Nokia and Pepsi in a futuristic film set in 2054 (*Minority Report*, 2002). He wanted to ensure that, on the one hand, the consumer understood that the action was supposed to take place on Earth and not in an unknown world, and on the other hand, that the familiarity that consumers have with these brands would enable them to believe that this future is not as distant as they might have thought.[33] When the director Jessica Bendinger filmed *Stick It* (2006) in the world of gymnastics, she used Gymnova equipment and filmed a championship sponsored by Neutrogena; and the film gained in credibility thereby.

We might think that if directors genuinely seek to make the surroundings of their film credible without appealing to advertisers, they can still obtain the products they need. They can design them, as Richard Linklater did in showing the Ayn Rand book *The Fountainhead* in his film *A Scanner Darkly* (2006), filmed in a highly original manner. But this is not always the case, and the use of special effects does not always provide a possible replacement. To strengthen the military environment for the Steven Soderbergh film *The Good German* (2006), the journalist played by George Clooney reads *The Stars and Stripes* newspaper. For the Phil Alden Robinson film *The Sum of All Fears* (2002), a large amount of material and military vehicles of all kinds were present onscreen.

The US Army has often collaborated with Hollywood studios, for understandable reasons relating to image. As early as 1915, for the famous film *The Birth of a Nation*, the director D W Griffith received strategic and logistical support from the army.[34] In the case of *The Sum of All Fears*, the army allowed the production access not only to F-16 fighter planes, CH-53E helicopters and B-2 bombers, but also to many military infrastructures, as well as the help of several liaison officers from different corps and services. In exchange, the army gained a window of communication to a large audience, within the context of a film where it was not being criticized.

There, indeed, lies the key to the exchange: a win–win relationship. In 1986, the US Navy helped to finance the Tony Scott film *Top Gun*, which allowed them to profit from an appreciable rise in recruitment.[35] However, by way of counter-example, although invited to participate in the film *Courage Under Fire* (Edward Zwick, 1996), the army chose not to do so, judging that it did

---

[33] Jean-Marc Lehu (2005) Le placement de marques au cinéma, proposition de la localisation du placement à l'écran comme nouveau facteur d'efficacité potentielle, *Décisions Marketing*, 37, January–March, pp 17–31. See also Wayne Friedman (2002) *Minority Report* stars Lexus, Nokia, *Advertising Age*, 17 June, and Ron Grover (2002) Hollywood product placement, circa 2054, *BusinessWeek*, 17 June.

[34] Lawrence H Suide (2002) *Guts and Glory: The making of the American military image in film*, 2nd edn revised and extended, University Press of Kentucky, Lexington, KY.

[35] Jonathan Duffy (2005) Well placed, *BBC News Magazine*, 30 March.

not portray a positive image, something that could have had a harmful effect on recruitment.[36] Furthermore, when the army does not perceive any benefit, but the military scenes do not negatively affect its image, certain placements are accepted, and are then purely and simply invoiced to the film production. Thus, it cost US$3 million to bring eight Black Hawk helicopters to Morocco for the purposes of filming Ridley Scott's *Black Hawk Down* (2001).[37]

These are the cases of which brands dream: those that are sought-after by the scriptwriter or the filmmaker with the precise goal of lending credibility to a particular environment. Brad Bird and Jan Pinkava didn't forget to show the Eiffel Tower to make sure the audience locate the animation movie *Ratatouille* (2007) in Paris. For these placements, they do not ask for financial or technical support, but only for authorization to use registered trade marks. Since this type of placement had been relatively rare until that point, some might have been surprised to find a Chanel boutique in the streets of Paris in the animated film by Don Bluth and Gary Goldman, *Anastasia* (1997). The directors wanted to emphasize the fact that the scene was indeed taking place in Paris in the 1920s. The placement is very positive: the heroine is left obviously very happy following several purchases. However, the placement was not sought by the French luxury brand, which merely gave its approval. Chanel became the guarantee of credibility.

Finally, certain films are voluntarily linked with a particular product or brand: for example, the (genuine) magazine *Confetti* (2005), which organizes a competition in the Debbie Isitt comedy of the same name, or FedEx express delivery in *Cast Away* (Robert Zemeckis, 2000), since the plot hinges on one of the company's employees. Even beyond the realism legitimately sought by the director, however, it is possible that some placements are judged to be indispensable for the story to appear credible, or simply to increase its authenticity. Certain critics have pointed the finger at what they judge to be too-obvious appearances of logos, brand names or even the commercial name of the airline Pan Am in the 2002 film directed by Steven Spielberg, *Catch Me If You Can*. We should bear in mind that the storyline is inspired by the true story of the life of Frank Abagnale Jr, whom the FBI had tracked over several years for having usurped various identities, principally to the detriment of Pan Am. Moreover, at the time the film was being made, the airline had already been out of business for a considerable length of time. The use of a fictitious name would have been possible, but the film's credibility would naturally have suffered as a result. An identical case concerns the now defunct

---

[36] The story in the movie tells the dramatic case of friendly fire causing the death of several soldiers. It further shows surviving soldiers contradicting themselves while explaining the accidental circumstances, and hiding some evidence.

[37] Katharine Q Seelye (2002) When Hollywood's big guns come right from the source, *New York Times*, 10 June.

car brand Tucker in the film *Tucker: The Man and His Dream* (Francis Ford Coppola, 1988), which tells the industrial saga of Preston Thomas Tucker. The same is true for Martin Scorsese's film *The Aviator* (2004): it would be impossible not to cite TWA, given that the film tells the life story of Howard Hughes, who was the company's owner.

In Peter Jackson's 2005 film *King Kong*, the story is set in 1933 and various scenes take place in the streets of New York. An alert viewer will have noted the care that Peter Jackson brought to the production. The shots of Times Square, which is habitually filled with brands and company names,[38] are in fact highly realistic; their sobriety is more appropriate to the year 1933. Likewise, it is possible to identify brand placements for Fisk tyres, and the frontage of a Woolworth store, for example: two brands that are now extinct in the US, but did exist in the era during which the film is set, and which contribute to the natural credibility of the film.

The creation of internal commercial synergies

In the Angela Robinson film *Herbie: Fully Loaded* (2005), one of the characters gains a 'super cool' job (sic) as assistant producer at ESPN, a channel devoted to sport and which belongs to the Walt Disney Company, also producer of the film. In the same film, Tropicana orange juice benefits from a highly visible and particularly positive placement. Tropicana is also the official sponsor of the Nascar stock car races, which are at the centre of the film.[39] In the majority

---

[38] Times Square in Manhattan lures an average of 40 million visitors each year. Kodak's research estimates that Times Square appears on more than 100 million photos every year. See in particular Abbey Klaassen (2006) Corona ads change Times Square's iconic view, *Advertising Age*, 16 February. For a real-time interactive check, connect for example to: www.earthcam.com/usa/newyork/timessquare/interactive. phpp

[39] Ross Johnson (2005) Product placement for the whole family, *New York Times*, 6 July. Other scenarios got inspiration from NASCAR, for example Tony Scott's *Days of Thunder* (1990), and in 2006, Adam McKay's *Talladega Nights: The ballad of Ricky Bobby*. In this case, the story is almost entirely focused on NASCAR. It was the opportunity for a 'few' brand placements such as 3M, 76 Lubricants, ACDelco, Advanced Auto Parts, Applebee's, Baby Einstein, Baccarat, Bain de Soleil, Barilla, Bell, Big Red, Bosch, Budweiser, Cadillac, Caterpillar, Checkers, Chevrolet, CitiFinancial, Clevite, Coca-Cola, Commit, Coors, Country Crock, Craftsman, Dickies, Dodge, Domino's Pizza, Dynacorp, EA Sports, ESPN, FedEx, Fig Newton, Food Lions, Ford, Fox, Gillette, Goodyear, Halliburton, Havoline, Honda, Hummer, Jenga, Jesel, Jim Beam, KFC, Kodak, Lowe's, Lucky Charms, M&M's, Mac Tools, mbna, McDonald's, Michelob, Mobil, Moog, Mopar, Motorola, Mountain Dew, MTV, NBC, NetZero, Nextel, Old Spice, Pepsi, Perrier, Playgirl, Powerade, Puma, QVC, Rally's Hamburgers, Re/MAX,

of sporting video games designed by Electronic Arts, 'EA Sports' logos are visible on the players' equipment or on advertising billboards inserted into the game. In 2005, in the series *Navy NCIS*, by Donald P Bellisario, the character Tony DiNozzo, played by Michael Weatherly, switches on a television series from the 1980s, and *Magnum P.I.* is being shown on repeat. It just so happens that that series was produced by Donald P Bellisario.

In 2006, in the animated film *The Ant Bully* (produced by Warner Brothers), John A Davis alludes directly to *Harry Potter*, another saga produced by Warner Brothers. The major international communications companies are often present in various media. The News Corporation group owns, for example, the film production studios 20th Century Fox, the magazines *Inside Out, The Weekly Standard* and *Big League*, HarperCollins publishers, the newspapers *The Times*, the *Daily Telegraph*, the *Sun* and the *New York Post*, and the television channels Sky, Fox and Star, to mention but a few. It is easy to imagine the innumerable synergies that it is possible to create within such an empire.

Synergies are sometimes expedited by the screenplay. *King Kong* (Peter Jackson, 2005) involves – a film director! The placement of production studios is therefore not incongruous. The choice of Universal Studios seems all the more logical given that it was also the production studio of the film itself.[40] These commercial synergy operations are very common, but are not necessarily perceived as such by the public at large, who are not always aware of the interactions between one group or one company and another. By way of example, an attentive viewer of *Killer Instinct*, produced and broadcast by Fox, might have noticed that on the desk of Lieutenant Matt Cavanaugh (played by Chi McBride), a mug regularly appears on which can be clearly seen the OLN logo, the initials of Outdoor Life Network, a smaller sister channel of the Fox network.

Still on the subject of Fox, some may have spotted the Fox channel in *Minority Report* (2002), or in *Fantastic 4* (2005), both of them produced and distributed by 20th Century Fox, of course! The magazine *Popular Science* (from the Time Warner Inc group) could be seen in the film *Scooby-Doo 2: Monsters Unleashed* (Raja Gosnell, 2004), a Warner Bros production (from the Time Warner Inc group). Mickey Mouse was mentioned in *Chicken Little* (Mark Dindal, 2005), a film produced by Walt Disney Pictures. In another animated film by the studio, *The Wild* (2006), the director Steve Williams takes his heroes through Times Square: he does not forget to place, among

---

Sharpie, Sony Vaio, Sparco, Speed Channel, Sprint, Subway, Sunoco, Taco Bell, Target, Tide, United Auto Workers (UAW), USG, Vanson Leathers, Visa, Waffle House, Wal-Mart, Winnebago, Wonder Bread, among the most prominent ones. See also Rich Thomaselli (2006) Movie gives wonder bread worth $4.3 million, *Advertising Age*, 7 August.

[40] RKO Pictures studios are also subject to a brand placement in the movie.

Toys'R'Us, McDonald's, Kodak, TiVo, Quaker and more logos, the ABC network logo, a subsidiary of the same group as the production studio. The CBS channel could be seen in Steven Spielberg's *War of the Worlds* (2005), since the channel and the production studios Paramount belong to the same group, Viacom.[41]

Such synergies can also occur between studios. In 2005, in the *Medium* series produced by NBC, a scene was rewritten especially to allow a group of friends to attend the premiere of the film *Memoirs of a Geisha*, by Rob Marshall, principally produced by Columbia Pictures. This rewriting of the script followed an agreement between NBC and Sony (owner of Columbia Pictures).[42]

The major groups can also create synergies by means of grouped placement contracts. For seasons 8–10 of *Survivor* (CBS), the Procter & Gamble group signed a contract regarding 20 of its brands, thereby becoming one of the show's four biggest advertisers. The contract comprised tie-in operations from *Survivor 8* onwards, and placements in *Survivor 10*. The promotional operation set up in parallel invited consumers to buy at least three of the products concerned within the framework of a game with questions based on the *Survivor* programme.[43]

Such grouped contracts allowed the creation of synergies between products, and, of course, the benefits of more favourable prices overall. The production studios now themselves identify the possible synergies between their activities and the products of subsidiaries of sister companies of their group. Looking for the brand of the television set in Professor Jules Hilbert's (played by Dustin Hoffman) office in the film *Stranger Than Fiction* (Marc Forster, 2006)? Sony, of course! Sony products, or the Japanese brand itself, could be identified recently in *Catch and Release* (Susannah Grant, 2007), *Underworld: Evolution* (Len Wiseman, 2006), *RV* (Barry Sonnenfeld, 2006), *The Da Vinci Code* (Ron Howard, 2006), *Silent Hill* (Christophe Gans, 2006),

[41] On 3 January, 2006 Viacom Group was split in two. Viacom Incorporated is responsible for publishing activities, cable networks and thematic television networks, as well as Paramount studios and DreamWorks studios, while CBS Corporation is responsible for CBS TV Network, UP Channel, and audiovisual production activities from Paramount and DreamWorks, including radio stations, billboard networks and entertainment parks. See in particular Eric Leser (2006) La scission Viacom-CBS pourrait ouvrir une nouvelle ère dans les media américains, *Le Monde*, 5 January.

[42] David Cohn (2005) TV writers must sell, sell, sell, *Wired Magazine*, 12 December.

[43] Concerned brands were Herbal Essences, Crest, Dawn, Infusium, Bounty, Pantene, Clairol, Olay, Cover Girl, Tide, Secret, Old Spice, Oral Care, Pepto-Bismol, Aussie, Charmin, Zest, Pur, Pringles and Downy. They came from different business sectors, which facilitated cross-selling to consumers. See in particular Jack Neff (2003) P&G announces 20 brand tie-in with *Survivor*, *Advertising Age*, 19 December.

Casino Royale (Martin Campbell, 2006), *The Pursuit of Happyness* (Gabriele Muccino, 2006), *Click* (Frank Coraci, 2006), *Talladega Nights: The Ballad of Ricky Bobby* (Adam McKay, 2006), *The Covenant* (Renny Harlin, 2006), *The Fog* (Rupert Wainwright, 2005), *Hitch* (Andy Tennant, 2005), *Bad Boys 2* (Michael Bay, 2003) *50 First Dates* (Peter Segal, 2004), *S.W.A.T.* (Clark Johnson, 2003), *Resident Evil: Apocalypse* (Alexander Witt, 2004), *You Got Served* (Chris Stokes, 2004), *Something's Gotta Give* (Nancy Meyers, 2003), *Identity* (James Mangold, 2003), *Charlie's Angels: Full Throttle* (McG, 2003), *Men in Black II* (Barry Sonnenfeld, 2002) and *Panic Room* (David Fincher, 2002), in particular: all of them are films produced by Sony Pictures or by one of the studios owned by the company. It is an approach with a perfect economic logic. In the animated film *Open Season* (Roger Allers, Jill Culton and Anthony Stacchi, 2006). Boog, one of the characters, watches *Wheel of Fortune* on the television. Of course, this choice of programme was not a random one. It is produced by Sony Pictures, whose subsidiary Columbia Pictures produced the cartoon.

Finally, there is a synergy tip of the hat when in the film *The Island* (Michael Bay, 2005), the actress Scarlett Johansson, playing the clone of a famous actress, realizes that she is a clone when she sees an advertising film by the actress in question. It is an advertising film created for the Calvin Klein brand. In reality, the actress Scarlett Johansson was at the time the muse of the perfume Eternity Moment by Calvin Klein (a licence now managed by the Coty group).

PART II

Advantages and methods of the use of product placements

4 Product placement: a competitive means of communication

Frames, engines steering columns, bodies, fenders, wheels, all drop into place in apparently the right color sequence and just at the moment they are needed. Since automobile production was at a standstill, this array of components parts was not available. To solve this riddle we borrowed a dozen new cars from the Chrysler company and disassembled them so that we would be able to reassemble them for the camera.

(King Vidor on the filming of *An American Romance* (1944), when car production had been halted because of the war. King Vidor (1954) *A Tree is a Tree: An autobiography*, Longmans,Green & Co, London)

If product and brand placement is now so sought-after by advertisers, it is because it brings with it numerous advantages, particularly if an advertiser has few resources in comparison to its competitors.[1] This is an important point, since contrary to received wisdom, product placement is not a communication technique reserved only for the world's leading brands. Both the smaller actors in a market and the challengers can also make skilful use of it. In *Hostel* (2005), by Eli Roth, we find placements for leading brands such as Coca-Cola, M&M's, Motorola, Puma and Canon, but also for the more

---

[1] H Ronald Moser, Layne Bryant and Katie Sylvester (2004) Product placement as a marketing tool in film and television, *National Social Science Journal*, 22(1), pp 76–86.

modest Speed 8, a food supplements brand. In *Glory Road* (James Gartner, 2006) big names such as Chrysler, Spalding, Esso, Pontiac, Converse and United Airlines feature prominently in the credits, as does the small El Paso Texan radio station, Krod-AM 600.

The Apple communications budget is tiny compared with that of HP, Dell, NEC or Microsoft. This is why, in line with its positioning, Apple has always tried to communicate differently. As it happens, product placement is one promising possibility. Apple appeared recently in *Trust the Man* (Bart Freundlich, 2006), *Big Momma's House 2* (John Whitesell, 2006), *Sahara* (Breck Eisner, 2005), *Monster-in-Law* (Robert Luketic, 2005), *Hide and Seek* (John Polson, 2005), *Dodgeball* (Rawson Marshall Thurber, 2004), *The Forgotten* (Joseph Ruben, 2004), *Elf* (Jon Favreau, 2003), *School of Rock* (Richard Linklater, 2003) *The Recruit* (Roger Donaldson, 2003), *Mr Deeds* (Steven Brill, 2002), *SwimFan* (John Polson, 2002), *The Ring* (Gore Verbinski, 2002), *Bridget Jones's Diary* (Sharon Maguire, 2001), *Ocean's Eleven* (Steven Soderbergh, 2001) and *Vanilla Sky* (Cameron Crowe, 2001) among others.

Not all brand and product placements match up to a standard procedure of insertion into a feature film.[2] It is not a question of brutally 'tattooing' the film with such and such a logo or brand. Consumers themselves are often unhappy about placements, if they find them distracting.[3] Logically, the nature of the placement should derive first and foremost from the advertiser's objectives. In the final reckoning, however, it also depends on the imperatives of the production and the director's wishes.[4] Finally, not all placements are welcome. In 2003, Allied Domecq rejected the placement of its Stolichnaya vodka, which was proposed for the Terry Zwigoff film *Bad Santa*: in it, Billy

---

[2] Jean-Marc Lehu (2005) Le placement de marques au cinéma, proposition de la localisation du placement à l'écran comme nouveau facteur d'efficacité potentielle, *Décisions Marketing*, 37, January–March, pp 17–31. One of the most comprehensive available works about the sum of academic knowledge on the subject has probably been presented by Siva K Balasubramanian, James A Karrh and Hemant Patwardhan in 2006, in their article Audience response to product placements: an integrative framework and future research agenda, *Journal of Advertising*, 25(3), Fall, pp 115–41. It is a comprehensive analytical work that clearly explains the characteristics of the process. More specifically it shows that the execution of the placement and the individual-specific factors as brand familiarity, judgment of the placement fit, and attitudes toward those placements, influence processing depth which in turn affects message outcomes. See also Ignacio Redondo (2006) Product placement planning: How is the industry placing brands in relation to moviegoer consumption? *Journal of International Consumer Marketing*, 18(4), pp 33–55.

[3] Claire Atkinson (2003) Merger of advertising and content worries consumers, *Advertising Age*, 6 January.

[4] Janet Wasko, Mark Phillips and Chris Purdie (1993) Hollywood meets Madison Avenue: the commercialization of US films, *Media, Culture, and Society*, 15(2), pp 271–93.

Bob Thornton was playing an alcoholic and violent character, who could very quickly have changed the brand's image.[5]

According to the analysis of Richard Heslin, professor of psychology at Purdue University, a viewer's anti-advertising 'defences' are lowered at the cinema, thereby offering brands an opportunity to communicate that may be very competitive.[6] Brand awareness can be concretely reinforced. The more the brand is seen or heard, the better the chances that it will be remembered. A relatively high frequency can induce the consumer to believe that the brand is very well-known and, in certain cases, that it is probably better.[7] Admittedly, some will be quick to say that this is not nearly enough. But even if the placement only contributed to increasing familiarity with the brand, this would facilitate its introduction to or its preservation on our 'mental

---

[5] Nevertheless, the director used a bottle of Stolichnaya vodka covering only its name, which was not at all to please the brand, as the bottle remained recognizable. The Distilled Spirits Council of the United States and the Beer Institute (the trade associations for the spirits and beer industries) recommend to their members to limit advertising and product placement to audiences which comprise no more than 30 per cent of individuals under the legal drinking age. See especially Gail Schiller (2005) Ties-in often sobering for liquor firms, *Hollywood Reporter*, 3 August.

[6] Heslin Richard (1999) Movies may carry a hidden pitch, *USA Today*, 1 December. Several research projects tend to prove that the placements do not need to be consciously recalled in order to influence the viewer's brand attitude. This is clearly an illustration of the mere exposure effect detailed by Robert Zajonc, especially if the placement is repeated during the film, show or other medium. See Robert B Zajonc (1968) Attitudinal effects of mere exposure, *Journal of Personality and Social Psychology Monographs*, 9, supplement 2, part 2, pp 1–27. For an application to product placements in television shows, see in particular Jörg Matthes, Christian Schemer and Werner Wirth (2006) More than meets the eye: investigating the hidden impact of brand placements in television magazines, paper presented to the Association for Education in Journalism and Mass Communication Conference, Advertising Division, 2–5 August, San Francisco, CA.

[7] See in particular research from Alan G Sawyer (2006) Possible psychological processes underlying the effectiveness of brand placement, in Comments, ed John Ford, *Journal of International Advertising*, 25(1), pp 107–14; See also William E Baker, J Wesley Hutchinson, Danny Moore and Prakash Nedungadi (1986) Brand familiarity and advertising: effects on the evoked set and brand preferences, *Advances in Consumer Research*, 13, ed Richard J Lutz, Provo, Utah, Association for Consumer Research, pp 146–47; James A Karrh (1995) Brand placements in feature films: the practitioner's view, *Proceedings of the Conference of the American Academy of Advertising*, ed Charles S Madden, AAA, Athens, GA, pp 182–88; and Shonall Sabherwal, Jim Pokrywczynski and Robert Griffin (1994) Brand-recall for product placements in motion pictures: a memory-based perspective, paper presented to the Association for Education in Journalism and Mass Communication Conference, 10–13 August, Atlanta, GA.

agenda', which is a considerable achievement in itself, given the competition supplied by all the other brands that surround us.[8]

However, a placement can also become an image vector. If the tailor Brioni dresses James Bond, 'The image never ages. What you are dressing is an icon. He is a symbol of eternal youth and the ideal connoisseur' said Umberto Angeloni, the chairman of Brioni.[9] Vans never imagined that it would be projected to the forefront of the scene, to the point of becoming the reference for skate shoes,[10] by being placed in the small teen comedy *Fast Times at Ridgemont High* (Amy Heckerling, 1982) with Sean Penn. However, not all product placements share the same fate. Despite all the efforts put into it, a film can be an enormous failure, ruining the hopes of its partners in just a few days of showing in cinemas. One of the examples quoted most often in this respect is from 1987: the Richard Fleischer film *Million Dollar Mystery*. The film's total takings barely reached US$989,033 (or just US$708.50 per cinema)! The film's storyline involved an important placement for Glad dustbin bags.

A technique accepted by the audience

The vast majority of studies conducted on the subject confirm an overall tolerance among audiences for the placement of products or brands, and even an appreciation of the approach in certain cases of successful integration,[11]

---

[8] For more information about the mental agenda and its role, see in particular Maxwell McCombs and Donald Shaw (1972) The agenda-setting function of mass media, *Public Opinion Quarterly*, 36, pp 176–85; and also Max Sutherland and John Galloway (1981) Role of advertising: persuasion or agenda-setting? *Journal of Advertising Research*, 21(5), pp 25–9. Also see Maxwell McCombs (1992) Explorers and surveyors: expanding strategies for agenda setting research, *Journalism Quarterly*, 69, pp 813–24. For a specific study about hotel name placements, see in particular Robert A Nozar (2001) Product placements help heighten brand exposure, *Hotel and Motel Management*, 216(9), pp 3, 5. About alcoholic beverages placements' efficiency, see in particular Mark Greer (2003) Going Hollywood: beverage companies are dealing with advertising overload with less traditional tie-ins, *Beverage Industry*, 1 May.

[9] Guy Trebay (2002) Buy like Bond; make it a Finlandia and 7Up, shaken not stirred, *New York Times*, 27 October.

[10] Alycia de Mesa (2004) Sports brands play at life style, *Brandchannel Newsletter*, 25 October.

[11] Israel D Nebenzahl and Eugene Secunda (1993) Consumer's attitudes toward product placement in movies, *International Journal of Advertising*, 12(1), pp 1–11; Rungpaka Tiwsakul and Chris Hackley (2005) Ethics and regulation of contemporary marketing communication practices: an exploration of the perceptions of UK-based consumers towards the ethical issues raised by product placement in British TV shows, research paper SoMo502, School of Management, London University, Royal Holloway, Egham, Surrey; Yayoi Anzai (2003) The perception of Japanese university

especially among regular viewers.[12] Following a survey among US consumers, MindShare observed that 80 per cent of respondents liked this new form of advertising.[13] In order to benefit from a positive perception, the most important thing is to respect the rule of a tolerable and justified presence. In 2005, in Canada, the cookery programme *The Next Great Chef* proposed, and obtained, a placement by the Knorr brand. There was a natural logic between the product and the nature of the programme.[14]

A well-orchestrated placement is therefore more likely to be positive not only for brand awareness, but also for the brand's image.[15] In *Author! Author!* (Arthur Hiller, 1982), Al Pacino plays the part of a playwright, who, along with all the cast members of his latest play, is waiting impatiently for a review by the *New York Times*, cited and presented as the absolute reference. In *Entrapment* (1999), by Jon Amiel, Sean Connery and Catherine Zeta-Jones play high-class thieves for whom precision is essential. The placement of a Casio G-Shock watch on the wrist of each is therefore a particularly judicious choice by the brand. It subtly expresses the quality of its precision, its reliability even in extreme circumstances, and in particular for burglars, for whom exactitude is essential.[16] In the film *I, Robot* (Alex Proyas, 2004), Will Smith does not

---

students concerning product placement in Hollywood movies, *Economic Journal of Takasaki City University of Economics*, 46(3), pp 107–16. See also Paul J Gough (2004) Consumers respond favourably to product placement of brands in TV, movies, *MediaPost*, 22 April. It is nevertheless legitimate to question this tolerance and ask whether it will stay positive in the future, especially if the number of placements continues to rise quickly and without control. See in particular the very interesting paper from Barbara B Stern and Cristel A Russell (2004) Consumer responses to product placement in television sitcoms: genre, sex and consumption, *Consumption, Markets and Culture*, 7(4) pp 371–94.

[12] Pola B Gupta and Siva J Gould (1997) Consumers' perceptions of the ethics and acceptability of product placements in movies: product category and individual differences, *Journal of Current Issues and Research in Advertising*, 20(1), pp 47–59.

[13] David Kaplan (2005) Product placement: well-placed among consumers, *MediaPost*, 25 March.

[14] Keith McArthur and Grant Robertson (2005) CRTC ponders impact of product placement, *Globe and Mail*, 1 November.

[15] See in particular the paper presented by Carol J Pardun and Kathy Brittain McKee (1996) What advertising agency media directors have to say about placing clients' products in motion pictures, Association for Education in Journalism and Mass Communication Conference, 10–13 August, Anaheim, CA, and the one from Daragh O'Reilly, Rachel Cripps, Efstathia Kazani, Reshma Patel and Angeliki Zarra (2005) Interpretation of product placement by UK movie-goers: a qualitative study, 34th European Marketing Academy conference (EMAC), Milan, 24–27 May.

[16] In 2003, for F Gary Gray's *The Italian Job*, the actor Mark Wahlberg also plays a burglar who uses a Casio G-Shock watch. It illustrates the relevancy of the brand's placements, with a consistent positioning, but also the property masters' interest in the product and the brand.

restrict himself merely to wearing Converse shoes, but clearly expresses his personal preference for them.

Certain brands like to be placed in films set in the past, in order to highlight their long existence, and sometimes exploit the nostalgia by providing or recreating old models or old packaging. Many other brands are equally interested in being placed in futuristic films. Gigantic outdoor advertisements for Pan Am, Bell, Coca-Cola and Atari appear in Ridley Scott's *Blade Runner* (1982), set in 2019; Coca-Cola also figures in the highly aesthetic *Renaissance* (Christian Volckman, 2006), set in Paris in 2054; Nike and Pepsi-Cola are present in the consumerist world of *Back to the Future* (Robert Zemeckis, 1989) showing the world of 2015; *USA Today* (becoming *Mars Today* for the purpose) is read on Mars in *Total Recall* (Paul Verhoeven, 1990), which takes place in 2084. Gap occupies an entire scene in *Minority Report* (Steven Spielberg, 2002), which takes place in 2054. FedEx is the referenced express messenger service for all kinds of deliveries in *I, Robot* (2004), which is set in 2035. Puma is the only shoe available in the complex of *The Island* (Michael Bay, 2005), set in 2019. The majority of these placements show prototype products that will never be sold. Not only is it a futuristic universe, which is positive for the perceived age of the brand, but the brand also sends an implicit message that in this future period – the time in which the story is set – it is likely that it will still exist and still form part of the daily lives of consumers, even if it has sometimes disappeared between now and then.

For car makers, the cost of making a prototype can run to millions of dollars, but it is also an opportunity to create an international shop window for their concept car. Ford joined in the game with a variant of the Taurus, for *RoboCop* (Paul Verhoeven, 1987), where the action takes place shortly before the year 2000; General Motors imagined the vehicle of the future for *Demolition Man* (Marco Brambilla, 1993), set in 2032; Lexus designed the car of the future in *Minority Report* and Audi the RSQ Sport Coupé in *I, Robot* (see Figure 4.1). In the latter case, the operation was initiated by the Genevan agency Propaganda, to which the German brand, enthused by the project, dedicated a team of engineers and technicians, who managed to complete the job in barely eight weeks. On the other hand, does a child of the twenty-first century still see a futuristic placement for Pan Am[17] in the now-past future of *2001: A Space Odyssey* (Stanley Kubrick, 1968)?

---

[17] Pan American World Airways was founded in 1926 by John Montgomery and Richard Bevier. It was the first air company in the world, but it finally went bankrupt on 4 December 1991. Since the end of the 1990s the Pan Am brand name has been sold and used by different businesses.

Figure 4.1 Prototype Audi RSQ Sport Coupé used in the film *I, Robot* (2004). Visuals reproduced by kind permission of Audi.

A potentially powerful vector of positive image

When Myrna Loy mentions the Cartier brand for Clark Gable to hear, in W S Van Dyke's *Manhattan Melodrama* (1934), the name of the jeweller is given as the absolute reference in the business. When the endearing character of Sam Wheat, played by Patrick Swayze, in *Ghost* (Jerry Zucker, 1990), wears Reebok trainers, the brand profits from his likeability. In *Meet the Fockers* (Jay

Roach, 2004), Robert De Niro boasts explicitly about the merits of his new Fleetwood coach. If James Bond is associated with the Evian brand in Lee Tamahori's *Casino Royale* (2006), it is positive for Evian because Agent 007 has a good image, sportive and elegant. It is also positive for James Bond, since the water of Evian is objectively known for its mineral qualities. Having the actor Michael Douglas boast of the qualities of the Gulfstream V jet while it is in flight, in *The In-Laws* (Andrew Fleming, 2003), yields more image points than a simple advertisement designed with the same objective. In *The Terminal* (Steven Spielberg, 2004), the character played by Tom Hanks buys a Hugo Boss suit in one of the brand's boutiques, and only minutes later talks up its price and quality to the actress Catherine Zeta-Jones. In each case, the brand image is clearly supported by the characters.

A great number of brands entered the twenty-first century with an image altered by years of crisis, heavily penalized by repeated price wars, handicapped by incomprehensible errors of strategy, wounded by unscrupulous, if not plain ignorant, brand managers, whose short-term objective was simply to achieve a significant result quickly, which would allow them to sell their services more highly elsewhere. It is true that we should not systematically condemn them, since the pressures of hierarchy and competition meant that they were (and still are) sometimes forced to make far-reaching decisions, with negative consequences for the brand's image capital. This is understandable, if not justifiable.

A product placement can lead to the generation of a positive attitude towards the product or the brand.[18] For a placement to become a vector of positive image for the product, it 'only' needs to be done well! Put in these simple terms, the observation seems undeniably naive. And yet! It is a question of giving the brand a full role in its own right, at the appropriate moment, and not simply a bit-part; a role that adds value both to the brand and the film; a role that adds value to the brand and the actor. In short, it needs an exchange whereby each of the parties can benefit from the placement operation, while additionally considering that they are dealing with increasingly wary consumers.[19]

According to Jean-Patrick Flandé, of Film Média Consultant, it is necessary for 'the product to be invited on board, the ideal viewer is the unwary viewer'. 'Our aim is to carry out a creative and gentle integration', explains

---

[18] Isabelle Fontaine (2005) Brand placement in movies: a matter of exposure, 34th European Marketing Academy conference (EMAC), Milan, 24–27 May. As a powerful potential image medium, the placement does not concern only a brand and/or a product, of course. The *CSI* TV series and the many films like Curtis Hanson's *Lucky You* (2007) that take place in Las Vegas have contributed a lot to the city's image all around the world.

[19] David Natharius (2004) When product placement is *not* product placement: reflections of a movie junkie, *Journal of Promotion Management*, 10(1/2), pp 213–18.

Ruben Igielko-Herrlich, one of two directors of the Swiss placement agency Propaganda.[20] At OMD USA, Ray Warren calls for it to be 'organic, building in our clients without it being too obvious to viewers'. The words of Brian Scott Frons, managing director of ABC Daytime, offer the perfect conclusion: 'The ultimate test for good integration is if the characters would do the same exact thing'.[21] It is not a question of imposing the brand, of tacking it on to a scene, but of integrating it as well as possible into the environment and inviting it to participate. Then, the association can become very positive.

The presentation of Dell Computers as a recruiter of young IT talents in the early scenes of *The Recruit* (Roger Donaldson, 2003) contributed to building its image in research and development, and more simply as that of an assembler of detached units destined to form a computer. A film tells a story. The opportunities for potential promotions are therefore numerous. The objective is not to sing the brand's praises, as in several excessive cases criticized by the American writers' guild towards the end of 2005[22] – the viewers themselves would be quick to criticize and reject this – but simply to make the brand appear in favourable conditions. However sometimes wild praise does work, as in the Ivan Reitman comedy *Evolution* (2001), in which David Duchovny foils an alien invasion with the help of Head & Shoulders shampoo. The approach can even have marketing advantages: although the location had aged somewhat, the film *Moulin Rouge!* (Baz Luhrmann, 2001) contributed to rejuvenating and affirming the image of the legendary Parisian cabaret, which had simultaneously adopted a genuine redynamization strategy.

An image, however, is by definition fragile and subject to fluctuations. Placing a Nokia telephone in the hands of the actress Halle Berry, bottles of Dasani water in her refrigerator, and having her use an Apple portable computer in *Catwoman* (Pitof, 2004), where she plays the leading role of the avenger, is positive for all these brands. In contrast, when the actress was awarded the 2005 Razzie award for worst actress for her performance in *Catwoman*, and she commented on the subject, 'I want to thank Warner Bros for casting me in this piece-of-s... movie',[23] this was not necessarily a positive

---

[20] Laetitia Wilder (2006) Propaganda, la PME genevoise reine de la pub subliminale, *Bilan*, 201, March, pp 42–45.

[21] Stuart Elliott (2004) There's no place to turn: more embedded pitches will lurk in TV shows, *New York Times*, 17 June. See also on this subject, research by Claire Sherman (2004) Product integration in television: an Australian industry perspective, recall, Australian and New Zealand Marketing Academy Conference (ANZMAC), Victoria University, Wellington, New Zealand, 29 November–1 December.

[22] T L Stanley (2005) Writers guild protest TV product placements, *Advertising Age*, 27 September. See also Jesse Hiestand (2006) Guilds picket over placement, *Hollywood Reporter*, 9 February.

[23] Xan Brooks (2005) Razzie Berry gives a fruity performance, *Guardian*, 27 February.

factor. That is not to mention undesired negative placements, such as that of Guy Georges, the seven-times murderer known as 'the beast of the Bastille', who arrived at his trial in Paris (France) before the cameras of television journalists, wearing a polo shirt carrying a large and unmistakable Umbro logo. Cases of parasitic placements are analysed later in the book.

A highly variable price, a relatively low cost

In 1975, Clairol apparently paid US$10,000 to have its goods appear in Michael Ritchie's film *Smile*. Ten years later, the California Raisin Board is thought to have paid US$25,000 dollars to be seen in Robert Zemeckis's *Back to the Future* (1985). In 1992, France Télécom apparently disbursed €450,000 for a divine telephone call in Claude Lelouch's *La Belle Histoire*. Ford apparently had to out-bid BMW by several million dollars (US$30–40 million in total, according to sources) to see an Aston Martin reappear in the adventures of James Bond, in *Die Another Day* (2002). In the final account, however, these prices have no meaning. The price of a placement is impossible to determine in absolute terms, at the risk of falling into the deepest incoherence. At one end of the scale, a sum is paid by the studio to the brand for some 'placements', because the screenplay requires a certain specific, and indispensable, prop or product. This was the case, for example, for access to a TGV (high-speed train) from the SNCF (French national rail company) in *Mission: Impossible* (Brian de Palma, 1996).[24] In the middle of the scale, there is no payment but simply provision of goods by the brand, as with Virgin Cola in the film *La Boîte* (Claude Zidi, 2001). At the other end of the scale, certain very favourable placements, planned for very large productions, can represent an investment of several million dollars for a brand wishing to participate in the project. To establish an average would not be very relevant when there is such variation.

It is therefore not possible to give exact prices for a 'standard' placement, given that there simply is no standard placement.[25] However, the following mathematical formula is often quoted by certain experts: if initially a 'classic' visual placement costs X dollars, the same placement with the spoken mention of the brand name will cost on average twice X dollars. As for the same placement, but with the product being used by one of the actors, it is safe to assume on average three times X dollars.[26] However, this rule is not so much

---

[24] Laurent Raphaël (2003) Casting de marques pour les longs métrages, *La Libre Belgique*, 3 January.

[25] Gail Schiller (2005) Industry seeks formula to value product integration, *Hollywood Reporter*, 30 December.

[26] Direct contacts between the actor and the brand, before the film pre-production, are considered here. For instance, before the shooting of Peter Howitt's *Sliding*

simple as simplistic: these same experts are often incapable of providing a precise calculation method, because the price will depend on so many variables.

Furthermore, the figures given in the press are often overall sums: this allows the media to exploit the shock effect. In reality, these sums bring together numerous items that are complementary, but differ widely one from the other, and are not necessarily linked to the placement itself. It may be a question of a logistical service, of a contribution in kind of products and props required for filming (computers, cars, jewellery, audiovisual equipment and so on), of preferential conditions for a loan of materials, of tie-in advertising when the film is released, and other issues. The multiple meetings carried out for this book with placement professionals brought to light that among the principal elements influencing the price are the factors listed below. Naturally, the disclosure of a possible surcharge should be considered, all other factors being otherwise constant and comparable.

Factors that can influence the cost of a placement

The brand's fame

The bigger this is, the higher the entrance fee will be. The strong awareness of an international brand, for example, can naturally legitimize a higher cost than a placement for a small local brand, for which sometimes only permission to use trade marks, if necessary, is requested. The University of Nevada, mentioned in *Dodgeball* (Rawson Marshall Thurber, 2004), does not necessarily have the same renown as MIT, mentioned in *National Treasure* (Jon Turteltaub, 2004).

Identification of the brand

Certain products are placed/used without, however, the brand being readily identifiable. This is the typical case with stealth placements. The more the brand is identifiable by name, the higher the cost can rise. In the film *Paycheck*

Doors (1998), Calvin Klein directly offered the main actress, Gwyneth Paltrow, the possibility of creating her entire wardrobe for the film. Pleased, the actress proposed the idea to the Miramax studios who were handling the project, and it was accepted. See in particular Craig Stephens and Regina Molaro (2005) Product screening, *License!* March, pp 22–27.

(John Woo, 2003), cars, motorcycles, the name, the logo and a dealer for the BMW brand are seen and mentioned.

The film's budget

Here again we find the small production/big production contrast, with at first glance a higher cost for the latter. You might be forgiven for thinking that large-scale productions, already richly endowed, would not be interested in a budget supplement from a placement. This is partly true, but they are always interested in placement contracts that will bring reciprocal promotion operations to support the film's release. For several years now, the promotional 'budget' offered by brands partnering a James Bond adventure has been equivalent to, if not greater than, its production costs.

The type and genre of the film

Placements can also sometimes be found in small, independent productions. The Windex[27] cleaner by SC Johnson is almost a central element in the comedy *My Big Fat Greek Wedding* (Joel Zwick, 2002). Naturally, however, even if some of these films achieve major international success, the initial financial ambitions of the producers can hardly carry the same weight as those of an extremely large international production. After the success of the first film, *Spider-Man 2* (Sam Raimi, 2004) was almost guaranteed a warm reception from the public. Result: Bloomingdale's, Burger King, Nike, Rolaids, Columbia University, D'Agostino, Dr Pepper, eBay, BMW, Fritos, Joe's Pizza, Canon, Mercedes, NASA, Steinway & Sons and Bloomberg, among others, placed their brands there.

---

[27] The brand and the product are seen many times in the film, as they seem 'essential' to the father of the bride. The movie production cost did not exceed US$5 million, making the film an unpretentious little production. However, domestic gross was US$241.438 million, to which we must add US$127.305 million from the international market, making a total of US$368.743 million (source Box Office Mojo LLC, November 2006). It was one of the top-grossing motion pictures of 2002. For a semiotic analysis of the placement, see the communication paper from Charles Leech and Kevin September (2004) Semiotic and narrative congruence: leveraging consumer insights through product placement, *Esomar Consumer Insight Conference*, Vienna, April 2004. About the influence of the movie genre and the fact that comedy may not systematically outrank the other genres on brand recall, as it is sometimes admitted, and about the surprising potential of the science fiction genre, see Steven David Garza (2005) The influence of movie genre on audience reaction to product placement, paper presented to the Association for Education in Journalism and Mass Communication Conference, 10–13 August, San Antonio, Texas.

The film's credits

The producer's name, as well as that of the director and the actors, has value. It is linked to his or her past films, salary, or simply his or her fame and image. Moreover, it is often capitalized on to promote the film. Consequently, it is understandable that this value comes at a price, and can in some cases contribute to raising the cost for a placement. The chance to appear alongside Denzel Washington, already an Oscar-winner, and in a Tony Scott film to boot, in *Man on Fire* (2004), attracted notably Puma, Coca-Cola, Mercedes, Motorola, Casio, Chevrolet, Tabasco and Brother.

The barter deal

In certain cases (the majority, in fact), the recompense for the placement is not financial. It is the company's decision which of the cost criteria should be used – intermediary concession price, market price, transfer cost, reconstituted cost – to determine the final cost of the placement. BMW did not pay for the placement of Mini cars in the film *The Italian Job* (F Gary Gray, 2003), but did, however, provide 32 vehicles matching the specific requirements of the production,[28] while General Motors notably supplied the set of *The Matrix Reloaded* (Andy and Larry Wachowski, 2003) with 24 prototype Cadillac CTS and Escalade EXP cars.

The importance of the placement

The more space the placement takes up onscreen (in close-ups, for example), the longer it remains on screen and the more scenes in which it appears, the higher the cost. In *Minority Report* (2002), Tom Cruise is in a race against time and regularly checks his Bulgari watch, always seen in the centre of the screen.

The location of the placement

As with a shop, not all scenes of a film, or all areas of a cinema screen, necessarily have the same potential for impact. If the placement takes place in a scene of great intensity, and likewise if the brand name is close to the centre of the screen, there may be a placement premium added to the cost. In *Sideways* (Alexander Payne, 2004), wine is a central element of the screenplay, and tasting sessions often provide the opportunity for a central close-up on the beverage.

---

[28] Scott Donaton (2004) *Madison+Vine, Advertising Age,* McGraw-Hill, New York.

Integration into the story

Because of the higher impact that it is thought to create, the integration of a placement into the story calls for a cost premium over the simple appearance of the brand in the background of a scene. In one case of integration, the journalist Polly Perkins, played by the actress Gwyneth Paltrow, uses a Leica camera in *Sky Captain and the World of Tomorrow* (Kerry Conran, 2004).

Contact with the principal actors

Integration can reach the point of use by one of the principal actors. Main actor John Cena chooses Coca-Cola from a fridge at a gas station, in *The Marine* (John Bonito, 2006). This contact often provides the opportunity for a testimonial (usually unspoken) by the actor, and the placement is therefore more expensive in most cases, since it is completed by the actor's implicit fee. In the film *Rain Man* (Barry Levinson, 1998), the character of Raymond Babbitt, played by Dustin Hoffman, refuses to travel by plane unless it is with the Australian airline Qantas, whose planes never crash (sic)! In certain cases, the testimonial is matched with a specific payment to the actor, particularly if his or her image is to be used later by the brand. For example, in *Someone Like You* (Tony Goldwyn, 2001), Ashley Judd confines herself to eating Ben & Jerry's ice cream onscreen. In another case, like Daniel Craig now, Pierce Brosnan wore an Omega watch in James Bond, and the Swiss brand used the actor simultaneously for its advertising communication. Such a case justifies the drawing-up of a specific parallel contract.

Exclusivity for the brand

As with other advertising media, too many placements risk the dissipation of the viewer's attention. The fewer different placements a film contains, the higher the cost may be. A cost premium is also possible if the brand can be assured that no competitor will be placed. Errors excepted, only the Ford brand is really identifiable in *Planet of the Apes* (Tim Burton, 2001). In *Sin City* (Robert Rodriguez and Frank Miller, 2005), in contrast, car placements are subject to ferocious competition: Cadillac, Porsche, Mercedes, Lincoln, Chevrolet, Chrysler, Ford, Jaguar and Ferrari, notably, are present onscreen.

Recurrent placements

Placements benefiting from a scene that is repeated in a film teaser or in one of the trailers used for the film's promotion, as well as brands appearing on the film's official website, can lead to higher prices. Before the film's release, Coca-Cola appeared in the trailer for *Millions* (Danny Boyle, 2004).

The distribution type

The greater the number of theatres planned for the film's release, and the higher the number of countries in which it will be shown, the more likely the placement is to be subject to a cost premium given the larger potential audience to which it is intended. *King Kong* (Peter Jackson, 2005) benefited from a production budget of US$207 million and was shown in 3,627 theatres in the United States alone on its release, while it was also released worldwide. We can imagine how before the film's success, such a multiplication of contact opportunities would have been irresistible to Nestlé, conspicuously present onscreen (see also, in Appendix 1, a press release detailing all the film's partnerships).

Accompanying communications

The more the advertiser agrees to organize and finance public relations operations, communications events, merchandising operations and advertising at point of purchase, and in some cases to co-finance the publicity campaign for the film's release, the more the specific cost of the placement will be reduced. Originally, the screenplay of the film *Must Love Dogs* (Gary David Goldberg, 2005) made generic mention of an internet dating site. It was modified to integrate as naturally as possible the site perfectmatch.com, which is central to the meeting between John Cusack and Diane Lane. However, there was no payment made for this placement. PerfectMatch provided the technical services required by the film and organized a reciprocal promotion (involving other partners such as the Lifetime channel and the flower delivery company 1800Flowers) upon its release, for an estimated budget of US$7 million.[29] Complementary partners such as MSNBC, iVillage and Drugstore. com participated in the accompanying communications, and in the tie-in games organized at the time.

The placement contract

Is it a 'straight' contract – that is, a contractually negotiated contract in exchange for payment – or is an agent commissioned to carry out the operation? The agent's fees are generally fixed as a percentage of the total contract.

---

[29] T L Stanley (2005) *Must Love Dogs* becomes product placement bonanza, *Madison+ Vine*, 13 July. About Perfectmatch.com product placement continuing strategy, see also Julie Bosman (2006) A match made in product placement heaven, *New York Times*, 31 May.

They vary, however (usually from a few per cent to as much as 30 per cent) according to the tasks entrusted to the agent, which might include:

- identification of placement opportunities;
- elaboration of an *ad hoc* contract;
- prior intervention to determine the technical modalities;
- legal validation;
- follow-up on execution during filming;
- advice on the editing;
- verification of reciprocal publicity on release;
- duration of contract.

The price can therefore vary enormously, but the provision is not at all the same.

These principal factors therefore constitute as many variables of a complex equation, the resolution of which may eventually give an 'idea' of the price of a placement. It is only an idea, however, since it does not factor in the numerous subjective or *intuitu personae* factors that can also play a part, such as the fact that the director likes the brand or product, that the producer has a personal relationship with one of the brand's managers, that the brand is indirectly linked to the production studio – all factors likely to reduce the price. It is easy to see that setting out a standard price is in reality meaningless.

In the vast majority of cases, however, proportionally, in terms of the net potential impact (number of individuals reached), the cost of a placement is still significantly lower than the referent systematically taken into consideration: the 30-second television spot, even if the prices have increased considerably over the last few years.[30] For even if the duration of a film's stay in cinemas is increasingly limited, one of the major advantages of product placements in the cinema is the extraordinary exponential multiplication of its potential impact.[31]

---

[30] No surprise at all. The demand is drastically increasing to reach to audiences lost from classic media, but the number of 'good' opportunities is not following the same trend. A savvy director perfectly knows that putting a full basket of brands in every scene might expand his/her production budget, but would not necessarily enhance the quality of the movie. See Gary Levin (2006) The newest characters on TV shows: product plugs, *USA Today*, 20 September.

[31] Emma Johnstone and Christopher A Dodd (2000) Placements as mediators of brand salience within UK cinema audience, *Journal of Marketing Communications*, 6, pp 141–58; James A Karrh (1994) Effects of brand placement in motion pictures, *Proceedings of the Conference of the American Academy of Advertising*, ed Karen Whitehill King, Athens, GA, pp 91–96; Joël Brée (1996) Le placement de produits dans les films: une communication originale, *Décisions Marketing*, 8, May–August, pp 65–74; Allyson L Stewart-Allen (1999) Product placement helps sell brand, *Marketing News*,

If we suppose that a film achieves a box office of 3 million spectators in France (which would make it a success), its success in cinemas would generally attract a large number of viewers on pay-per-view channels, then on VoD or video on demand, then on its transition to general channels, then on re-showings. Eventually, there will be tens of millions of viewers who have seen the film at least once. It is easy to see, therefore, what the same exponential multiplication might mean for a successful US film with a starting base of several tens of millions of viewers, associated with an international exploitation on a large scale, and this over a period of years. It is clear that if we had the means to precisely relate the total cost of the placement to the number of persons exposed to it, the net profitability of this vector would not be in doubt.

Of course, not all films are successful, and the profitability ratio is not always so high. Many studies conducted before writing this book, however, show that the perception of brands placed grows on the second exposure (for example, watching the DVD after having seen the film at the cinema). This may be explained by the fact that viewers already know the film, and consequently the intrigue of the storyline absorbs less of their attention, allowing them to give more of their time to other elements, such as the props, including notably product placements.

A possible influence on purchasing behaviour

For the Stephen Frears film *Dirty Pretty Things* (2002), the set designer bought a Staples wall clock in a London flea market, on the instructions of the chief set designer, Hugo Luczyc-Wyhowski. The aim was to contribute to the US style of a room.[32] There was no placement contract; just a prop intended to guide the viewers' imaginations. Some months later, the clock, which sold for US\$8.98, became one of Staples' best-selling products.

Following the release of *Sideways*[33] (2004), in which two men at a crossroads in their lives go on a trip through the wine-growing valley of Santa Ynez in

---

3(8), 15 February, p 8. About how long the film is presented in theatres and the movie lifecycle, see Jean-Jacques Montel (1990) Le cycle de vie des films au cinéma, *Congrès de l'Association Française du Marketing proceedings*, La Baule, 10–11 May, pp 585–609.

[32] Coeli Carr (2003) Cue the stapler! *Time Magazine*, 11 August.

[33] The movie used a US\$16 million budget for its production. Proportionally talking, it was a real success. Domestic gross raised US\$71.503 (plus US\$37.831 million from the international markets), making a total of US\$109.334 million (source Box Office Mojo LLC, November 2006). See also research from Hudson and Ritchie about the potential of film tourism, in particular Simon Hudson and J R Brent Ritchie (2006) Film tourism and destination marketing: the case of *Captain Corelli's Mandolin*, *Journal of Vacation Marketing*, 12(3), pp 256–68 and Simon Hudson and JR Brent

California, business increased by 30 per cent at the restaurant 'The Hitching Post' which appeared in the film, bringing a general increase in tourism in California. More importantly, sales of pinot noir wine leapt up 22 per cent on the US market in the months of December and January alone (the film having opened in cinemas on 22 October).[34] As for the pinot noir brand Blackstone, it was rewarded with an increase in sales of almost 150 per cent!

Of course, a single case has never been enough to construct a theory, and certain studies carried out by the Find/SVP agency in 2005 tended to show a lower effectiveness, in terms of influence on buying behaviour, of branded entertainment in general compared with classic television advertising.[35] Even if the exception does not prove the rule, however, it is fairly easy nowadays, based on the numerous cases of successful placements, to convince an advertiser of the considerable potential influence of product placement on the buying behaviour of a segment of the audience.

The sale of Milk Duds confectionery rose unexpectedly after Marlon Brando offered them to George C Scott in *The Formula* (John Avildsen, 1980).[36] The sales of another brand of sweets, this time Reese's Pieces, improved by more than 65 per cent after the actor Henry Thomas used them to attract E.T. in the Steven Spielberg film *E.T. The Extra-Terrestrial* (1982).[37] The sunglasses brand Ray-Ban is said to have experienced difficulties in meeting demand, following a sudden 50 per cent rise in its sales, the year following the release of the Paul Brickman film *Risky Business* (1983), in which Tom Cruise sports

---

Ritchie (2006) Promoting destinations via film tourism: an empirical identification of supporting marketing initiatives, *Journal of Travel Research*, 44, May, pp 387–96.

[34] Adam Sauer (2004) Brandchannel's 2004 product placement awards, *Brandchannel Newsletter*, 21 February.

[35] Wayne Friedman (2005) Study finds ads more persuasive than product placement, *MediaPost*, 22 August. It is important to note that the research used a sample of 1,000 people questioned on the subject. It was then a 'declared' behaviour, with the usual limits that implies. Other studies suggest that short-term buying intentions may be better stimulated by other means than advertising. See in particular a communication by Terry Daugherty and Harsha Gangadharbatla (2005) A comparison of consumers' responses to traditional advertising and product placement strategies: implications for advertisers, AMA Winter Educators' Conference, San Antonio, TX, 11–14 February.

[36] Janet Maslin (2005) Plugging products in movies as an applied art, *New York Times*, 15 November.

[37] Mary-Lou Galician and Peter G Bourdeau (2004) The evolution of product placements in Hollywood cinema: embedding high-involvement 'heroic' brand images, *Journal of Promotion Management*, 10(1/2), pp 15–36. See also Dale Buss (1998) A product-placement hall of fame, *BusinessWeek*, 11 June, and Daniel Rosen (1990) Big-time plugs on small-company budget, *Sales and Marketing Management*, 142, December, pp 48–55.

Figure 4.2 The Seamaster 300M model, limited 007 edition. It is notice-able that the official 007 logo is repeated across the whole of the watch face. Reproduced by kind permission of Omega France.

the classic Wayfarer model.[38] Never have as many berets been sold to US women as at the end of the 1960s, following the release of the film *Bonnie and Clyde* (Arthur Penn, 1967), where Faye Dunaway proudly sports her beret throughout the length of the film. In 1995, after one of its models had appeared on Pierce Brosnan's wrist in Martin Campbell's *GoldenEye*, Omega is thought to have registered a 40 per cent increase in its watch sales.[39] In

[38] Abram Sauer (2005) Product placement: making the most of a close-up, *Brandchannel Newsletter*, 26 September, and also published in *BusinessWeek*, 29 September 2005. Ray-Ban's parent company Luxottica revamped the famous model in 2006–07, placing it in movies and music videos. See Christina Passariello (2006) Ray-Ban hopes to party like it's 1983 by relaunching its Wayfarer shades, *Wall Street Journal*, 27 October.

[39] Allyson L Stewart-Allen (1999) Product placement helps sell brand, *Marketing News*, 3(8), 15 February, p 8.

1993, the sales of Red Stripe beer doubled almost instantaneously following the release of the Sydney Pollack film *The Firm*, in which Gene Hackman asks Tom Cruise to give him a bottle of that brand.[40] In 2005, Staples participated in the programme *The Apprentice* (with Donald Trump) on NBC, featuring its new rotating storage system for offices. In less than 15 minutes, more than 100 units were sold, and within three days the list of e-mail orders held more than 10,000 names.[41] The record for improvement unquestionably belongs to the Etch-A-Sketch toy, whose sales increased by more than 4,000 per cent after a free appearance in the John Lasseter animated film *Toy Story* (1995)![42]

The influence of a placement is sometimes spontaneously generated without the help of a brand, and for products that, on the face of it, no one would even have troubled to do a marketing feasibility study for! In 1999, Edward McAvoy was chief set designer on the filming of Mike Judge's *Office Space*, with Ron Livingston and Jennifer Aniston in the principal roles. Since many scenes took place in offices, multiple props and office furnishings were necessary. The screenplay specified that one of the characters, Milton, was deeply attached to his stapler.[43] In order to make it more original, the chief set designer had the idea of choosing one in fire engine red. Having made enquiries and called the Swingline brand, he learnt that there was no stapler corresponding to his requirements. He therefore obtained permission from Swingline to paint one of their models. On the film's release, several clients requested a red stapler, which Swingline did not manufacture. The demand was such that Bruce Neapole, president of Swingline, took the decision to produce a model in fire engine red. The Rio Red Stapler model is now an integral part of the catalogue, and has already seen 'collector's editions', not to mention the internet forums, indeed whole virtual communities that, since the film's release, have formed around a simple stapler.

---

[40] Neither the bottle nor its label were clearly seen on the screen. The choice for Red Stripe was perfectly relevant. The beer is brewed in Jamaica, and the action took place in the Caiman islands. See also Norm Marshall and Dean Ayers (1998) Product placement worth more than its weight, *Brandweek*, 39(6), 9 February, pp 16–17; and Mitchell Alan (1996) The power of a plug, *Management Today*, February.

[41] Luc-André Cormier (2005) Mesurer l'impact du placement de produit, *Bulletin de l'Association Canadienne des Annonceurs*, May–June, p 5.

[42] The toy was chosen by the director because it reminded him of his youth. Slowing sales were slowly driving it toward the market exit, but the placement in the film thoroughly rejuvenated it. Another toy placed in *Toy Story* (1995), Mr Potato, benefited from an increase of 800 per cent in its sales. Slinky, a big soft spring invented in 1943 by Richard James – in a military context – disappeared from the shelves a long time ago, but consumers' demand was so strong that it was relaunched. The same year *Toy Story* was released, the Slinky toy was placed in the Steve Oedekerk film *Ace Ventura: When nature calls*.

[43] Coeli Carr (2003) Cue the stapler! *Time Magazine*, 11 August.

On the classic principle of identification and the desire to look like such and such a star, a (sometimes significant) part of the audience is often quick to wish to own the same accessories, to dress in the same way or to consume the same products as the star in question. In 2002, the jewellery designer Mia & Lizzie was beset with requests for a necklace in the shape of a horseshoe with diamonds, simply because the actress Sarah Jessica Parker had worn one in an episode of the fourth season of the television series *Sex and the City*.

Amplifying the effect and tracking the impact of online placement

In 2005, having realized the potential impact of a placement, Asics set up tie-in communications operations (advertising, internet site, promotional links and so on), for the release of the Karyn Kusama film *Æon Flux*, in which the lead actress Charlize Theron wore the Fencing LA model. An internet site is the ideal link for a placement.[44] It can be set up before the film's release to receive the traffic of web users who have seen the trailer on another site. It makes it possible to inform visitors to the brand's website of the placement: their informed minds will then pick it up more easily when they go to see the film. It also allows promotional operations to be organized in tandem with the film's release. The most important aspect is that it represents not only a communication space accessible at low cost, whatever the moment and place of connection, but above all a communications space under the full and complete control of the brand.

The internet is not only a powerful potential bridge. The forums that it houses offer advertisers an exceptional opportunity to gauge the placement's impact, particularly when the product placed is not necessarily easy to identify. The case of sunglasses brands is a case in point. In fact, without an extreme close-up on a name or a logo, it is often impossible to recognize the brand. Like all accessories worn by a star, sunglasses are often the subject of avid and rapid searches by fans upon the film's release. Touring various discussion forums throughout the web, it is arresting to discover the number of questions posed on the network immediately after a film's release, to find out sometimes the brand, sometimes the model, sometimes where it can be purchased. For the brand placed, following these exchanges allows it to glean some clues on the attractiveness of the placement and the impact it has had. For instance, this could be examined for the pair of sunglasses protecting

---

[44] Fred S Zufryden (2000) New film website promotion and box-office performance, *Journal of Advertising Research*, 40(2), pp 55–64. See also Ray LeMaistre (1999) What's in a name? *Communications International*, 26(12), pp 40–44.

Nicolas Cage in *Lord of War* (Andrew Niccol, 2005), for the very sophisticated pair worn by the agent Ethan Hunt, played by Tom Cruise, in *Mission: Impossible II* (John Woo, 2000), the sunglasses used by Will Smith and Tommy Lee Jones in *Men in Black II* (Barry Sonnenfeld, 2002), the sunglasses of the blind superhero played by Ben Affleck in *Daredevil* (Mark Steven Johnson, 2003), the famous yellow lens sunglasses of Brad Pitt and Angelina Jolie in *Mr & Mrs Smith* (Doug Liman, 2005), the 'burning' pair worn by the actor Chris Evans, playing Johnny Storm in *Fantastic 4* (Tim Story, 2005), the protective goggles worn by Paul Walker in *Eight Below* (Frank Marshall, 2006), and the different models worn by Matthew McConaughey, Penelope Cruz and Steve Zahn in *Sahara* (Breck Eisner, 2005).[45]

The majority of the 'big' brands today possess (or at least should possess) internal or external functionalities that allow them to follow what is said about them and about their products. The objective is to counter as much as possible the dissenting comments to which they can be subjected. Furthermore, discussion forums have a near-universal reach, so important that the greatest attention must be paid to the opinions exchanged there. If it is rarely possible for brands to intervene directly on dissenting sites, but they can on the other hand infiltrate the forums to glean information, and sometimes cleverly diffuse counter-messages, like a submariner launching countermeasures to escape an approaching torpedo. Brands should take care not to be found out, though! This approach is necessary nowadays, however, since certain placements deemed too commercial can sometimes suffer stinging criticism, particularly on sites dedicated to the cinema and its fans. These criticisms may not only harm the film, but also cause the brand placed to lose several image points.

Such observation of the network of networks can also help to identify a positive placement impact. Following the good old principle of identification with the star, certain viewers are quick to join the hunt for products (accessories, clothing and others) seen in a film, all the more so if they are perceived to be original. The case of shoes is an enlightening one, since they are a generally accessible good, an integral part of an outfit, and therefore a sign of status. Some consumers therefore seek to own them to look like the star, do as they do, or have the illusion of following in their footsteps. On the

---

[45] Persol PO 2679S in *Lord of War*; Oakley X-Metals model in *Mission: Impossible II*; Ray-Ban Predator II model in *Men in Black II*; Ray-Ban Predator Olympia Gunmetal for Ben Affleck in *Daredevil*; Oliver Peoples 'Nitro' series, 'shooting yellow' limited edition in *Mr & Mrs Smith* (Angelina Jolie also wears the Ray-Ban 3025 model in the desert scene); Arnette AN3016 model in *Fantastic 4*; Scott large model with anti-frost lens, Ray-Ban Aviator model for Penelope Cruz, Ray-Ban Orbs Titanium Classic model for Matthew McConaughey and Ray-Ban Predator Shot Extreme model for Steve Zahn in *Sahara*.

release of the Quentin Tarantino film *Kill Bill Vol. 1*, in 2003, the demand from consumers who had seen the yellow and black Onitsuka Tigers tai chi shoes in the film impelled the Japanese manufacturer Asics to increase their production. Monitoring exchanges on internet discussion forums can also make it possible to evaluate the real potential of such demand, in order to distinguish the fashion effect from the real trend.

In this respect, we should mention the original case of the Wes Anderson film, *The Life Aquatic with Steve Zissou* (2004). In one of the scenes, the leading actor Bill Murray talks up the merits of a shoe model whose three lateral stripes alone make it easy to identify the manufacturer Adidas. However, in this precise case, the model did not exist. It was in fact a 'makeover' of the Adidas ROM Classics model of 1959 (relaunched in 1979), for which the shoe maker had given the director permission.[46] Despite the requests, Adidas stated that it did not intend to relaunch the model, particularly not with the appearance shown in the film. Some weeks later, however, various internet forums were exchanging tips and advice on transforming an existing ROM Classics model into a 'Steve Zissou model'![47]

Tie-in possibilities

The majority of large film productions nowadays enjoy a marketing budget equivalent to, or often greater than, that dedicated to their production alone.[48] Tie-in operations rest on contracts allowing an advertiser to make reference to a film in which its brand or products are placed. They may be specific products linked to the film and marketed by the brand. For example Mattel created a special series of Barbie dolls resembling Reese Witherspoon to tie in with the film *Legally Blonde 2* (2002) by Charles Herman-Wurmfeld, and a limited series of 10 007 Omega Seamaster watches was issued, recalling the watch maker's association with the adventures of James Bond. These operations can take the form of special children's meals, with free toys based on the film or its characters, at Burger King or McDonald's. It is first and foremost a question of tie-in advertising.

---

[46] For a previous movie, *The Royal Tenenbaums* (2001), Wes Anderson had already made contact with the brand, dressing three characters including actor Ben Stiller in prominently labelled Adidas sport apparel through the entire movie.

[47] S Wloszczyna (2005) Steve Zissou's cool shoes prove tough to fill, *USAToday*, 13 January.

[48] Charles A Lubbers and William J Adams (2001) Promotional strategies utilized by the film industry: theatrical movies as product, *Journal of Promotion Management*, 6(1/2), pp 161–80.

Figure 4.3 An example of the partnership between the DaimlerChrysler brand and the film *Sahara* (Breck Eisner, 2005).

Source: Jeep®, 2005. Reproduced by kind permission of DaimlerChrysler.

These operations also contribute to compensating for the relative increase in film production budgets.[49] The studio is assured of participation in, or even a total assumption of responsibility for, the film's marketing budget (press relations operations, launch campaign, promotional relaunch, specific events and so on). As for the advertiser, it can in this way prolong the effect of the

---

[49] Charles A Lubbers and William J Adams (2004) Merchandising in the major picture industry: creating brand synergy and revenue streams, *Journal of Promotion Management,* 10(1/2), pp 55–63.

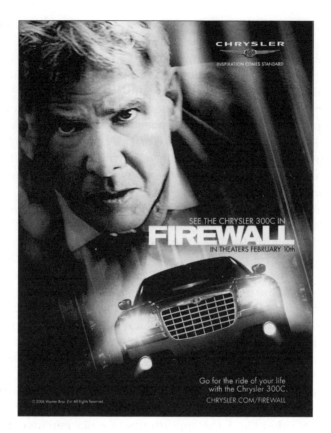

Figure 4.4 Advertisement for the Chrysler 300C on the release of the film *Firewall* (2006), by Richard Loncraine. Reproduced by kind permission of DaimlerChrysler.

placement outside the film, and even sometimes allow an identification that would otherwise have gone unnoticed. In *Die Another Day* (2002), it is difficult to know how much of Halle Berry's beauty is due to Revlon cosmetics; but it is a typical case of stealth placement, revealed by the tie-in operation.

For the film studio, the additional advantage lies in the fact that these advertisements for the brands placed will mention the film's title and thereby contribute to its promotional launch campaign. When the Dr Pepper soft drink releases a communication announcing the release of the Sam Raimi film *Spider-Man 2* (2004), it is just as much an advert for the film. Better still, at the time of the release of *X2* (Bryan Singer, 2003), the brand, which was both a placement partner and tie-in partner, produced a series of special soft drinks cans reproducing the images of characters from the film.

Perfectly orchestrated, this synergy can help to massively expand the impact of both the film's and the brand's communications.[50] In the feature film *Garfield* (Peter Hewitt, 2004), the famous slogan of the collective campaign by milk producers in the United States, 'Got milk?', is spoken by Garfield the cat in the first minutes of the film. The character was used after the film's release for the advertising campaign. This approach can involve several brands in parallel. Appendix 1 reproduces the press release from Universal Studios announcing the full list of partnerships for Peter Jackson's *King Kong* (2005). It is an example of a coherent assembly of partner brands at different levels, with an appropriate orchestration of the whole, which accompanies the film's cinema release.

The technique is not a recent one. From the earliest days of cinema, a great many brands have courted stars for their advertising. In 1932, Paul Muni played the title role in *Scarface,* directed by Howard Hawks. United Artists signed a tie-in contract for US$250,000 with the cigar brand Owl, enabling it to base its advertising on the fact that the lead actor in *Scarface* smoked its brand of cigars.[51] At the time, the implicit tie-in was almost automatic. The stars 'belonged' to the studios. In order to use them in advertising, authorization from those same studios was required. Almost all advertisements based on testimonials during the first half of the twentieth century systematically mentioned the latest film of the star shown in the advertisement, as well as the production studio.

The progressive independence of stars, who came to take control of their own destinies and their advertising choices, spelt the end of this automatic practice. On the other hand, the opportunities for placements combined with tie-in operations are now increasingly studied far in advance. For the film *Baby Boom* (Charles Shyer, 1987), in which motherhood plays an important role, Kimberly-Clark considered well in advance, in addition to the placement of its Huggies nappies, the possibility of organizing a special couponing operation and a competition on the film's release.

It is also important, if possible, to anticipate the inclusion of a clause in the star's contract, in order to enable him/her to appear in advertisements (particularly point-of-purchase advertising, or POPA). POPAs used by opticians and referencing the Ray-Ban brand, placed in *Sahara* (Breck Eisner, 2005), would not have the same impact in-store without the photos of the

---

[50] Scott Robert Olson (2004) The extension of synergy: product placement through theming and environmental simulacra, *Journal of Promotion Management,* 10(1/2), pp 65–87. See also Ronald Grover (2002) The trouble with tie-ins, *BusinessWeek,* 3 June.

[51] The cigars smoked by Paul Muni in *Scarface* were not actually Owl brand. But at this time consumerism and advertising ethics watchpeople were still very few and their action quite limited.

three lead actors from the film. It is noticeable that the brand also took care to choose a photograph of the actors wearing sunglasses. It seems like a self-evident detail, and yet in 2005, the watch brand Hamilton mounted a tie-in campaign of this type for the release of John Stockwell's film *Into the Blue*. Since the film is set in the Bahamas, and partly at sea, the visual showed the lead actors together in the same shot, in diving gear and bare arms. One small problem: none of them were wearing watches!

Daryl Hannah discovered while watching television that certain scenes from the film *Roxanne* (Fred Schepisi, 1987) in which she had played the lead alongside Steve Martin, had been inserted into an advertising spot for Diet Coke without her permission. The actress was quite rightly offended by this: her audience might have thought that she was promoting the product, whereas she had never been asked either for her opinion or for her permission. The production studios, Columbia Pictures, apologized and came to an amicable settlement with the actress.[52]

Those known as 'A-list' stars are today generally reluctant to associate their image with a tie-in promotional operation, fearing that it could devalue them.[53] When it is possible, however, all the professionals questioned confirmed the attraction of the association, both for the film and for the brand. In 2005, the actor John Travolta played the game to the full on the release of the F Gary Gray film *Be Cool*, in which Cadillac cars had a choice placement. He agreed to participate in the campaign, which included a competition parallel to the film's release. It is almost a textbook example of perfect symbiosis. First of all, John Travolta took part in short films presenting the competition, playing Chili Palmer, his character in *Be Cool*. Mentions of the film were also inserted into the short films. Second, the competition invited participants to create a five-second short film online, and the director F Gary Gray was part of the judging panel.[54]

---

[52] For the record, Columbia Pictures studios, established in 1920, was bought back by the Coca-Cola company in 1982 (before being sold to Sony Corporation in 1989). Of course, the placement should have been proposed to the actress before, but one may understand that in this case, synergies could have been spontaneously suggested. See in particular, Ronald Alsop (1988) Consumer products become movie stars: marketers gain as film makers try to cut costs, *Wall Street Journal*, 29 February.

[53] Jean Halliday (2005) John Travolta's product placement fever, *Advertising Age*, 21 February.

[54] The officially imposed time was five seconds, to meet Cadillac's objective: going from 0 to 60 miles per hour in five seconds. The website received 2,648 short films, and the winner was inserted in a 30-second commercial run during the Grammy Awards ceremony. See in particular Kris Oser (2005) Five-second online films for Cadillac, *Madison+Vine*, 13 July.

Although tie-in operations can complement placements, not all of them necessarily follow a product or brand placement in the feature film. Those franchises whose success is often 'scheduled' have no difficulty in attracting partners. For the reappearance of Superman (whose franchise was born in 1938) on the big screen in *Superman Returns* (Bryan Singer, 2006), Warner Bros enjoyed the support notably of Burger King, PepsiCo Inc (most particularly Pepsi-Cola, Mountain Dew, Aquafina and Sierra Mist), Perfectmatch.com, Quaker State and Duracell, to accompany the film's release. In an original and innovative case, in 2006, the Starbucks Entertainment subsidiary of Starbucks coffee houses announced that it had signed a partnership with Lionsgate for the United States launch of Doug Atchison's film *Akeelah and the Bee*. This type of partnership is original since, in return for promoting the film in some 5,500 points of purchase in different ways (posters, events, promotion on the WiFi network, satellite radio programme, private premieres and so on), Starbucks had negotiated a percentage of the profits from the film's box-office and DVD takings, and from sales of the soundtrack on CD.[55]

Sometimes, however, these promotional operations without prior placements stem from the fact that a placement is simply impossible. Burger King restaurants and M&M confectionery, for example, signed a contract of this type with *Star Wars Episode III: Revenge of the Sith* (George Lucas, 2005), whereas, of course, even watching the film frame by frame, you will not find a single branch of the fast-food chain on Coruscant, and the Jedi Masters are not known for their regular consumption of M&M's.

Nor do they sip Minute Maid or Coca-Cola in *Harry Potter*: nevertheless, in 2001, the Atlanta giant signed an exclusivity contract of US$150 million with Warner Bros to be able to use images from the film on its packaging, within the framework of promotional operations. Churlish spirits rose up against the association of a children's hero with a soft drink full of sugar and therefore calories. An internet site, www.saveharry.com, was even born to interrogate J K Rowling. In an interview with the *Daily Mail*, however, the author of the famous wizard's adventures explained that she was happy with the contract, since Harry's image was not directly used, and all the more so since the contract came with a US$18 million subsidy from Coca-Cola to the

---

[55] The Starbucks Entertainment name and logo appeared in the main title, in the trailer and on the movie poster, in the same conditions of those of the other producers, Lion's Gate and 2929 Entertainment. See also Gail Schiller (2006) Starbucks brews film deal, *Hollywood Reporter*, 13 January. It was not the first step for Starbucks in the entertainment and show business: the coffee shops chain was also involved in music production. Among others, it has co-produced Ray Charles's *Genius Loves Company*. See Scott Galupo (2005) Starbucks sells 'Genius' with the joe, *Washington Times*, 11 February, and Stanley Holmes (2005) Strong lattes, sour notes at Starbucks, *BusinessWeek*, 20 June.

Figure 4.5 Screen shot of the US internet site for the Alienware brand, a partner of the film *Æon Flux* (Karyn Kusama, 2005). Reproduced by kind permission of Alienware Corporation.

educational programme 'Reading is Fundamental', encouraging children to read.[56]

In tie-in cases of this type, it is more the film 'brand' that is integrated into the communication of its partner brands. Although Burger King restaurants and Baskin-Robbins ice creams did not feature in the animated film *Spirit: Stallion of the Cimarron* (Kelly Asbury and Lorna Cook, 2002), they certainly

---

[56] Olinka Koster (2001) Harry Potter and the not-so-wizard Coca-Cola wheeze, *Daily Mail*, 18 October. See also Mary-Lou Galician (2004) Harry Potter, Coca-Cola and the Center for Science in the Public Interest: an interview with Michael F Jacobson, *Journal of Promotion Management*, 10(1/2), pp 227–31. Concerning the limits of the contract, see in particular Ronald Grover (2001) Harry Potter and the marketer's millstone, *BusinessWeek*, 15 October.

Figure 4.6   Screen shot of the US internet site for M&M's. Promotional operation on the release of the film *Star Wars: Episode III, Revenge of the Sith* (George Lucas, 2005). © Mars Incorporated (2006) – http://us.mms.com/us/mpire/index.jsp. Reproduced by kind permission of Masterfoods France.

participated in the launch publicity campaign and organized promotional operations linked to the film. It is important that the promotional operation coincides with the film's release, and that, if possible, it is carried by all communications vectors of the partner brand, in particular nowadays on its internet site.

The coincidence of the promotion and the release of the film can easily become a source of logistical and marketing problems. In fact, from the moment the contract is signed, the signatories have no control over possible direction and production delays, or over the postponement of the release to avoid a head-on confrontation with another studio's film, or simply because the number of available screens is not suitable, or because the film is not thought to be good enough to risk the cost of a cinema release. It is sometimes an advantage for the brand, which can then prolong its promotional operation.[57]

---

[57] Todd Wasserman (2005) The metrix revolutions, *The Hollywood Reporter*, 27 September.

Figure 4.7 Screenshot from Burger King's website supporting a tie-in operation with *Scooby-Doo2: Monsters Unleashed* (Raja Gosnell, 2004) produced by Warner Bros. Pictures.

In the vast majority of cases, however, this quickly becomes catastrophic, if the delay lingers on or if the film goes straight to video. To illustrate this type of problem, experts often mention the film *Over the Top* (Menahem Golan, 1986) with Sylvester Stallone. In this film, the eau de cologne Brut, by Fabergé, enjoyed a relatively important placement, and this placement was supposed to be accompanied by a major tie-in operation for the New Year celebrations, along with the film's release. Unfortunately, the film release was postponed until February 1987.

Finally, tie-in operations do not necessarily follow the film everywhere it is shown, if only because the advertiser placed is not necessarily present everywhere in the world, or because the cost of such an operation would be too great. For example, the tie-in part of the partnership contract signed between Warner Bros studios and the fast-food chain Burger King for the Raja Gosnell film *Scooby-Doo 2: Monsters Unleashed* (2004) only covered US territory. Warner Bros could therefore sign similar international promotional operations with the competitor company KFC without any real risk of telescoping.

Measuring the effectiveness of a placement

'Product placement isn't about sales; it's about brand awareness,' claims expert Samuel Turcotte.[58] However, the advertisers of the twenty-first century are legitimately nervous about this effectiveness. In fact, who could claim to have identified, for example, the impact of the character Popeye on the world consumption of spinach since his appearance in the *Thimble Theatre* cartoon strip by Edgar C Segar on 17 January 1929?[59] The only certainty in terms of measuring the effectiveness of product or brand placement is that there is a strong and urgent call from advertisers to know whether their investment is profitable. To date, however, there is no reliable and complete standard measuring tool.[60] In the light of the observations of the experts interviewed for this book, it seems probable that there will never be one – which does little to reassure advertisers about their investments[61] – if only because when they talk about placement effectiveness, advertisers do not always mean the same thing. Where they seek to know at least the CPM (cost for an audience of 1,000 viewers), television and film producers look for finance as far in advance as possible. In reality, everything initially depends on the objective given to the placement. Is it to increase awareness of the brand, to improve its image, to confirm or modify its positioning, to make known its advances in

---

[58] Samuel Turcotte is associate manager at Internet Media (Sun Microsystems). See Mary-Lou Galician (2004) A rising independent filmmaker argues for product placement: an interview with Samuel A Turcotte, *Journal of Promotion Management*, 10(1/2), pp 223–26. Samuel Turcotte is also the author of a Master's thesis about product placement regularly quoted: *Gimme a Bud! The feature film product placement industry,*1995, University of Texas, Austin, TX.

[59] It was in 1932 that producer Max Fleisher (Fleisher Studios in association with Paramount Pictures), signed with Hearst's King Features Syndicate for the rights to adapt the comics on screen. During those cartoon adventures the power of spinach was stressed. See in particular Fred Grandinetti (2004) *Popeye: An illustrated cultural history*, 2nd edn, McFarland, Jefferson, NY. About brand and product placements in comic books, see Brian Steinberg (2006) Look-up in the sky! product placement! *Wall Street Journal*, 18 April.

[60] Jim Edwards (2005) The tracker: will product placement get its own dot-comeuppance? *Brandweek*, 25 July, and Dan Glaister (2005) US networks cash in as advertisers turn to product placement, *Guardian*, 30 September. See also why academic research has to be careful, as explained by Michael R Solomon and Basil G English (1994) Observations: the big picture – product complimentary and integrated communications, *Journal of Advertising Research*, 34, January–February, pp 57–63.

[61] Beng Soo Ong and David Meri (1994) Should product placement in movies be banned? *Journal of Promotion Management*, 2(2/4), pp 159–75.

research and development, to launch a new product, or to increase its sales? This latter point is naturally the most sensitive.

Admittedly, as mentioned above, there have been cases of a clear impact on sales. However, these emblematic cases should not lead us to believe that there is a simple 'mechanism' enabling such an effect to be guaranteed. In comparison with the context of a simple advertising film, for a feature film the audience is a prisoner of a screen for a longer period and also partly bounded by the other films shown on the screen. This means that the environment in which the placement is effected often allows a greater contextual intensity of the communication. Its likelihood of potential recurrence, though, is poor, and much more distant in time, when compared with a classic 30-second spot, which will be shown many times. Systematically contrasting spot and placement, however, is simplistic and dangerous, since although their marketing objectives are sometimes similar, they still remain complementary. In the vast majority of placement cases, even if it is known that a placement can encourage the act of purchasing,[62] it is brand awareness above all that is to be reinforced, and brand image that is to be enhanced.[63] Numerous research projects have supplied ammunition on certain aspects of the effectiveness of placements. As for measuring with any certainty their impact on sales, however, the number of exogenous variables is too great and their nature too uncontrollable.

Communications consultancies and placement consultancy agencies, as well as large research bodies and new, small original structures, today offer sometimes highly sophisticated tools for the tracking and analysis of the impact of product and brand placements (particularly in the cinema and on television). The market caters for all appetites: Nielsen Media Research with Place*Views and Nielsen BuzzMetrics, NextMedium, Image Impact, IAG Research with In-Program Performance Service, Intelliseek, Millward Brown, Marketing Evolution, E-Poll, Brand Advisors and TNS Media Intelligence with Branded Entertainment Reporting Service, among others, have clearly perceived the potential of branded entertainment, and above all their clients' desire to know what exactly was the return on their investment.[64]

---

[62] Cynthia R Morton and Meredith Friedman (2002) 'I saw it in the movies': exploring the link between product placement beliefs and reported usage behaviour, *Journal of Current Issues and Research in Advertising*, 24(2), Fall, pp 33–40.

[63] Laurie A Babin and Sheri Thompson Carder (1996) Viewers' recognition of brands placed within a film, *International Journal of Advertising*, 15(2), pp 140–51.

[64] Gail Schiller (2005) Industry seeks formula to value product integration, *Hollywood Reporter*, 30 December. See also Karen J Bannan (2006) No end to placement data services, *Advertising Age*, 6 February; Laura Blum and Steve McClellan (2006) Lack of ROI tools stalls overseas placements, *Adweek*, 24 July; and Patti Summerfield with Lisa D'Innocenzo (2006) So your brand's a TV star: what's it worth? *Strategy Magazine*, February, p 26.

The tools developed are, however, very different from one another, and do not necessarily always measure the same thing (the criterion might be visibility, brand perception, resulting awareness points, image points, help with positioning, identified impact on sales and so on). The great difficulty for a reliable model is linked to the fact that the nature and context of a placement (every film is unique) can vary considerably from one case to the next. Long before the professionals, academic research had begun to mull over this hybrid communications technique.[65]

The vast majority of professionals are united in admitting that even if numerous tools exist and provide sometimes-reliable information, it is still largely incomplete, because the mechanism of communication based on product and brand placement is so complex. It is possible to determine precisely the nature (size, duration, number of occurrences, type of appearance and so on) of the placement; it is also possible to calculate awareness or image scores, but as for calculating the exact effectiveness on sales (present and future) resulting from all these factors, that is a different matter.

Among the most original measuring tools, we may note that offered by the iTVX company, a recognized US specialist in branded entertainment. This allows simultaneous real-time measuring of placement effectiveness on the basis of 50 variables. It concludes with the calculation of a ratio (Q-ratio) expressed in relation to the comparable cost of a 30-second advertising spot, where a Q-ratio of 1.0 is equivalent to 100 per cent of a 30-second spot. This evaluation tool (Media Pro Valuator) also offers a reader enabling the simultaneous analysis of the visual quality of the placement (mode of appearance and clarity), the clarity of the pronunciation of the brand name in a citation, and the degree of integration of a placement into the storyline.[66] The iTVX solution offers a high degree of precision for calculating the 'quality' of the placement on the basis of the retained variables.

Even so, what might be deemed a high-quality placement may not necessarily have the commercial impact expected in the light of this judgement, and may not make it possible to anticipate when returns will be shown. The effect of a placement can sometimes be very slow to appear. This depends of course on the product concerned and of the purchasing opportunities, but also, once again, on the nature of the placement. Moreover, many actors are not unhappy about the persistent fuzziness surrounding the 'real commercial

---

[65] Siva K Balasubramanian (1994) Beyond advertising and publicity: hybrid messages and public policy issues, *Journal of Advertising*, 23(4), pp 29–46; James A Karrh (1998) Brand placement: a review, *Journal of Current Issues and Research in Advertising*, 20(2), Fall, pp 31–49; Isabelle Fontaine (2002) *Étude des réponses mémorielles et attitudinales des spectateurs exposés aux placements de marques dans les films*, Management PhD thesis directed by Professor Joël Brée, Paris IX Dauphine University.

[66] A demo of how the tool works is available on the iTVX's website: www.itvx.com.

effectiveness' of the placement, since it enables them to organize global 'placement plus promotion plus advertising plus public relations' operations that interact between themselves. If one day a standard model is devised, such operations will become more compartmentalized and will no longer necessarily be accepted for all their components. Furthermore, another model is beginning to emerge, concerning the price of the placement this time: it is a matter of determining the variables to be taken into consideration for evaluating it with greater precision and relevance.

5 Professional recommendations for effective placements

We may state without fear of correction that it is not (yet) possible to determine in advance the exact conditions that will ensure, at the end of the day, a product placement or a brand integration that will guarantee an increase in sales or an automatic improvement in brand awareness or image. There are too many uncontrolled variables in the model; too much instability in the environment; too many uncertainties regarding audience reactions and the time lapse of these reactions.

In 1988, McDonald's and Coca-Cola invested heavily in the Stewart Raffill film, *Mac and Me*, which was a resounding flop with total box-office receipts of just US$6.424 million. Branded entertainment is not a trade of simple modalities. For the professionals of this sector, however, it is a trade where confidence must try to compensate for the uncertainty of success that is intrinsically linked with the world of show business.[1] Nevertheless, as with

---

[1] Cristel Antonia Russell and Michael Belch (2005) A managerial investigation into the product placement industry, *Journal of Advertising Research*, 45(1), pp 73–92. See also James A Karrh, Katty Brittain McKee and Carol J Pardun (2003) Practitioners' evolving views on product placement effectiveness, *Journal of Advertising Research*, 43(2), pp 138–49.

Interview with Catherine Emond, founder of the Casablanca agency

What is the attraction of a product or brand placement in the cinema for advertisers nowadays?
Placement in the cinema offers a brand natural and noticeable visibility, for a very profitable investment (a cost per thousand below €3). Furthermore, it is a medium that is still very uncluttered, with an average of five to ten brands per film. It allows the development of the brand's likeability, by establishing a trust relationship with the viewer who chose this film, who feels close to the theme and the actors. The potential is enormous because the film carries the brand into all distribution channels.

Are there not still some limits?
For an advertiser, the cardinal error to be avoided is thinking that you can put an advertisement in a film, whereas the idea of a placement is to integrate naturally. Then you must be careful up until the final cut. You must never forget that in France it is the director who has the final cut. For the producer, it's important not to rely on the placement for finance, because the presence of brands is still unpredictable. As for the agency, it must be careful never to force the director's hand, or the team's. That never works.

How do these recommendations take shape in real life?
In 1998, for the Tonie Marshall film *Vénus beauté (institut)*, (Venus Beauty (Institute)) Gatineau and Mavala benefited from a placement. The brands were chosen when the institute was constructed, the screenplay was modified as a consequence, the aestheticians trained the actresses: the result was successful and realistic. It is also necessary to supplement the placement. In 2004, for the Jérôme Salle film *Anthony Zimmer*, it was the director who chose the watch brand IWC. It gives the character a unique and refined air, even as it plays a fundamental role in the film. Still in 2004, for the Julie Lipinski film *Le plus beau jour de ma vie* (The best day of my life), the Liérac brand was sold in the pharmacy of the heroine, played by Hélène de Fougerolles. Liérac took advantage of this to put on parties in pharmacies themed on the film, with invitations to local press agencies, and 1,500 pharmacies highlighted a themed consumer promotion (with point of sale material, the shop window and counter all transmitting the range). Finally, Liérac invited its VIPs to the film's premiere.

any genuine commercial transaction, there are certain principles that allow the definition of the most favourable context for the placement. The delicate operation of bringing a brand or a product into a world of entertainment such as a film is not simple. The type and nature of the environment in which the product or the brand is to appear – or better, be used – are of fundamental importance, since, as academic research has shown, this environment largely conditions the impact of the placement.[2]

Defining the objective and the attraction of the placement

Even today, many placements follow the 'classic' format, simply aspiring to create, nurture or regenerate awareness of a brand. Should we blame them for this? Emphatically not: according to the firm Accenture, an average individual was exposed to around 650 commercial messages per day in 1985.[3] This commercial exposure has exceeded 3,000 messages per day since 2002. Everyone knows this phenomenon: information overkill. How can we imagine that a normal individual would be able to consciously perceive and, above all, memorize so much information – particularly commercial information – each day? Herein lies the justification for the approach that seeks to remind people of the brand name as much as possible, if only to enable it to maintain its place in the great crowd evoked in the minds of target individuals.[4] Nevertheless, with the increasing awareness of the attraction of branded entertainment, we can see a certain professionalization of this approach.[5]

---

[2] See in particular research works from Moonhee Yang, Beverly Roskos-Ewoldsen and David R Roskos-Ewoldsen (2004) Mental models for brand placement, in L J Shrum (ed), *The Psychology of Entertainment Media: Blurring the lines between entertainment and persuasion*, Lawrence Erlbaum Associates, Mahwah, NJ, pp 79–98.

[3] Accenture (2002) *Mind The Gap*.

[4] In the evaluation/decision process followed by an individual, the evoked set gathers the different alternatives offered to him/her. Then, in a buying process, the evoked set includes all the products and the brands considered by consumers when they make their choice. As the consumer's memory storage capacity is limited, the size of the consideration set is also limited (source: *L'Encyclopédie du Marketing*, Éditions d'Organisation Publishing, 2004, Paris, p 312).

[5] Jean-Marc Lehu (2005) Le placement de produits au cinéma: hiérarchie des critères d'utilisation ou hiérarchie des étapes? Une étude exploratoire qualitative auprès d'agents professionnels anglo-saxons, 4th Congress of Marketing Tendencies, Paris, 21–22 January.

Nikon's objective is not the same when it places a camera in the Gary Winick film *13 Going on 30* (2004) as when it places one in the hands of Julia Roberts in *Stepmom* (Chris Columbus, 1998) or ensures that one is shown in *The Interpreter* (Sydney Pollack, 2005). *13 Going on 30* is a light comedy, and the compact camera Nikon Coolpix is placed in the context of a festive occasion, at a wedding ceremony. In *Stepmom* it is a professional digital Nikon camera used by a professional photographer (Julia Roberts) for a fashion photoshoot. In *The Interpreter*, again it is a professional Nikon camera, but this time given to a major journalist, who witnesses a murder in an African country. In the latter two cases, Nikon is nurturing its preferential position among professionals in the studio and in the field, with all the technological connotations of quality requirements that this implies.[6] In *13 Going on 30*, it expresses its accessibility to the public at large. It is the same brand, but there are different products, different placements and therefore different messages.

The attraction of a placement must be justified as naturally as possible. In order to do this, it must fully respect the characteristics of the product and the brand. In the first part of the film *Just My Luck* (Donald Petrie, 2006), everything goes right for the character of Ashley (Lindsay Lohan): it is therefore logical to associate her with upmarket products from the food shop Balducci's. In contrast, the association in the United States between Home Depot (the world leader in DIY) and the successful television programme by Mark Burnett, *The Contender,* is often named by professionals of branded entertainment as a case of out-and-out failure, since no coherence between the brand and the programme was ever found: in this case, even the awareness objective may be missed.[7]

According to professional analysis, the classic placement aims to be seen, and if possible liked, by the viewing audience. Nonetheless there is another aim, much less widely known, but which an advertiser interested in placement may follow: that of reaching its *internal* audience. This second objective is often neglected, but it can sometimes represent the primary target. It can be motivating and affirming for a company's employees (even in a DIY company) to see it in a particular successful television show or in a feature film. Certain

---

[6] In 1980, when Nikon was contacted for Ronald Neame's *Hopscotch* movie, the brand took care that the CIA secret agent played by Walter Matthau was competent. Even if it was a comedy, the purpose was to be sure not to put the Nikon camera in a dummy's hands.

[7] The show runs on the NBC network in the United States and on different channels around the world. Each scene is considered as a placement opportunity. If some brands are naturally linked to sports in general or to boxing in particular, for all the other branded participants, like Toyota and Home Depot, the objective is more about awareness, to favour the brand's recall.

studies even claim that this can lead to an improvement in morale and productivity,[8] not to mention that some employees can be led to participate actively in filming. Thus, in Steven Spielberg's *The Terminal* (2004), not only did United Airlines, placed in the film, allow the use of its aeroplanes and its VIP Red Carpet Club lounge, it also allowed 40 of its employees to take part as extras.[9]

Ensuring a positive presence onscreen

In 1968, the computer manufacturer IBM was a partner in the Stanley Kubrick film *2001: A Space Odyssey* – until it realized that a malfunction in the computer would transform it into an implacable murderer of the astronauts in the space ship. IBM immediately pulled out of the project, and Stanley Kubrick renamed his computer HAL, an acronym formed of the letters preceding the IBM initials in the alphabet.[10] Ensuring a positive presence onscreen is simply essential! Pepsi-Cola was institutionalized in *One, Two, Three* (Billy Wilder, 1961); Cheerios were the cereal of choice in *Mommie Dearest* (Frank Perry, 1981); a ruby brooch from Fred's is extolled in *Pretty Woman* (Garry Marshall, 1990); Chanel is venerated in *Tacones Lejanos* (High heels) (Pedro Almodóvar, 1991); France Telecom is indispensable in *La Belle Histoire* (The beautiful story) (Claude Lelouch, 1992); Pontiac is praised to the skies in *xXx* (Rob Cohen, 2002); Napster is 'personalized' in *The Italian Job* (F Gary Gray, 2003); perfectmatch.com is endorsed in *Must Love Dogs* (Gary David Goldberg, 2005); Timex Iroman Triathlon is the watch in *Stranger Than Fiction* (Marc Forster, 2006). All these placements are very positive for the brand image.

The Robert Zemeckis film *Cast Away* (2000) is often mentioned as a counter-example to the standard placement, because of the omnipresence throughout the film of the express delivery service FedEx and a Wilson volleyball.[11] It is

---

[8] Cristel Antonia Russell and Michael Belch (2005) A managerial investigation into the product placement industry, *Journal of Advertising Research*, 45(1), pp 73–92.

[9] Michael McCarthy (2004) And co-staring United, *USA Today*, 21 June.

[10] Robert Philpot (2004) Brought to you by ... product placements becoming increasingly harder to escape, *San Diego Union-Tribune/New York Times*, 27 June. See also Andrea Petersen (2001) If product's invisible, can it be placed? *Wall Street Journal*, 9 April.

[11] Naomi Aoki (1004) With ads easier to dodge, companies eye new ways to get out the message, *Forbes*, 30 August. For a detailed analysis of this specific case, see in particular Ted Friedman (2004) *Cast Away* and the contradictions of product placement, *Journal of Promotion Management*, 10(1/2), pp 171–83.

true that both enjoy particularly prominent placements throughout the film. However, in 2000, the use of a fictitious brand would certainly have given rise to more questions. FedEx is present because the actor Tom Hanks plays the role of one of its employees, and because multiple scenes give excuses to see the logo, the company, its packaging, its employee uniforms, its trucks, its aeroplanes – and because in reality, FedEx is a company well versed in brand management. The presence of Wilson is explained by the fact that once washed up on his desert island, the character played by Tom Hanks begins to converse with a Wilson volleyball, and that the brand name can also be used as a first name.

These two placements are without doubt an illustration of what is at first glance a positive presence, even if some found it a little extreme. If we look closer, however, there was also an element of risk for FedEx. In fact, the storyline shows one of the company's transport aeroplanes crashing, the loss of almost all its cargo, the unauthorized opening of certain packages by an employee (although admittedly he is 'cast away' on a desert island!) and the delivery, some years later, of a lost parcel. Some years later! The company's advertising promises deliveries in just a few hours, from one corner of the planet to another, and the quality of its service is one of its main sales points. There could therefore have been a risk of wrong interpretation. This was not the case, because of a staging that removed all suspicions in the matter. This example, however, does help to illustrate the necessary precautions that a brand interested in a placement owes it to itself to take, especially in extreme cases like this one.

Maximal exposure can also sometimes be hazardous. When, in 1988, the Nestlé group bought the Rowntree company, it found, in the confectionery company's brand portfolio, the rights to a little-known chocolate brand, Wonka. The Swiss group surely had no idea at that time that in 2005, the director Tim Burton would wish to remake the Mel Stuart film, *Willy Wonka & the Chocolate Factory* (1971). In 2000, the sales of Wonka chocolate bars had fallen so low that the brand's termination was planned. Seeing an opportunity for a relaunch, however, Nestlé did not hesitate to participate in the filming of *Charlie and the Chocolate Factory* (2005), supplying Tim Burton with hundreds of chocolate bars and more than 100,000 fictitious products. Even if the initial version in 1971 had not been a great cinematic success, Warner Bros did not hesitate to invest US$150 million in the production of the Tim Burton film, which was a genuine commercial success in cinemas.[12]

The placement in the film is a genuine piece of special pleading in favour of chocolate, which caused a reaction among certain consumer associations

[12] Theatre grosses were US$474.968 million: US$206.459 million in the United States and US$268.509 million from the international market. Source: Box Office Mojo, LLC, November 2006.

fighting obesity in children.[13] Notwithstanding, the brand was redynamized in all the markets where it was present. In the original book by Roald Dahl,[14] the eccentric character Willy Wonka opens the doors of his factory to five consumers who had been lucky enough to find a Golden Ticket in the wrapping of their chocolate bar. It was only natural that Nestlé, seeing the Wonka brand taking the lead role in the film, should organize a major promotional campaign along the same lines for the film's release. Everything was put in place to make this case a marketing success: 60 million cases in support of the competition, 30,000 retail outlets equipped with special display cases, a media advertising campaign and dedicated internet site, a tie-in promotional link between Warner Bros and Nestlé, signs in cinemas, a makeover for the product packaging with the child characters from the film, and the association of complementary partners, such as the distributors Wal-Mart, Albertson's, Kroger and Target, the bookshop Barnes & Noble, and American Express.[15]

The advertisers interested in the placement and their agents must both ensure a positive presence.[16] This involves the painstaking study of the means

---

[13] See in particular Anita Awbi (2006) EU food manufacturers get go-ahead for product placement, *Food & Drink Europe*, 2 March. The subject raises many other questions: see also Aaron Baar (2005) FTC rules against product placement disclosure, *Adweek*, 10 February; Rebecca Segall (2003) The new product placement, *The Nation*, 24 February; Ted Lempert (2005) Childhood obesity fuelled by marketing tactics, *San Francisco Chronicle*, 27 April; Caroline E Mayer (2005) TV ads entice kids to overeat, study finds, *Washington Post*, 7 December; Michelle R Nelson and Laurie Ellis McLeod (2005) Adolescent brand consciousness and product placements: awareness, liking and perceived effects on self and others, *International Journal of Consumer Studies*, 29(6), pp 525–28; Gary Ruskin and Juliet Schor (2005) Every nook and cranny: the dangerous spread of commercialized culture, *Multinational Monitor*, 26(1/2), published at http://www.multinationalmonitor.org/mm2005/012005/ruskin.html; Ira Teinowitz (2006) Sen. Harkin launches fresh attack on fast food, *Advertising Age*, 6 April.

[14] For the original edition, see Roald Dahl (1964) *Charlie and the Chocolate Factory*, illustrations by Joseph Schindelman, Alfred A Knopf, New York.

[15] Those brands were promotion partners when the movie was released. Brandchannel (Interbrand Group) identified amongst the placed brands Converse, Golf World, LYPC, Marshall, Nike, Oprah Winfrey and Rockem Sockem Robots. For more information about this case, see in particular T L Stanley (2005) 'Charlie and the Chocolate Factory' goes sweet with ties-ins, *Madison+Vine*, 8 June; Michelle Griffin (2005) Nestle hopes its Wonka brand will turn into a golden ticket, *The Age*, 29 August; Mark Sweney (2005) Willy Wonka chocolates relaunch with *Charlie and the Chocolate Factory* film tie-in, *Marketing*, 9 March, and A O Scott (2005) Looking for the candy, finding a back story, *New York Times*, 15 July.

[16] Sharmistha Law and Kathryn A Braun (2000) I'll have what she's having: gauging the impact of product placement on viewers, *Psychology & Marketing*, 17, December,

of placement and the drawing up of the most detailed placement contract possible (see below). Any disagreement during filming or after the film's release can lead to negative publicity for the brand.

Points to consider in establishing a placement contract

Subject and storyline of the film

There must be a rigorous analysis to determine whether the film is compatible with the brand's history (historical coherence with the brand, compatibility of positionings, tolerable level of violence,[17] possible pornographic nature of the screenplay and so on). The contract must specify that any modification during filming could lead to the withdrawal of the placement initially considered. For instance the placement of the arcade games brand Galaxian in the film *Doom* (2005) by Andrzej Bartkowiak, itself inspired by a video game, seems natural because the film's environment lends itself perfectly to it.

The product placement policy of the production studios

It is important to take into consideration the studio's previous experiences, its contractual rigour, the possibilities of control offered to brands, possible validation of the contract after viewing of the finalized version of the film, and so on. Most of the major studios – 20th Century Fox, Warner Bros, MGM and United Artists (Sony), Universal, Walt Disney, Paramount, Columbia (Sony) and so on – have had their own departments for several decades dedicated to organizing product placements.

---

pp 1059–75. See also Samuel A Turcotte (1995) *Gimme a Bud! The feature film product placement industry*, Master's thesis, University of Texas, Austin, TX, exploring the negative association between Coca-Cola and violent images included in Oliver Stone's *Natural Born Killers* (1994); see also Jack Feuer (2001) Unwelcome guest, *Adweek*, 22 October about wired associations.

[17] A violent content is a sensitive variable, but this is not necessarily a reason to avoid the project. On the contrary, in 1998 Jeffrey Goldstein listed 17 distinct explanations justifying why spectators are lured by violent programmes. See Jeffrey Goldstein (1998) *Why We Watch: The attractions of violent entertainment*, Oxford University Press, New York. Therefore, the brand has to be fully conscious of the violence index and of the possible negative impact on its image.

The director

Issues to be taken into account include his/her reputation, personal image, previous films, attitude towards the placement and the brand in question, and possible active participation in the integration of the products or brand. The association of a name such as Steven Spielberg's, for example, acts from the beginning, quite apart from his likely brilliance in directing the film, as a proof of serious intent for the production, and it also virtually guarantees the film will be given media coverage. This is what encouraged Hitachi to sign with Paramount for Spielberg's *War of the Worlds* (2005). In the final account, however, the products placed were not clearly identifiable, and the brand was apparently disappointed.[18]

Actors likely to be associated with the brand

There should be an analysis of the awareness and above all the image of the actors, apart from the role they play, in order to ensure that there are no potential incompatibilities with the brand. Agencies such as E-Poll Market Research or GlamourSpeakers are able to calculate awareness, image, attraction and influence scores for a star on many attributes, which give the advertiser an idea of the 'marriage' they will be exposing themselves to.[19] The association of Palm Pilot with Jodie Foster in *Flightplan* (Robert Schwentke, 2005) and Lacoste and Coca-Cola with Will Smith in *Hitch* (Andy Tennant, 2005), for example, carries an implicit guarantee for the brands because of the stature of these actors.

---

[18] Gail Schiller (2005) Attention-grabbing film promotions were the exception and not the rule, *Hollywood Reporter*, 7 September. For a detailed research about attitude towards the placed brands, see Isabelle Fontaine (2006) Etude du changement d'attitude pour les marques placées dans les films: persuasion ou effet d'exposition?, *Recherche et Applications en Marketing*, 21(1), pp 1–18.

[19] See B Zafer Erdogan, Michael J Baker and Stephen Tagg (2001) Selecting celebrity endorsers: the practitioners perspective, *Journal of Advertising Research*, 41(3), May–June, pp 39–48; Michael A Kamins (2004) Does fame alone really sell? The effectiveness of celebrities in advertising, *Marshall Magazine*, Spring, University of Southern California, Los Angeles, CA, pp 47–49; M Ellen Peebles (2003) And now, a word from our sponsor, *Harvard Business Review*, 81(10), October, pp 31–42; David Iddiols (2005) Fame game, in K. Suresh (ed), *Celebrity Endorsements*, ICFAI University Press, Hyderabad, pp 12–17.

Contractual incompatibility

There may be incompatibilities between a desired placement and the contractual engagements of an actor outside the film: this may involve two competing brands, for example. Perhaps the actor is the advertising spokesperson for brand A and is asked to wear, or even to praise, brand B onscreen. As Milla Jovovich and Andie MacDowell are ambassadors for L'Oréal, for example, it would be a 'sensitive' issue if another cosmetics manufacturer was to request placement in a film in which they appeared.

The film's dialogue

The aim of this is to verify that any possible misuses of language are not likely to alter the brand's image. For example there might be mentions of political or trade union commitment, lewd remarks or remarks with sexual, racist or xenophobic connotations, which may be necessary to give credibility to the character or the story, but association with which might be damaging to the brand. In *Rain Man* (Barry Levinson, 1988), Tom Cruise denigrates the supermarket chain Kmart in talking to Dustin Hoffman. Alan Arkin rails about chicken dinners while packaging from the restaurant Dinah's, a poultry specialist, is clearly visible on the meal table, in *Little Miss Sunshine* (Jonathan Dayton and Valerie Faris, 2006).

The story's characters

Again, it is important to verify that the characters do not act in ways contrary to the brand's values. It stands to reason that brands will normally wish to avoid association with a murderer, pervert, unscrupulous thief, traitor, liar or loser. Tom Cruise he might be, but the direct association or otherwise of Compaq, Michelob, Nokia and Bacardi with his character as an implacable hired killer in *Collateral* (Michael Mann, 2004) nonetheless carried a degree of risk.

The screenplay and shooting schedule

There should be analysis of the modes of appearance onscreen, or of integration into the screenplay, the types of placement (visual, verbal, combined), the nature of hands-on placement (considering the means, occasion, visibility, actor(s) involved and so on), the number and length of scenes with placements, the importance of the placement, the location onscreen and so on. In the case of a verbal placement, it is recommended that an extract from the script with the lines mentioning the product be literally written into the contract. In *Forrest Gump* (Robert Zemeckis, 1994), Tom Hanks says very clearly, regarding a visit to the White House: 'Now, since it was all free, and I wasn't hungry but thirsty, I must've drank me 15 Dr Peppers.'

The locations used during filming

Another important issue is to check the exteriors or countries where the story is supposed to be set. Verify the possible cases where the brand is censored in one country, or the presence of a competitor's manufacturing or distribution sites makes promotion difficult. For the series *Ally McBeal* and *The Practice* from producer David E Kelley, Starbucks agreed to build an entire set reproducing a coffee shop.[20]

The music used

Music and songs are often present in the cinema, to the point where they sometimes become essential to the film.[21] As such an influence can act positively or negatively on the placement, it is important also to ensure their compatibility with the positioning and image of the brand (considering both the type of music and the lyrics). Brands such as Schott, New Skool, Ecko, Adidas, UnLtd and Mecca worked perfectly with the music of the group B2K in *You Got Served* (2004), by Christopher B Stokes, because their (young) targets were compatible.

Management of the placement

This involves confirming with the studio the general conditions of the placement, issues of exclusivity (in total, by sector and so on), the placement guarantee (assurances that it will not be lost in editing), legal conformity, the length of the shoot and of the production as a whole, the final fixing of the film's release date, and other similar issues. The contract will also mention the person in charge of monitoring the execution of the contract in the interest of both parties. Contracts can be highly detailed, such as that associating Samsung with 20th Century Fox for the film *Fantastic 4* (Tim Story, 2005). The reason was that 90 different Samsung products, from a refrigerator to a plasma screen, were to benefit from a placement.[22]

---

[20] Jim Edwards (2006) The tracker: the fine line between placement and payola, *Brandweek*, 30 January.

[21] Morris B Holbrook (2004) Ambi-diegetic music in films as a product-design and placement strategy: the sweet smell of success, *Marketing Theory*, 4(3), pp 171–85.

[22] Kenneth Hein (2005) Tie-ins: Samsung recharges with *Fantastic 4*, *Brandweek*, 20 June.

Supplying the production

This aspect needs consideration if the contract is based on the provision of materials, products or services. The number, nature, any specificities required by the studio, and delivery methods (and in certain cases the recovery methods) for the products and services must be clearly defined in the contract. For example, for David Fincher's film *The Game* (1997), the specific aerial cameras were supplied by Spacecam Systems Inc, while the Hydroflex company provided the underwater cameras and lighting.

Financing

If the contract anticipates payment, the methods and schedule (total amount, down payment, balance, due dates) must be clearly detailed. It is preferable for the balance payment to coincide with the end of shooting, the end of post-production or, better still, the film's cinema release. This last condition, however, is rarely possible in actuality. Long before the release of *Superman Returns* (Bryan Singer, 2006), Warner Bros had sold the rights to Electronic Arts, in order to enable the release of a multi-platform videogame inspired by the film at the same time as the film was released. In 2005, Volkswagen and NBC Universal announced the signing of a contract thought to be worth US$200 million, guaranteeing the car maker that its cars would be placed in the studio's films and series, as well as the opportunity to participate in various promotional operations.[23] It was impossible at that time to precisely describe the films and series. Such financing, however, offered the possibility of making sure of these opportunities.

The film's credits

The brand may ask to be acknowledged in the end credits of the film, in order to free itself from the possible advertising connotations of the placement. It is important to specify this point in the contract, particularly as regards the terms used and the location of the acknowledgement. For instance, in the end credits to Martin Scorsese's *Casino* (1995), particular thanks are given to the Jockey Club of Ontario and the Casino Hotel Riviera.

---

[23] Nat Ives (2005) That abundance of Volkswagens on TV shows will be product placement, not coincidence, *New York Times*, 13 January. See also Caroline Talbot (2005) Ces marques qui colonisent les programmes, *Stratégies*, 1365, 14 April.

The accompanying communications

All tie-ins, public relations, supporting advertising campaigns and so on, both at the time of the film's release and after, must be anticipated before the contract is signed, and governed by detailed particular clauses. To neglect this point exposes the brand to blockages and possible financial pressures. It is not unusual for these operations to be governed by a discrete contract, joined to the placement contract. If the box-office takings of *Godzilla* (Roland Emmerich, 1998) were not a huge success, the tie-in operations contained in the contract, organized by the restaurant chain Taco Bell, were in contrast highly effective.[24]

The duration of the contract

Delays can be highly unpredictable in the world of cinema. It is therefore preferable to specify the length of the contract. This naturally takes effect from the moment of signature or on the date specified. It usually ends at the end of the legal duration of the film makers' rights. Other methods are possible, however. It may be helpful to make arrangements for the video release or for television broadcasting, to ensure for example that the agreed edit will be retained.

Brand protection and litigation

Any placement contract must clearly stipulate that all rights attached to the brand in question remain the property of the brand. This is particularly in order to avoid uncontrolled additional uses or mentions. In consideration thereof, the contract must clearly stipulate the brand's agreement to the use of its name and its products for the film, in accordance with the contract's terms. As in any professional contract, the courts with competence to settle any possible litigation will be mentioned. Trials are very rare, since they are generally damaging to both parties in image terms. In the vast majority of cases of disagreement, an amicable settlement is eventually reached.

---

[24] Charles A Lubbers and William J Adams (2004) Merchandising in the major motion picture industry: creating brand synergy and revenue streams, *Journal of Promotion Management*, 10(1/2), pp 55–63. About the specific case of the movie, see in particular Tim Carvell (1998) How Sony created a monster, *Fortune*, 137(11), pp 162–70.

Confidentiality

The precise conditions of a placement are rarely disclosed to the media. More often than not, the partners commit to respecting a confidentiality clause (which might or might not include penalties for non-observance), with the basic aim of avoiding amplifying the commercial connotations of the contract. Such a confidentiality clause will also apply to the brand representatives and to the characteristics of the film (storyline, script, actors, locations and so on), in order to avoid disrupting the communications orchestrated by the studio. It is in fact rare that the financial conditions of a contract are revealed to the media.

Designing and studying the methods for a placement possibility is therefore far from simple. Major brands that are well versed in placement techniques, such as Coca-Cola, possess extremely rigorous specifications to validate all checklists in advance. Certain brands sometimes even decline invitations. In 2004, Jonathan Frakes directed the film *Thunderbirds*, inspired by the famous puppet series of the 1960s by Gerry Anderson. One of the charismatic characters, Lady Penelope Creighton-Ward, had the habit of driving around in a pink Rolls-Royce, very futuristic for that era. In 2004, the car brand had become the property of BMW. When contacted to participate in the making of the film, the German car maker declined the offer, not for financial reasons, but for fear that such a transformation, as well as the association with the colour pink, could harm the brand's image.[25] It is not uncommon for car makers to be invited to participate in filming.

The cost of a car, especially a luxury car, can be significant for a production budget, and more particularly if the screenplay calls for its destruction or major adaptations. This is why it is common for car makers to add a clause to their partnership contracts indicating that their cars shall not be given to the bad guys in the story (assassins, rapists, mafiosos, gang members, kidnappers, terrorists, paedophiles and so on), since it is preferable that they not be assimilated into the brand's image. BMW preferred its Minis to be driven by Mike Myers as *Austin Powers in Goldmember* (Jay Roach, 2002), and by Charlize Theron and Mark Wahlberg in *The Italian Job* (F Gary Gray, 2003), rather than by Patrick Wilson, who played Jeff Kohlver, a 32-year-old man who meets a 14-year-old girl online and invites her to come to his house so he can take photographs of her, in *Hard Candy* (David Slade, 2006).

This preference is by no means systematic. In some cases, a brand may wish to 'slum it', or simply give itself a more rebellious edge. In those cases, however, it makes arrangements to monopolize all the 'roles', good and bad,

---

[25] Alan Wilkes (2004) Product placement puts you in the pink, *Irish Independent*, 28 March.

in order to avoid any confusion, as the Ford group did in the adventures of James Bond, and Toyota did in *Terminator 3* (Jonathan Mostow, 2003). Arnold Schwarzenegger drove a Toyota Tundra whereas the 'villains' rode in a Lexus SC 430. When the Bayer group is called upon for a product placement, the positive aspect of the placement is clearly indicated in the agreement. The remarks made about the product must be perfectly compatible with the brand's arguments, the product must be involved in a context that does not in any way harm the brand or the company, and it must benefit as much as possible from an advantageous placement from a competitive point of view.[26]

Maximizing the prominence and visibility of the placement

Some brands have no hesitation in adapting their product and their signing (for instance, the shapes, colours and size of the logo) in order to give their placement greater visibility. This is what the Avaya brand, a specialist in corporate communications,[27] did when it was placed in *Just Like Heaven* (Mark Walters, 2005) and *The Bourne Supremacy* (Paul Greengrass, 2004). It may be that the props master hides logos during filming, but he or she might not do so systematically if they do not interfere with the scene. Various studies show that some brands placed in films are never noticed by the audience.[28] In order to avoid this pitfall, an HP printer is filmed in full frame while it enables actress Kristen Bell to reconstitute the photo of a spirit in *Pulse* (Jim Sonzero, 2006).

[26] Robin Kitzes Silk (2001) From *E.T.* to *Cast Away*: product placement in film, *International Trademark Association Bulletin*, February.

[27] Abram Sauer (2005) Product placement: making the most of a close-up, *Brandchannel Newsletter*, 26 September.

[28] Jean-Marc Lehu (2005) Le placement de marques au cinéma, proposition de la localisation du placement à l'écran comme nouveau facteur d'efficacité potentielle, *Décisions Marketing*, 37, January–March, pp 17–31. The placement prominence variable is more and more privileged, including in productions from Brazil, Thailand, India and South Korea. See research by N Devathan, Michelle Nelson, J McCarty, S Deshpande, H J Paek, R Punnahitanond, S E Stein, A M Vilela and R Yaros (2003) Product placements go global: an examination of contacts across five countries, *Advances in Consumer Research*, 30, ed Punam Anand Keller and Dennis W Rook, AAA, Atlanta, GA, pp 170–71.

The prominence of a placement essentially concerns three factors that must be considered together: the space taken up on screen, the length of time onscreen and the number of occurrences. All these factors are of course naturally favourable when it comes to audience recall of the placement.[29] A placement can be prominent if it takes up a large physical space onscreen or if it is repeatedly mentioned in the characters' dialogues. Research on placements has shown that when it is possible to bring an appearance and a verbal mention together in a placement, this provides an even greater opportunity for memorization.[30] The producers are sometimes more reluctant to agree to a verbal mention, since the advertising connotation can rapidly take over if the placement is not well integrated into the storyline. In 1988 the producer Michael Peyser refused a request from Eastern Airlines to modify the dialogue, when it wished to improve its placement in Jim Abrahams's *Big Business*.[31] A placement can also be considered pre-eminent if the length of the product's or the brand's exposure onscreen is significant.[32]

Finally, prominence can also be analysed by considering the number of scenes in which the brand or product are present. The combination of these three factors can give the placement an unmissable aspect, and can open wide the doors of perception and, in some cases, memorization. Taking into account the parallel distracting factors linked to the story or the direction, prominence must therefore be considered as an essential aspect, to be taken into account when the contract is signed.

Ultimately, if the brand is supposed to appear onscreen, it is of course preferable for it to be seen (or heard) on that same screen.[33] Prominence should also be analysed in a relative manner, however: that is, in relation to the number of other placements present in the same space (same film, same novel, same programme and so on). It can be argued that a higher number of

[29] Pola B Gupta, Siva K Balasubramanian and Michael L Klassen (2000) Viewer's evaluations of product placements in movies: public policy issues and managerial implications, *Journal of Current Issues and Research in Advertising*, 22(2), pp 41–52.

[30] See in particular Cristel Antonia Russell (1998) Toward a framework of product placement: theoretical propositions, *Advances in Consumer Research*, 25, ed Joseph W Alba and J Wesley Hutchinson, AAA, Atlanta, GA, pp 357–62.

[31] Ronald Alsop (1988) Consumer products become movie stars: marketers gain as film makers try to cut costs, *Wall Street Journal*, 29 February.

[32] Ian Brennan, Khalid M Dubas and Laurie A Babin (1999) The influence of placement type and exposure time on product placement recognition, *International Journal of Advertising*, 18(3), pp 323–37.

[33] Pola B Gupta and Kenneth R. Lord (1998) Product placement in movies: the effect of prominence and mode on audience recall, *Journal of Current Issues and Research in Advertising*, 20(1), Spring, pp 48–59.

placements contributes to the realism of the scene, but the trap of intolerable over-exposure can quickly open wide, as we shall examine later.[34]

It is also important to ensure the visibility of the placement. The prominence of the placement is important, but visibility makes sure that the brand can be correctly identified. This is unquestionably a difficult aspect to manage, and one that requires the possibility of a placement to be studied as far in advance as possible. For *Rocky III* (Sylvester Stallone, 1982), a scene was rewritten to allow the character of Rocky Balboa (played by Stallone) to clearly recommend that his son eat the cereal of champions, Wheaties.[35] As far as possible, the placement's visibility must transcend the simple context of the film to improve this visibility.

If an internet site is planned, it is wise to study the possibility of mentioning the partnership underlying the placement and to request a hyperlink between the film's site and the advertiser's site. When the Karyn Kusama film *Æon Flux* (2005) was announced, a promotional internet site (see Figures 5.1 and 5.2) was opened to show the trailer, and give information on the film with the aim of making site visitors keen to see it in the cinema. The site had a page dedicated to those partners whose products or brand had been placed. In return, as we have seen, the partner brand's website can also profit from the image of the film and communicate its release. Such a tie-in communications operation allows the placement's visibility to be increased. Likewise, if a videogame based on the film is planned, the advertiser should consider whether it is also relevant to use it as a bridge and to integrate into it, always keeping in mind that the placement operation should be visible and coherent. The study of target compatibility (brand/videogame) will therefore be important in the decision. This particular case will, however, be analysed later in the book.

---

[34] Several different academic research reports have supplied indications about the average number of placements for each movie studied: 11.6 for Sapolsky and Kinney, 18.2 for Troupe, for instance. But the calculation basis differs and observed standard deviations are often very high. See in particular Barry S Sapolsky and Lance Kinney (1994) You oughta be in pictures: product placements in the top grossing films of 1991, in Karen Whitehill King (ed), *Proceedings of the Conference of the American Academy of Advertising*, AAA, Athens, GA, p 89; and M L Troupe (1991) *The Captive Audience: A content of product placements in motion pictures*, Master's thesis, Florida State University, Tallahassee, Fla, quoted by Ian Brennan and Laurie A Babin (2004) Brand placement recognition: the influence of presentation mode and brand familiarity, *Journal of Promotion Management*, 10(1/2), pp 185–202.

[35] Janet Maslin (1982) Plugging product in movies as an applied art, *New York Times*, 15 November.

Figure 5.1 Screen shot of the promotional internet site for the Paramount film *Æon Flux* ((Karyn Kusama, 2005). By kind permission of Asics.

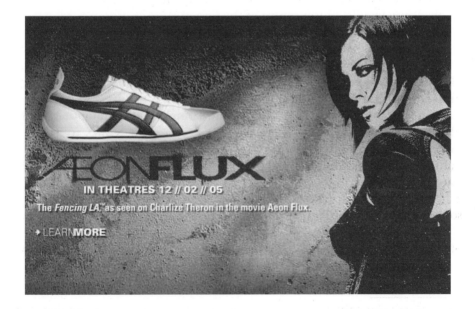

Figure 5.2 Screen shot showing a hyperlink on the Asics website, to the site for the film *Æon Flux* (2005). Reproduced by kind permission of Asics.

Obtaining a central location onscreen

In the film *Hardball* (Brian Robbins, 2001), a placement is made for the newspaper *The New Yorker* and another for the *New York Post*. Only the latter enjoyed a central placement. Tests carried out on these two placements among a sample of video viewers of the film were able to identify a spontaneous memory for the *New York Post* but not for *The New Yorker*.

Not all product or brand placements appear systematically in the same area on the screen. According to the nature of the product or brand, the requirements of the screenplay and the integration process followed, the conditions of appearance will be very different. The power of potential impact is not the same on all areas of a screen. Without taking into account the other characteristics of the placement, the central location onscreen seems to be clearly the best.[36] This can be partly explained by the fact that this is generally where the action takes place and where the viewer's attention is naturally drawn. Tests carried out on different films such as *Men in Black II* (Barry Sonnenfeld, 2002), *Minority Report* (Steven Spielberg, 2002) and *Intolerable Cruelty* (Joel and Ethan Coen, 2003) showed that placements that were more prominent (in both time onscreen and space occupied by the placement), but distant from the central position, occasioned a much weaker spontaneous memory than those that had enjoyed a central position. When actor Nicolas Cage transforms a bottle of Aquafina into a magnifying glass in *National Treasure* (Jon Turtletaub, 2004), the scene places the bottle and its label, clearly legible, in the centre of the screen.

All advertisers whose product to be placed is of small size are particularly vigilant about obtaining this central position. It is sometimes their only chance to be truly noticed. This occurs most frequently through the necessity of genuinely integrating the product into the storyline, so that it will appear in its own shot, even briefly. Directors appear to be relatively well disposed to wrist watch placements, as long as the commercial connotation of the placement remains limited. In fact, when the director wishes to precisely indicate the notion of the time to the viewer, there's nothing like a character naturally looking at his or her watch, and a camera shot that focuses on the watch for a few seconds. Therefore in most cases, the central placement is achieved. There are a great many cases but, once again, it is because they seem so natural that very often the integration goes down well with the audience.

We may note in particular, among the great names of watchmaking, James Stewart's Tissot watch in *Rear Window* (Alfred Hitchcock, 1954), Gregory

---

[36] Jean-Marc Lehu (2005) Le placement de marques au cinéma, proposition de la localisation du placement à l'écran comme nouveau facteur d'efficacité potentielle, *Décisions Marketing*, 37, January–March, pp 17–31.

Peck's Gruen Precision in *The Guns of Navarone* (J Lee Thompson, 1961), Sean Connery's Rolex Submariner in *Goldfinger* (Guy Hamilton, 1964), Kirk Douglas's Bulova Accutron in *Seven Days in May* (John Frankenheimer, 1964), Catherine Zeta-Jones's Casio G-Shock in *Entrapment* (Jon Amiel, 1999), the Panerai of Jason Statham in *The Transporter 2* (Louis Leterrier, 2005) and in *The Italian Job* (F Gary Gray, 2003), the Panerai again, on the wrist of the actor DMX in *Exit Wounds* (Andrzej Bartkowiak, 2001), and on Hugh Grant's wrist both in *Bridget Jones's Diary* (Sharon Maguire, 2001) and in *Two Weeks Notice* (Marc Lawrence, 2002), Kurt Russell's Breitling Sirius in *Stargate* (Roland Emmerich, 1994), Clint Eastwood's Rolex GMT in his own *Firefox* (1982), Tommy Lee Jones's Hamilton Venturas in *Men in Black* (Barry Sonnenfeld, 1997), which becomes a Hamilton Pulsar in *Men in Black II* (Barry Sonnenfeld, 2002), Roger Moore's Seiko TV watch in *Octopussy* (John Glen, 1983), Alan Alda's Raymond Weil in *Murder at 1600* (Dwight H Little, 1997), Alec Baldwin's Omega Seamaster in *The Edge* (Lee Tamahori, 1997), Tom Cruise's futuristic Bulgari in *Minority Report* (Steven Spielberg, 2002) and his IWC Mark XV in *Vanilla Sky* (Cameron Crowe, 2001), Gary Sinise's Omega Speedmaster Professional in *Mission to Mars* (Brian de Palma, 2000), and Pierce Brosnan's Omega Seamaster Professional, notably in *GoldenEye* (Martin Campbell, 1995), Eric Bana's Hamilton in *Hulk* (Ang Lee, 2003), and Arnold Schwarzenegger's Panerai Marina Luminor in *Eraser* (Chuck Russell, 1996).

The common feature of these different examples of well-directed watch placements is that they benefited from a close-up. Placing it at the centre of the screen, the shot enables viewers to acquaint themselves with what the character is supposed to see on his or her watch; it is a shot that lends itself to good audience identification. Exposure is sometimes even more powerful, as for the Omega Seamaster Professional watch shown in full screen in the opening credits of *Tomorrow Never Dies* (Roger Spottiswoode, 1997), and the Adanac used by the American government, which occupies a similar place in the opening credits of *Gone in Sixty Seconds* (Dominic Sena, 2000). Although the cases of association between watches and the cinema are ancient and numerous, certain brands are more involved than others.[37]

The TAG Heuer manufacturer is especially present on the big screen. This is a real axis of communication, reinforced by its advertising campaigns which are based on various celebrities from the world of sport or cinema, such as Brad Pitt, Uma Thurman and Steve McQueen (see Figures 5.3 and 5.4). TAG Heuer appeared recently in *The Departed* (Martin Scorsese, 2006), *Babel* (Alejandro González Iñárritu, 2006), *Crank* (Mark Neverdine and Brian Taylor, 2006), *Something New* (Sanaa Hamri, 2006), *Fun with Dick and*

---

[37] In George Melford's *The Sheik* (1921), as in George Fitzmaurice's *The Son of the Sheik* (1926), actor Rudolph Valentino wore a Cartier Tank watch.

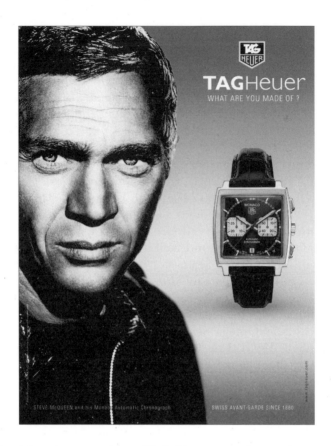

Figure 5.3 Advertisement for a TAG Heuer watch, model Monaco Automatic Chronograph, with the actor Steve McQueen (2005). Reproduced by kind permission of TAG Heuer SA, Marin, Switzerland.

Jane (Dean Parisot, 2006), *Zathura: A Space Adventure* (Jon Favreau, 2005), *The Island* (Michael Bay, 2005), *In My Country* (John Boorman, 2004), *Be Cool* (F Gary Gray, 2005), *Bewitched* (Nora Ephron, 2005), *Four Brothers* (John Singleton, 2005), *First Daughter* (Forest Whitaker, 2004), *Closer* (Mike Nichols, 2004), *Collateral* (Michael Mann, 2004), *Ils se marièrent et eurent beaucoup d'enfants* (They got married and had many lots of children) (Yvan Attal, 2004), *The Bourne Supremacy* (Paul Greengrass, 2004), *Secret Window* (David Koepp, 2004), *Win a date with Tad Hamilton!* (Robert Luketic, 2004) and *The Recruit* (Roger Donaldson, 2003).[38] It can be seen that these films are all very

---

[38] Many recent examples of TAG-Heuer placement could be given. The TAG-Heuer brand could be seen in 1971, in Lee Katzins' movie, *Le Mans*, as a sponsor of a racing car driver played by Steve McQueen. He wore the famous Monaco model launched in 1969.

Figure 5.4 Advertisement for a TAG Heuer watch, model Link Diamonds Watch, with the actress Uma Thurman (2005). Reproduced by kind permission of TAG Heuer SA, Marin, Switzerland.

different and consequently reach audiences that are equally varied, which can be very attractive to a brand such as TAG Heuer, to enlarge its original connotations of luxury and sport.

The question of the central screen position takes a different turn when it relates to a place. If that place is clearly identified, and character development takes place there, then the placement is considered to be central. Hence the multiple grants that a director can sometimes receive if he/she chooses to film in one town in preference to another, or prefers one region to another. This is not only because this often constitutes, for some viewers, an explicit or non-explicit invitation to go there themselves, but also because many people are already assiduous practitioners of cinema tourism, visiting locations in order to relive the experiences of one character or another in the exact places seen in the film or the series. *March of the Penguins* (Luc Jacquet, 2005) was responsible for an increase in visitor numbers at many aquariums across the world, since these had a section dedicated to sphenisciforms, or in other words, to one of the 18 existing species of penguin.[39] In France, the successful series *Dolmen*, set in Brittany, did a great deal for local tourism. However, it is the Provence-Alpes-Côte d'Azur region of France that heads the list of directors' and producers' choices.

Negotiating and controlling integration into the story

This recommendation is without doubt the most important of all: it is the Holy Grail of placements! Integration into the screenplay is the necessary connection for passing from perception to persuasion. It is essential to see (or hear) the product or the brand placed in the film, because this is the starting point of the process. It is increasingly important, however, for this product or brand to reveal a need or arouse a desire in the viewer. As we have already mentioned, a brand or product placement's success with the audience can never be guaranteed. For a brand to try its luck, however, it must avoid the numerous snares that lie in wait. An integration that has not been properly thought through and is irrelevant is one of them. Placing a Philips electric razor in the hands of the actor Will Ferrell, so that he can shave onscreen, in *Bewitched* (Nora Ephron, 2005), is preferable to inserting a simple advertising board for the brand in the background. The objective is therefore to give the product a genuine role.[40] Before we can really talk of integration, however, this role must appear to be natural, logical, and even, in some cases, vital. The impact of the placement can then be much greater, as academic research has confirmed.[41]

---

[39] See in particular Abram Sauer (2006) Brandchannel's 2005 product placement awards, *BusinessWeek*, 2 March and Jennifer Carter (2005) Penguins waddle into spotlight, *Dallas Morning News*, 13 August.

[40] Mary R Zimmer and Denise E DeLorme (1997) The effects of brand placement type and a disclaimer on memory for brand placements in movies, paper presented to the Association for Education in Journalism and Mass Communication Conference, 30 July–2 August, Chicago, IL.

[41] See in particular Alain d'Astous and Francis Chartier (2000) A study of factors affecting consumer evaluations and memory of product placements in movies, *Journal of Current Issues and Research in Advertising*, 22(2), pp 31–40. About the 'product assimilation' technique, when the brand becomes the central character of the show, see Kim Bartel Sheehan and Aibing Guo (2005) 'Leaving on a (branded) jet plane': an exploration of audience attitudes towards product assimilation in television content, *Journal of Current Issues in Advertising*, 27(1), Spring, pp 79–91.

Pick up the trail!
The case: Pink Panther. +++ The car: smart fortwo.

Figure 5.5   Screen shot of the internet site www.smart.com, during the promotional operation set up by Smart on the release of the film *The Pink Panther* (Shawn Levy, 2006). Reproduced by kind permission of DaimlerChrysler.

The most interesting case of a brand integrated into the screenplay occurs when the principal actor uses the brand or the product. In *The Cannonball Run* (Hal Needham, 1976), while drinking, actor Dom DeLuise tells Burt Reynolds that he is drinking Dr Pepper. Goldie Hawn frequently uses her Mastercard in *Bird on a Wire* (1990) by John Badham. Charlie Sheen drives a BMW 325is throughout *The Chase* (Adam Rifkin, 2004). Matthew Modine, Paul Reiser and Randy Quaid eat at McDonald's in *Bye Bye Love* (Sam Weisman, 2005). Mike Myers uses a Motorola telephone in *Austin Powers in Goldmember* (Jay Roach, 2002). Diane Lane travels to Italy on a United Airlines flight in *Under the Tuscan Sun* (Audrey Wells, 2004). A Smart ForTwo car is the almost ideal accompaniment for Inspector Clouseau in *The Pink Panther* (Shawn Levy, 2006). See also Figure 5.5. In all these cases, the brand or the product, or even the service, is integrated into the screenplay. In different ways, admittedly: but at a given moment, they are all useful to the scene.

What is even more advantageous for the brand is that it also enjoys the actor's implicit recommendation. This recommendation can be a simple positive image factor, but in some cases it also has a direct impact on sales of the product in question.[42] The sales of Ray-Ban's Aviator sunglasses rose by

---

[42] In 2006, the Smart car's placement in *The Pink Panther* was followed by Ron Howard's *The Da Vinci Code*, David Zucker's *Scary Movie 4*, Tim Hill's *Garfield 2* and Ridley Scott's *A Good Year*, revealing a clear and clever marketing strategy from Mercedes-Benz for its little car. See Hamish Pringle (2004) Succeeding with celebrities, *Market Leader*, 24, Spring, pp 40–45. See also Allyson L Stewart-Allen (1999) Product placement helps sell brand, *Marketing News*, 33(4), p 8.

40 per cent in the seven months following the release of *Top Gun* (Tony Scott, 1986), after viewers had seen Tom Cruise wear them.[43]

Regarding the integration of Yahoo, Apple's iPod and Microsoft's Xbox in the film *Transformers* (Michael Bay, 2007), producer Lorenzo di Bonaventura declared to *Advertising Age:*

> The script was designed to incorporate some of these things ... as opposed to jamming a soda machine in somewhere after the movie's done. Hopefully smart filmmakers will start [talking to promotional partners] earlier. The earlier the dialogue begins, the sooner they can integrate you in ways that are legitimate as opposed to being thrown in there, which is where product placement becomes problematic.[44]

Integration into the storyline, or plot placement, has been confirmed on numerous occasions by academic research to offer a potential impact much greater than a simple appearance in the background of the set.[45] It is still necessary, however, for what is written in the contract to appear onscreen. Not only can the director wish to change the screenplay during filming and possibly thereby alter how the brand is integrated, but he/she may also ultimately decide, in the editing suite, that the scene in question is not interesting (any more), or that it breaks up the rhythm of the film. Cue deletion, pure and simple! We should bear in mind that whereas, in the United States, the final decision (right of final cut) rests with the producer, in a country such as France, where the artist's moral rights are of great importance (unlike the United States where they do not exist), the director maintains complete control of his/her *oeuvre*.

Even more frustrating for the advertiser, however, is that the scene may be shot in a favourable manner and retained during editing, but the post-production delays on the film are protracted and all other complementary promotional activities are confused, or must even be cancelled. What is the point of an operation such as a linked event at point of purchase, for example, if the film has not been released? Worse still, if it is not even scheduled for release?

---

[43] J D Reed (1989) Plugging away in Hollywood, *Time Magazine*, 2 January. See also Kerry Segrave (2004) *Product Placement in Hollywood Films: A history*, McFarland, Jefferson, NC.

[44] See the very relevant article from T L Stanley and Marc Graser (2006) Content integration works better before the cameras start rolling, *Advertising Age*, 27 September.

[45] Cristel Antonia Russell (2002) Investigating the effectiveness of product placements in television shows: the role of modality and plot connection congruence brand memory and attitude, *Journal of Consumer Research*, 29, December, pp 306–18.

Such cases are rare today, but the release of the film *Die Hard 2* (Renny Harlin, 1990) gave rise to legal proceedings concerning a placement, or rather a non-placement. The leading maker of portable power tools had signed a US$20,000 contract with 20th Century Fox to ensure that a Black & Decker Univolt cordless drill would be used in the film.[46] Unhappy with the scene afterwards, however, the director removed it from the final cut, and thereby removed the product placement. Black & Decker had prepared a promotional campaign based around this placement. The case ended in an amicable settlement between the parties, shortly before the court case was due to begin.

When a film's storyline concerns sport, whether directly or indirectly, many brands are ready to appear on the poster. Thus, in the film *The Benchwarmers* (Dennis Dugan, 2006), we can see Adidas, Under Armour, Nike, Easton, Wilson and Mizuno, among others, who were all happy with their placement. In 1997, however, Reebok was less lucky, and did not hesitate to take the studio Tristar Pictures to court for failure to comply with its placement contract.[47] Originally, the two parties had reached an agreement stipulating that the Reebok brand should be presented in a positive manner in the film *Jerry Maguire* (Cameron Crowe, 1996). Throughout the film Cuba Gooding, Jr plays an American football player who wants his agent to obtain an advertising contract for him. In exchange for the commitment to feature its products, Reebok had provided more than US$1.5 million worth of props, equipment and advertising support. The film should have ended with acknowledgement of Reebok's assistance in the film's end credits, which was not the case, hence the legal proceedings.[48] As part of the settlement of these differences, when the film was first broadcast on television in the United States on the *ShowTime* channel on 17 January 1998, the cut scene was replaced in the film's end credits. These two examples illustrate the advantages of drawing up a detailed contract and the importance of meticulously observing the process of integrating the product or brand into the scene.

---

[46] Steven Colford (1990) Lawsuit drills Fox, Cato, *Advertising Age*, 3 December.

[47] Stuart Elliott (1997) Reebok's suit over *Jerry Maguire* shows risks of product placement, *New York Times*, 7 February.

[48] Adam Sandler (1996) Reebok sues TriStar over *Jerry* tie-in, *Variety*, 24 December. Reebok got US$10 million in compensation after an out of court settlement. See in particular Dale Buss (1998) A product-placement hall of fame, *BusinessWeek*, 11 June and Robert Philpot (2004) Brought to you by ... product placements becoming increasingly harder to escape, *San Diego Union-Tribune/New York Times*, 27 June. In 2006, the appliance company Emerson initiate a lawsuit against NBC, accusing the network of placing its In-Sink-Erator (garbage disposal) brand without consent in the *Heroes* series. The Emerson brand logo was removed from the re-broadcasts of the series. See Jim Edwards (2006) The tracker: in-sink-erator's background placement jumps to forefront, *Brandweek*, 6 November.

Signing a detailed partnership contract as far in advance as possible

It is not uncommon these days for brands to bypass their traditional advertising agency to sign a contract directly with the film producers.[49] According to placement professionals, there are two main explanatory factors: on one hand, it reduces the cost by cutting out the middle party; on the other, an advertising consultancy may not always have the personnel in house, or even the state of mind, to envisage such partnerships with the very specialized world of cinema.

Jeep® became a partner of Bristol Bay Productions on *Sahara* (Breck Eisner, 2005), two years before the film's release.[50] Miramax studios have a contract with Coors Brewing; Kmart has one to supply wardrobes for several Warner Bros Television Network series. Burger King enjoys a partnership with Dreamworks studios. McDonald's profits from a partnership agreement with the *Spy Kids* franchise, and a long-standing one with Walt Disney. Starbucks is associated with Lion's Gate.[51] Ford is committed to Revolution Studios. Procter & Gamble, heavily involved in branded entertainment, has signed a partnership contract with Warner Bros for the series *What I Like About You*, within the framework of a US$300 million partnership with Viacom since 2000.[52] For its part, NBC Universal has a similar partnership with the car maker Volkswagen.[53] The production studios Weinstein Co has agreed to a two-year marketing partnership with the L'Oréal group, and signed a comparable alliance, for US$25 million,[54] with the communications company WPP, which also has a co-production agreement with ABC, notably for *The Days*. This is not a fad, but a genuine trend!

Such contracts offer three major advantages. First, they enable the placers concerned to consider an intelligent integration strategy into the screenplay

---

[49] Melanie Wells (2001) Who really needs Madison Avenue? *Forbes*, 29 October.

[50] Stuart Elliott (2005) Lessons taught by *Lara Croft* help Paramount and Jeep to a smooth ride across *Sahara*, *New York Times*, 10 March. Todd Wasserman and Karl Greenberg (2005) Tie-ins: Jeep, Ray-Ban to heat up Paramount's *Sahara*, *Brandweek*, 21 February.

[51] Kate MacArthur (2006) Starbucks partners with Lion's Gate for movie deal, *Advertising Age*, 12 January.

[52] John Consoli (2006) Buyer: begin placements with creators, *MediaWeek*, 8 February.

[53] A US$200 million contract concerning films and television series as well. Ives Nat (2005) That abundance of Volkswagens on TV show will be product placement, not coincidence, *New York Times*, 13 January.

[54] Marc Graser and T L Stanley (2005) Weinstein organizes brand integration studio, *Madison+Vine*, 9 November.

for the product or the brand. This enables them to study the nature of the film, its positioning and therefore the target audience it is aimed at. British Airways therefore linked up with the film *Proof of Life* (Taylor Hackford, 2000) because the film's profile meant that it was aimed at a clientele likely to be interested in its first and business classes. The company can expect to have better control over the placement methods and therefore over the appearance of its products and brands onscreen.[55] The objective is no longer to negotiate the maximum prominence at the expense of the film, but to achieve a rise in value for the placement and the film. In other words, it is to respect the elementary principle of a partnership: a win-win scenario. It also involves avoiding a win-lose scenario: having read a script of an episode of the television series *G vs E* (1999–2000), the bus company Greyhound, although it has always participated in films and television series, declined a partnership offer when it realized that the plan was to blow up a bus terminal.

Second, these contracts leave enough time to organize the life of the placement after the film is launched. The filming of an advertising spot alluding to the film in one form or another, the organization of a press relations campaign, the creation of a dedicated interactive internet site, the planning of an event at point of purchase, and the like are all operations that will require time for creation and coordination.

Third, these contracts can also be signed over the longer term, and can simply integrate the juxtaposition of placement tactics as they go along, film after film. A communications agency or an advertiser that holds such a contract with a production studio will find itself to be the first, even the only partner sought out for future projects.

In 2005, in the United States, General Motors participated in the programme *The Apprentice: Martha Stewart* to present its Lucerne model. This is held up in the specialist press as one of the worst examples of branded entertainment, since throughout the programme, Mercedes and Maybach models contributed by carrying the star to the placed brand.[56] Although investments in product placements continue to grow, the 'interesting' projects are not necessarily more numerous each year. It is therefore worthwhile to master them.

If a tie-in publicity campaign is envisaged for the film's release, it is also important to ensure that all permissions have been obtained in advance: not only to avoid the lack of them blocking the campaign, but also to avoid possibly seeing prices raised under time pressure. This is especially the case for the actors themselves, with whom, as we have already discussed, it is

---

[55] Ian Brennan, Khalid M Dubas and Laurie A Babin (1999) The influence of placement type and exposure time on product placement recognition, *International Journal of Advertising*, 18(3), pp 323–38.

[56] Marc Graser and T L Stanley (2006) Best and worst M&V deals, last half of 2005, *Madison+Vine*, 4 January.

sometimes necessary to sign a parallel contract for the use of their image, if their character is supposed to appear in point-of-purchase advertising, or in an advertising film. In the United States, certain contracts go so far as to secure the actor's commitment to not disparage the product or brand in interviews. The perfectly controllable star only exists in the hands of Al Pacino in *S1mOne* (Andrew Niccol, 2002) where the 'star' is a virtual reality actor. All other stars are and remain human beings, whose personality, character or simply mood are not always perfectly in accord with the management of the brand's image.

The contractual aspect of product and brand placements in cinema is not a recent one. Nevertheless, the new contracts are much more detailed, in order to avoid the snares of the past. How many placements, although they appeared on camera, have remained prisoners of the editing suite, disappearing totally in the final version of the film shown, or did not achieve the role promised to them? Hence the interest for advertisers (and sometimes for communications agencies themselves) in using professional placement specialists, not only to establish the most effective contractual relations possible in advance, but also to supervise the proper execution of the contract throughout the production process. Beyond the expected return on investment, generally nowadays the reputation of the brand is at stake. Therefore there is no question of neglecting the manner in which it will be presented. One unfortunate appearance, and all or part of its image capital risks going up in flames in a few brief seconds.[57]

The advantage of placement specialists is that they think for the brand and for the film (or any other placement vector), in order to find the most symbiotic association possible, or in other words the one likely to best serve the objectives (technical, logistical, marketing, commercial, financial and strategic) of both partners. Considering as early as possible the most suitable methods of integrating the brand can enable to a great extent the elimination of possible surprises and drawbacks, which are always potentially fraught with bad consequences for the brand should they occur.

---

[57] Evelyn Nussenbaum (2005) Products slide into more TV shows with help from new middlemen, *New York Times*, 6 September.

6 Respect for a legal framework and the desire for ethical practice

In the United States, in a television programme (particularly live), it is not uncommon to hear guests, preferably celebrities, boast of the merits of such and such a product, or such and such a brand, in one of their answers to the presenter's questions, especially if this product has a medical connotation. Thus, the audience might have thought that Lauren Bacall herself used Visudyne to combat muscular degeneration, and that she mentioned it quite naturally, following her own satisfaction with it.[1] They might have believed that the actor Rob Lowe was promoting Neulasta to combat the secondary effects of cancer, because his character Sam Seaborn, in the series *The West Wing*, was pressuring the Administration to achieve a cure for cancer inside 10 years, or because he had become the ambassador for the association *By My Side, Taking Charge of Cancer Treatment*, following his father's cancer.[2] Then again,

---

[1] Daniel Eisenberg (2002) It's an ad, ad, ad, ad world, *Time Magazine*, 2 September. See also articles from David P P Hamilton (2002) Celebrities help 'educate' public on new drugs, *Wall Street Journal*, 22 April and Melody Petersen (2002) Heartfelt advice, hefty fees, *New York Times*, 11 August.

[2] Adele Slaughter (2002) Rob Lowe campaigns for cancer patients, *USA Today*, 13 September.

perhaps it was because he had also become the advertising spokesperson for Amgen laboratories, makers of Neulasta. Where does testimonial end and advertising begin? Everyone knows the selling power of a celebrity, so where is the ethical, or even the legal line that must not be crossed?[3]

In the United States, it seems that almost anything is permissible in placement terms. To date, the protests of consumer or corporatist associations have never been truly taken on by legislators. This is simply because the public in general seem not to complain. In Europe, Commissioner Viviane Reding proposed a relaxing of the 'Television without borders' directive of 3 October 1989[4] at the end of 2005.[5] This advance was significant, since the original text did not consider product placements as such. This proposal by Commissioner Reding had a triple interest. She was implicitly making an observation that there was a degree of legislative anarchy on this subject between the different Member States, with more or less restrictive but nonetheless real bans in countries such as France, Great Britain and Germany, unlike others.[6] The Commission argued even then that only Austria had a clear legal framework in place regarding the use of product placements. With broadcasting via cable, satellite or telephone line of television programmes from all over the world in the different countries in question, these gaps in the legal regime could set local actors, themselves subject to possible restrictions, at a disadvantage.

Second, the Commission's analysis showed that in consequence, the lack of a framework contributed in fact to depriving European producers of content of an important source of finance.[7] Third, the professionals were well aware

---

[3] Hamich Pringle (2004) *Celebrity Sells*, Wiley, Hoboken, NJ. See also research by Michelle L Roehm, Harper A Roehm Jr and Derrick S Boone (2004) Plugs versus placements: a comparison of alternatives for within-program brand exposure, *Psychology & Marketing*, 21(1), pp 17–28; and a book by Graeme Turner (2004) *Understanding Celebrity*, Sage, London.

[4] Proposal for a Directive of the European Parliament and of the Council amending Council Directive 89/552/EEC on the coordination of certain provisions laid down by law, regulation or administrative action in Member States concerning the pursuit of television broadcasting activities presented by the Commission (13/12/2005).

[5] Softening did not concern prescription drugs and tobacco, but no restrictions were mentioned for alcohol. And placement prominently targeted at children would not be allowed. See in particular Leo Cendrowicz (2006) EU broadcast rules spark debate, *Hollywood Reporter*, 21 February.

[6] See Dan Sabbagh (2006) Product placement meets strong opposition in EU, *The Times*, 16 October. See also Doreen Carvajal (2005) EU's proposed ad rules back product placement, *International Herald Tribune*, 13 December and Colin Grimshaw (2005) Media analysis: Kit-Kats in Corrie?, *Marketing*, 2 June, for an analysis of the legal British framework.

[7] Steven Castle (2005) Brussels opens the door to the US-style product placement in TV programmes, *Independent*, 14 December.

that traditional advertising was losing ground in terms of impact.[8] Above all, she spelt out the consequences of an upheaval in the media environment, as described in the first part of this book, and clearly acknowledged that product placement was a separate form of communication. It was a lucid analysis, taking into account what had already been happening for several years on the other side of the Atlantic, and the damaging consequences that this could have on European production. In an interview with the *Financial Times*, Viviane Reding rightly defended the idea of product placement, claiming that such a recognition would contribute to creating jobs in Europe, and that this would stimulate production within the Union, while allowing the development of new techniques.[9]

The European Commission also indicated that it planned, understandably enough, to ban placements aimed at misleading the consumer, and to ensure that consumers were better informed of the nature of placements contained in the programme. This proposition was nevertheless criticized by various associations and even from within the Commission itself,[10] as a green light for out-and-out commercialism, not to mention excess liberalism.[11] And yet product and brand placements exist everywhere in the world, including in less developed or developing countries. Denying it, or attempting to protect ourselves at any cost, would be completely absurd, a demagogic fantasy without the shadow of a logical foundation. In contrast, calling for consumers to be better informed about these same placements would be a step in the right direction, and would enable the technique to develop in a healthier context, since possibilities for getting around the law remain.

The possibility of 'legally' getting around the law

Brands did not wait for the development of formal product placement before finding ways to 'legally' get around the ban on advertising communications, in

---

[8] Sarah Laitner (2005) Brussels studies shake-up in TV adverts, *Financial Times*, 25 October. See also the interesting analysis from Brinsley Dresden and Lewis Silkin (2006) EU TV rules could alter US cash flow, *Brandweek*, 13 March, which moderates a little bit the possibilities for the European industry facing the US branded entertainment paradise.

[9] Sarah Laitner and Tobias Buck (2005) Brussels to liberalise television advertising, *Financial Times*, 12 December.

[10] Benjamin Ferran (2005) Bruxelles veut ouvrir les vannes de la publicité à la télé, *L'Expansion*, 13 December.

[11] Raphaël Garrigos and Isabelle Roberts (2005) 'Télévisions sans frontières': le raid libéral de Reding, *Libération*, 26 September.

whatever form.[12] Placement did, however, make things much easier, particularly for certain sensitive sectors, all the more so since the introduction of digital communications, which made insertion easier without always troubling about the medium.[13] Some argue for the strengthening of the ethical boundaries that must not be crossed.[14] For, although television sponsorship in most countries is required to clearly identify the sponsor or sponsors, product placement still avoids this obligation in many cases, particularly in films.

There seems to be no easy solution to the problem. If sponsorship was scrupulously applied to programmes and television series, it would eventually also affect feature films shown on television. Is it reasonable to suppose that during a film or a television series, banners should appear onscreen to warn the viewer that paid-for placements are to appear? Nevertheless, placements suspected of being 'clandestine advertising' pose an additional problem, when the product concerned is banned from advertising elsewhere: all the

---

[12] Jean-Marc Lehu and Jean J Boddewyn (1996) La communication interdite, *Revue Française du Marketing*, 1996(1), pp 23–36. We may observe that many legal frameworks are becoming tougher when it comes to marketing communications, especially when targeting children, and more precisely when it concerns obesity risks. Regarding this, see Laurel Wentz (2006) Europe stops school soft-drink marketing, *Advertising Age*, 31 January. Product placement may offer the possibility of continuing to communicate while respecting the law, as confirmed by research from Kraak and Pelletier: Vivica Kraak and David L Pelletier (1998) How marketers reach young consumers: implications for nutrition education and health campaigns, *Family Economics and Nutrition Reviews*, 11(4), pp 31–41.

[13] See in particular Lawrence A Wenner (2004) On the ethics of product placement in media entertainment, *Journal of Promotion Management*, 10(1/2), pp 101–32; Amit M Schejter (2004) Product placement as an international practice: moral, legal, regulatory and trade implications, paper presented to the 32nd conference on Research in Communication, Information and Internet, October, National Center for Technology & Law, Law School, George Mason University, Arlington, VA. Rungpaka Tiwsakul and Chris Hackley (2005) Ethics and regulation of contemporary marketing communication practices: an exploration of the perceptions of UK-based consumers towards the ethical issues raised by product placement in British TV shows, Research paper SoMo502, School of Management, London University, Royal Holloway, Egham, Surrey, UK. For a detailed study of the US case, see Miguel Valenti, Les Brown and Laurie Trotta (eds) (2000) *More than a Movie: Ethical decision making in the entertainment industry*, Westview Press, Boulder, CO, and for a study of the Australian case, see in particular Stacey Brennan, Philip J Rosenberger III and Veronica Hementera (2004) Product placements in movies: an Australian consumer perspective on their ethicality and acceptability, *Marketing Bulletin*, 15, article 1, http://marketing-bulletin.massey.ac.nz

[14] Ching Ho Yu (2002) Ethical issues of product placement and manipulation, unpublished research paper, 21 November, Arizona State University, Temple, AZ.

more so since consumers themselves seem to be sensitive to the question.[15] The four main sectors in question are pharmaceuticals and weapons, and above all tobacco and alcohol.

The problem with pharmaceuticals stems from the fact that communication in this field is severely restricted in the majority of developed countries. The advantage of a placement is therefore that it avoids having to emphasize the directions for use, contra-indications, composition and other issues, and allows the product to be placed in situations that are positive for its awareness and image. Thus Lipitor is present in *Something's Gotta Give* (Nancy Myers, 2003), Pfizer's Zoloft appears in *The Sixth Sense* (M Night Shyamalan, 1999), while Vicodin is in *The Ring* (Gore Verbinski, 2002). However, since anything that is sexual in nature can be used in multiple manners, the most numerous placements of pharmaceuticals of past years are probably those of Pfizer's Viagra, present for example in *The Pink Panther* (Shawn Levy, 2006), *Diary of a Mad Black Woman* (Darren Grant, 2005), *The Dukes of Hazzard* (Jay Chandrasekhar, 2005), *Something's Gotta Give* (Nancy Meyers, 2003), *Barbershop* (Tim Story, 2002) and *SwimFan* (John Polson, 2002). Such placements naturally trigger questions as to the audience's interpretation, and even the self-medication that they may be tempted to practise in certain cases.[16]

Weapons placements rarely concern television, except for certain extreme fiction or documentary programmes, which may give rise to the mention of a specific brand or model. And regularly films, such as *American Gun* (2006) by Aric Avelino, denounce arms proliferation. On the other hand, it is not uncommon for arms manufacturers to seek positive placements for their products and brands in films. The violence linked to the use of these weapons on screen is a legitimate source of worry for many consumer and

---

[15] Rungpaka Tiwsakul, Chris Hackley and Isabelle Szmigin (2005) Explicit, non-integrated product placement in British television programmes, *International Journal of Advertising*, 24(1), pp 95–111. Research about warnings tend to prove that when 'preceding the movie, they serve as an additional memory cue and hence makes the information more accessible in memory'. See Michelle Bennett, Anthony Pecotich and Sanjay Putrevu (1999) The influence of warnings on product placements, in Bernard Dubois, Tina M Lowrey, L J Shrum and Marc Vanhuele (eds), *European Advances in Consumer Research*, Vol. 4, Association for Consumer Research, Provo, UT, pp 193–200. See also Margaret C Campbell, Peeter W J Verlegh and Gina E Slejko (2005) Fortification or trojan horse? the impact of warnings on the effectiveness of product placements, paper presented at the 33rd Association for Consumer Research Conference, San Antonio, TX.

[16] See in particular the analysis by Christopher R Turner (2004) Product placement of medical products: issues and concerns, *Journal of Promotion Management*, 10(1/2), pp 159–70, concerning the specific *Chicago Hope* series case, which takes place in an hospital environment.

viewer associations: they see it as an example of promotional use, knowing that the dividing line between reality and fiction is sometimes very narrow.[17]

There are historical cases of emblematic titles, such as *Winchester 73* (Anthony Mann, 1950), *Magnum Force* (Ted Post, 1973), *Police Python 357* (Alain Courneau, 1976) and *Le Gang des Otages* (The hostage gang) (Édouard Molinaro, 1973, and released in Italy with the title *Quelli della banda Beretta*), not to mention the many film titles including the brand name Colt. Since these brands are not attached to more common consumer products, the audience perhaps pays them less attention. This does not make them any less present onscreen, and these mentions are much more common than one might think.

Among others, we can note the recent placement of the Walther brand in *Die Another Day* (Lee Tamahori, 2002), Heckler & Koch in *Underworld: Evolution* (Len Wiseman, 2006), Beretta in *Four Brothers* (John Singleton, 2005), *Mr & Mrs Smith* (Doug Liman, 2005), *Sin City* (Robert Rodriguez and Frank Miller, 2005) and *Training Day* (Antoine Fuqua, 2001), Winchester in *Blade II* (Guillermo Del Toro, 2002) and *The Last Samurai* (Edward Zwick, 2003), Smith & Wesson in *Exit Wounds* (Andrzej Bartkowiak, 2001), Holland and Holland in *Sahara* (Breck Eisner, 2005), Steyr in *Sin City* (2005), and the Magnum brand heavily present in *Dawn of the Dead* (George A. Romero, 2004), *Four Brothers* (2005), *The Pacifier* (Adam Shankman, 2005), *Bruce Almighty* (Tom Shadyac, 2003), *Charlie's Angels: Full Throttle* (McG, 2003), *The Rundown* (Peter Berg, 2003) and *Blade II* (2002).

The producers included the warning message shown in Figure 6.1, similar to those found on cigarette packets, because the character of James Bond used a packet of Lark cigarettes in a highly ostentatious manner as a detonator. In many countries, advertising communication is now banned for tobacco and alcohol, or in any case stringent conditions are imposed. In addition, the Master Settlement Agreement (MSA), signed in November 1998 between the major cigarette manufacturers in the United States and the US authorities, contained specific bans on product placements in films, television programmes, theatre productions, live shows, music videos and videogames. Even today, however, it is not uncommon to see cigars, cigarettes and cigarette brands in films.[18]

---

[17] See in particular George Comstock (2004) Paths from television violence to aggression: reinterpreting the evidence, in L J Shrum (ed), *The Psychology of Entertainment Media: Blurring the lines between entertainment and persuasion*, Lawrence Erlbaum Associates, Mahwah, NJ, pp 193–211.

[18] Lise Feirud and Dick Mizerski (1998) The effects of cigarette product and brand placements in a movie, *Australian and New Zealand Marketing Academy Conference proceedings (ANZMAC)*, Otago University, Dunedin, New Zealand, pp 731–36. See also research from Christine A Edwards and her colleagues (2004) Out of the smokescreen: does an anti-smoking advertisement affect young women's perception of smoking

> # As tobacco products are used in this film, the Producers wish to remind the audience of the SURGEON GENERAL'S WARNING: "SMOKING CAUSES LUNG CANCER, HEART DISEASES, EMPHYSEMA, AND MAY COMPLICATE PREGNANCY."

Figure 6.1 The original warning included in the end credits of *Licence to Kill* (John Glen, 1989).

Although she is reminded that smoking is prohibited by Dr Michael Glass (played by the actor David Morrissey), Catherine Tramell (Sharon Stone) continues to smoke in *Basic Instinct 2* (Michael Caton-Jones, 2006). Among the significant examples subsequent to the signed agreement, we may find the case of the Boots brand in *Man on Fire* (Tony Scott, 2004), the Marlboro brand in *Four Brothers* (John Singleton, 2005), *Men in Black II* (Barry Sonnenfeld, 2002) and *Driven* (Renny Harlin, 2001), Bolivar cigars in *Black Hawk Down* (Ridley Scott, 2002), the Kool brand in *Driven* (2001) and *Training Day* (Antoine Fuqua, 2001), the Silk Cut brand in *Bridget Jones's Diary* (Sharon Maguire, 2001), the Newport brand in *8 Mile* (Curtis Hanson, 2002), and the 'textbook' case of Phil Alden Robinson's *The Sum of All Fears* (2002), where Marlboro, Kool, Camel, Parliament and Winston, in particular, are all identifiable!

The cigarette has always been used by directors as an attitude and ambience prop, and the examples of films where it is used are numerous in the history of the Seventh Art.[19] The great Howard Hawks classic, *The Big Sleep* (1946), opens on credits showing two shadowy figures smoking, while two cigarettes are shown in the foreground, an image reprised in the end credits. Other early precursors were *The Cigarette Girl* (William Parke, 1917) and *Road House*

---

in movies and their intention to smoke? *Tobacco Control,* 13, pp 277–82; as well as Cornelia Pechmann and Chuan-Fong Shih (1999) Smoking scenes in movies and antismoking advertisements before movies: effect on youth, *Journal of Marketing,* 63, July, pp 1–13. About the MSA itself and a 1999–2002 analysis, see Eric Ruel, Niranjana Mani, Anna Sandoval, Yvonne Terry-McElrath, Sandy J Slater, Cindy Tworek and Frank J Chaloupka (2004) *Health Promotion Practices,* 5(3), pp 99–110.

[19] William D McIntosh, Doris G Bazzini and Stephen M Smith (1998) Who smokes in Hollywood? Characteristics of smokers in popular films from 1940 to 1989, *Addictive Behaviour,* 23, pp 395–98.

(Jean Negulesco, 1948), which was distributed in France with the title *La Femme aux cigarettes*, both of them entirely representative.

Beyond the communication for the brand, the fundamental appeal for tobacco manufacturers is that if stars are filmed smoking, then it partially removes the stigma among potential consumers, particularly the young.[20] Young smokers are particularly vulnerable to this type of signal.[21] All these brands also requested the actors to give testimonials in parallel for use in advertising campaigns in the first half of the twentieth century. These testimonials are much less common nowadays, however (with the exception of certain cases in Asia, including some with Western stars), some celebrities having realized that it could be harmful to their own image.

Furthermore, many associations for the prevention of smoking have become much more responsive and militant; they recently complained that in over 65 per cent of cases, the cigarettes visible on the US big screen are linked to the presence of the lead actor, whose prescriptive powers, spoken and unspoken, are well attested.[22]

---

[20] See in particular Jason Edward Lavender (1998) Tobacco is a filthy weed and from the devil doth proceed: a study of the government's efforts to regulate smoking on the silver screen, *Hastings Communications and Entertainment Law Journal*, Fall, 21(1), pp 205–37; James D Sargent, Michael L Beach, Madeline A Dalton, L A Mott, Jennifer T Tickle, M Bridget Ahrens and Todd F Heatherton (2001) Brand appearances in contemporary cinema films and contribution to global marketing of cigarettes, *The Lancet*, 357(9249), 6 January, pp 29–32; Janet M Distefan, John P P Pierce and Elizabeth A Gilpin (2004) Do favourite movie stars influence adolescent smoking initiation? *American Journal of Public Health*, 94(7), pp 1239–44; Madeline A Dalton, M Bridget Ahrens and James D Sargent (2002) Relation between parental restrictions on movies and adolescent use of tobacco and alcohol, *Effective Clinical Practice*, 5, January–February, pp 1–10; James D Sargent, Madeline A Dalton, Todd Heatherton and Mike Beach (2003) Modifying exposure to smoking depicted in movies: a novel approach to preventing adolescent smoking, *Archives of Paediatrics & Adolescent Medicine*, 157(7), July, pp 643–48; Jennifer J Tickle, James D Sargent, Madeline A Dalton, Michael L Beach and Todd F Heatherton (2001) Favourite movie stars, their tobacco use in contemporary movies, and its association with adolescent smoking, *Tobacco Control*, 10, Spring, pp 16–22; Judith P P McCool, Linda D Cameron and Keith J Petrie (2003) Interpretations of smoking in film by older teenagers, *Social Science & Medicine*, 56, pp 1023–32.

[21] Melanie Wakefield, Brian Flay, Mark Nichter and Gary Giovino (2003) Role of the media in influencing trajectories of youth smoking, *Society for Study of Addiction to Alcohol and Other Drugs*, 98, pp 79–103. See also comments from Stanton Glantz (2003) Smoking in movies: a major problem and a real solution, *The Lancet*, 10 June, pp 1–2. And also Stanton Glantz (2001) What to do about Hollywood, tobacco's smoldering affair, *Los Angeles Times*, 2 June, and Amy Bellin's Master's thesis (2003) *Product Placement of Alcohol in Teen Movies: A qualitative analysis of perceptions and attitudes of high school students*, University of Florida, Gainsville, FL.

[22] Mireya Navarro (2005) Where there's smoke, there's a star, *New York Times*, 18 September.

The cinema is not alone in being targeted for its contentious placements. In December 2005, in France, the association Droits des Non-Fumeurs (Non-Smokers' Rights) secured the conviction of the magazine *Le Point* and the newspapers *Le Monde* and *Les Echos* before the 31st chamber of the Tribunal Correctional of Paris, for having illustrated an article with photographs showing racing-car drivers in their racing overalls, which carried the logos of cigarette brands (Mild Seven and Marlboro). The fines, of €800 for *Le Point* and €1,000 each for *Les Echos* and *Le Monde,* were rounded out by a total of €2,800 in damages in favour of the plaintiff association. It is highly unlikely that this was a case of conscious brand placement by these publications, merely a case of clumsiness. The limited amounts of the fines confirm this. This case, however, illustrates the vigilance of various bodies and associations, consumer or otherwise, in order to avoid such placements, whether conscious or not. They are in any case against the law.[23] The CNCT (French National Anti-Smoking Committee) is regularly led to draw the attention of the authorities to the re-broadcasting of sporting events, such as for example the Paris–Dakar race.

The same analysis could be made for alcoholic beverages.[24] An often-quoted example is Katharine Hepburn on board the *African Queen,* tipping Humphrey Bogart's Gordon's gin overboard into the Ulanga River, to prevent his excessive drinking (*The African Queen,* John Huston, 1951)! This type of case is rare, however. Appendix 2, which shows recent examples of alcoholic beverage placements in the cinema, shows the extent to which alcohol brands, for which the field of advertising expression is subject to legal restrictions elsewhere, have perfectly assimilated the exceptional opportunity that a placement can represent.

In this case, when a superhero appears in the titles, the (tacit) target of young consumers is never forgotten. We find Bacardi and Budweiser at Batman's side in *Batman Begins* (Christopher Nolan, 2005), Pabst and Corona alongside the four heroes in *Fantastic 4* (Tim Story, 2005), Kahlua alongside *Catwoman* (Pitof, 2004), Budweiser alongside *Hellboy* (Guillermo Del Toro, 2004), Heineken alongside *Daredevil* (Mark Steven Johnson, 2004), Foster's alongside the X-Men in *X2 – X-Men United* (Bryan Singer, 2003), Carlsberg and Budweiser alongside *Spider-Man* (Sam Raimi, 2002) – all of them powerful and invulnerable characters! All of them deliver connotations that alcohol brands could never claim in the context of their traditional promotional communications. They also represent incomparable vectors of de-stigmatization for a young target audience, which can then identify with

---

[23] See in particular article 3511-1 of the French Public Health Code.

[24] See also Amy Bellin (2003) *Product Placement of Alcohol in Teen Movies: A qualitative analysis of perceptions and attitudes of high school students,* Master's thesis in arts and communication, University of Florida, Gainesville, FL.

the actor, experience the scene by proxy at the time and aspire to repeat it later.[25]

Finally, it is even possible to get around legal prohibitions. This is the case for a drink such as Red Bull, which is not only deprived of communication, but is also banned from sale in France, as a result of a 2003 decision by the French food standards agency, the AFSAA, concerning in particular the effects of the taurine contained in the drink. It is a health warning on the basis of the precautionary principle. The product, however, can clearly be seen, in particular in *Boogeyman* (Stephen T Kay, 2005), in *Hellboy* (2004), in *Mean Girls* (Mark Waters, 2004), in *Ocean's Twelve* (Steven Soderbergh, 2004), in *Dickie Roberts: Former Child Star* (Sam Weisman, 2003), in *Just Married* (Shawn Levy, 2003), in *American Pie 2* (James B Rogers, 2001), in *Legally Blonde* (Robert Luketic, 2001), in *Save the Last Dance* (Thomas Carter, 2001) and in *The Fast and The Furious* (Rob Cohen, 2001); naturally, without any warning message at the beginning or end of the film.

Placement of causes

Literary works of fiction have long provided the opportunity to support a cause, as is shown by Christopher Buckley's anti-drug novel *Wet Work* (1992), and his anti-smoking novel *Thank You for Smoking* (1994).[26] Back in 1983, the comic artist Morris decided to substitute the emblematic cigarette of his star character, Lucky Luke, with a wisp of straw.[27] This unpaid placement for the cigarette dated from 1946, the date of the famous cowboy's first appearance. Some placements in the cinema and on television, however, also argue in favour of what is generally known as a 'good' cause. In 1995, in the *ex post facto* episode of the science-fiction series *Voyager*, a human member of the space exploration vessel explains to an alien that his people on Earth stopped smoking centuries ago, having realized the fatal consequences. The story is supposed to take place in 2371!

Another case: in one of the scenes from the remake of *The Italian Job* (F Gary Gray, 2003), while in a car stopped at a traffic light, the actor Jason Statham promptly jettisons his cigarette on seeing the joint poster campaign by the American Lung Association, the American Heart Association and the

[25] Murray Smith (1995) *Engaging Characters: Fiction, emotion and the cinema*, Oxford University Press/Clarendon, Oxford, UK.

[26] Christopher Buckley (1991) *Wet Work*, Knopf, New York. Christopher Buckley (1994) *Thank You For Smoking*, Random House, New York. See also Eamon Javers and Lorraine Woellert (2006) It's hard out here for a lobbyist, *BusinessWeek*, 20 March.

[27] Cartoonist Morris was honoured by the World Health Organization in 1988, for this highly symbolic decision, during the World No Tobacco Day.

American Cancer Society, where an electronic counter shows the number of tobacco-related deaths since the beginning of the year (286,708 when the scene takes place). Having retained the message, he explains to his partners, later in the film, that smoking killed five people while he was between two traffic lights. Finally, in the James L Brooks film *As Good as It Gets* (1997), Helen Hunt plays a single mother struggling against the shortcomings of her health insurance, which does not allow her to care for her son properly. This placement reflects a sociopolitical position influenced by militant groups who pressurize the government to improve the health system.

Such placements are not uncommon in the United States, where consumer associations have completely understood the influential power that they can have over the public.[28] Thus, Donald Faison, playing the doctor Christopher Turk in the series *Scrubs,* and Noah Wyle, in the role of Dr John Carter in the series *ER,* each appeared in an episode wearing a t-shirt with an enormous Amnesty International logo. In the series *Chicago Hope,* a Red Cross poster can be identified. The 'Right Decision – Right Now' campaign, funded by the cigarette maker R J Reynolds to prevent underage smoking, has also appeared in one form or another in series such as *ER, Seinfeld, Party of Five, Sabrina, The Teenage Witch* and *Sister, Sister.* The Robert Wood Johnson Foundation also managed to get its message across in favour of universal health coverage in popular series such as *Law & Order: Special Victims Unit* and *Passions* on NBC.[29] Such messages are criticized for being comparable to a form of hidden propaganda.[30] Caution is advisable in the application of this more or less direct proselytism. In fact, as Charles Rosin, a producer of television series, remarked: 'People turn on the television to be entertained. They do not expect to be given a civics lesson.'[31] The desired effect can quickly suffer a fatal reverse if the public perceives too great a desire to manipulate, regardless of the apparent justice of the cause.

Adapting the creation to better serve the product

When the Aquafina bottled water brand is placed in *Broken Flowers* (Jim Jarmusch, 2005) or in *The Manchurian Candidate* (Jonathan Demme, 2004),

[28] David Drum (1997) Product placement matures into placement of non-profit causes, *Variety,* 17 November.

[29] Laurie McGinley and Emily Nelson (2003) TV scripts highlight plight of uninsured, *Wall Street Journal,* 4 March.

[30] David A Ridenour (2003) *National Policy Analysis,* 456, March.

[31] Stuart Elliott (1994) Borrowing the methods of product placement, a campaign asks young people to avoid violence, *New York Times,* 6 October.

it uses its usual packaging. In contrast, when it is placed in the futuristic film *The Island* (Michael Bay, 2005), it is modified to give it a futuristic aspect, since the story is set in 2019. Conversely, when an old brightly shining Ford appeared in *Sweet Land* (Ali Selim, 2006), and when advertisements for the drink Dr Pepper were placed in *Idlewild* (Bryan Barber, 2006), set at the beginning of the twentieth century, during Prohibition in the United States, the brand's graphics from that period were revisited. The product and the brand adapt to make the placement more relevant.

For the requirements of communication, however, it is sometimes necessary to adapt the placement support. Having signed a partnership agreement with Mazda, the NBC channel reshot certain scenes from its series *E-Ring*, *Surface* and *My Name is Earl* in order to integrate the Mazda 5 and MX-5 models as stated in the agreement. In *The Sentinel* (Clark Johnson, 2006), a chase scene takes place in a shopping mall. In order to film it, it was important that while meeting all the director's needs, the camera positions allowed certain shops to be clearly visible onscreen, such as the clothing brand Esprit.

Others see the formula 'marketing respect for the artistic creation' as an ordinary oxymoron. It must be admitted that the objectives are not always perfectly compatible. Auteurs will always demand, above all else, complete freedom to express their artistic creation. This freedom, however, does not always mesh perfectly with the marketing ambitions of the advertiser in search of an effective product or brand placement. In 1998, Nora Ephron presented her latest film, featuring Tom Hanks and Meg Ryan. At the heart of the story is an anonymous exchange via e-mail. The film's title? Initially, it was *You Have Mail*. The messaging medium for this exchange, however, was not fictional: it was the world's leading instant messaging service, America On Line (AOL). The expression used by this software to alert the user to a new e-mail message was 'you've got mail'. In order to use the exact title, and to allow for a better identification of the placement, AOL and Warner Bros (the film's producers) managed to convince the director of the 'mutual' advantages of adapting the name of the film, which was finally distributed as *You've Got Mail*. Even Neil Simon agreed to modify the text of his play *Sweet Charity* (1966) for a 2005 revival, so that the monologue 'a double Scotch on the rocks' became 'a Gran Centenario tequila'.[32]

We should bear in mind that the primary reason for resorting to product or brand placements is financial, and that few arguments can stand up to money! Certain adaptations may therefore be necessary. The aim is not to divert support to ostentatiously commercial ends, at the risk of losing sense and credibility, but to proceed with a few small adjustments in the mutual interest of the producers of the film and the product champions. Ian Fleming

---

[32] Robert P P Laurence (2005) Product placement: the plot sickens, *San Diego Union-Tribune*, 4 November.

Figure 6.2 Bollinger advertisements used in connection with the release of James Bond films. Reproduced by kind permission of Bollinger Champagne.

described the spy James Bond 007 as enjoying many forms of alcoholic drink, and in particular vodka martinis. Numerous brands of drink are mentioned in the James Bond films. The first film introduced champagne – Dom Pérignon (1946), Bollinger, Krug or Veuve Cliquot, even if the loyalty of Bollinger's appearances (see Figure 6.2) and its ever-relevant integration into the plot certainly gave it the edge – and the bar was extended with each actor. From *Dr No* (Terence Young, 1962) onwards, the brands Black & White, Red Stripe and Smirnoff added themselves to the list. With each subsequent film more would appear onscreen: J&B, Carlsberg, Black Velvet, Absolut, Michelob, Busch, Cutty Sark, Stolichnaya, Heineken, Finlandia (see Figure 6.3), Guinness, Jim Beam, Courvoisier, Suntory, Cinzano, Johnnie Walker, and many different wines and cocktails.

Fleming never described James Bond as being at the wheel of a Citroën 2CV, a Lotus or a BMW Z3[33] in his works, any more than he made him wear Seiko or Omega watches, but placements for these brands nonetheless exist in the films. And do the audience reproach the producer or the director for this? Not according to the evidence. They do so even less if, once again, the brand or the product are intelligently integrated into the film. The associations are clear. The highly specific James Bond 007 'genre' is respected, even if it has been able to adapt itself over the decades.[34]

There is another case of adaptation that could possibly raise the question of ethics, this time regarding placements in books. In fact, novels are not the only books affected by this technique: a controversy arose in the United States in the second half of the 1990s, when it was discovered that high-consumption product brands had been integrated into school textbooks. In its 1999 revised version, *Mathematics: Applications and connections* (McGraw-Hill) contained, for example, different mathematical problems based on brands such as Disneyland, Sony, Nike, Barbie, Kellogg's, Spalding, Burger King, McDonald's and Gatorade. The editor explained that no money had been received and that these products had been mentioned only to facilitate learning in mathematics. The companies had not made any payment: they had only been asked for authorization to reproduce logos, which had, of

---

[33] The BMW driven by agent 007 was not always the same in the James Bond saga. He drove a Z3 model in *Goldeneye* (Martin Campbell, 1995), a 750i in *Tomorrow Never Dies* (Roger Spottiswoode, 1997), a Z8 in *The World Is Not Enough* (Michael Apted, 1999), and even a R1200 motorcycle in *Tomorrow Never Dies* (1997). For a detailed study of the Z3 launch in *GoldenEye*, see in particular Susan Fournier and Robert Dolan Jr (1997) *Launching the BMW Z3 Roadster, HBS Case 9-597-002, revised 8 January 2002*, Harvard Business School Publishing, New York.

[34] Guillaume Evin (2002) *Goldmaker*, Fayard, Paris. See also the very illustrated book by Alastair Dougall and Roger Stewart (2000) *James Bond: The secret world of 007*, Dorling Kindersley, London, for an overview of all the products and accessories used by the famous secret agent.

Figure 6.3 Finlandia advertisement developed for the release of *Die Another Day* (Lee Tamahori, 2002). Reproduced by kind permission of Finlandia.

course, been granted without difficulty. Students were asked to calculate the number of weeks they must save their pocket money to afford a new pair of Nikes, or to take into account the diameter of Oreo cookies to work out a simple fraction. The book had furthermore been approved by the specialist commissions of some 15 states. However it was strongly criticized by parents' associations, who had been up in arms since 1989, the year that Channel One arrived in many US schools. This educational channel was offered to the establishments for free, but intermittently broadcast advertising messages.[35]

We are far from finding a simple solution to the problem thus raised. On the one hand, any initiative to encourage students to learn an essential subject,

---

[35] Constance L Hays (1999) Math book salted with brand names raises new alarm, *New York Times*, 21 March.

and one which is often little liked, should be encouraged. On the other hand, how can we not be disturbed by the evident underlying commercial connotations?

The argument from showbusiness professionals

In 2005 the US Attorney General, Elliot Spitzer, attacked Sony, accusing it of having paid US radio stations to play songs by its artists. An amicable settlement was reached, for the sum of US$10 million. Was this not, however, a form of product placement, permitted elsewhere in multiple forms?[36] The same year, the professional associations Writers' Guild of America and Screen Actors Guild, representing screenwriters and cinema actors respectively, were strongly moved by the rising power of product placements, particularly in television programmes.[37] An internet site (www.productinvasion.com) was born to denounce this proliferation of placements and the 'manipulation' of screenplays that could ensue. It enabled dissenters to develop their point of view and to offer web users a little interactive film making fun of certain placements.

The actors' representatives were particularly critical of producers and broadcasters for not paying the presenters who used or presented these products on television, all the more so since, in the majority of cases, they saw these placements as stealth advertising, since the products were not officially part of the programme.[38] The writers also bemoaned the fact that constraints were imposed on the screenplay in advance, often imperatively, and that it fell to them to integrate these products into the series narrative or into the programme, not to mention last-minute contracts that imposed a forced and often 'bolted-on' placement. On the one hand, the producers clearly perceived a considerable financial windfall to be exploited. On the other, the advertisers knew that they could demand much more in return for their support than for placements in feature films – particularly for placement

---

[36] See in particular Max Sutherland (2006) Product placement regulators gone AWOL, in Comments, ed John Ford, *Journal of International Advertising*, 25(1), pp 107–14; David Teather (2005) Spitzer lid on payola at radio stations, *Guardian*, 26 July.

[37] Brian Lowry (2005) Hidden message in product placement fight, *Variety*, 15 November. See also Vincent Porter (2006) EU television product placement directive is by no means clear-cut, *Financial Times*, 14 January; Doreen Carjaval (2006) Placing the product in the dialogue, too, *New York Times*, 17 January, and Jesse Hiestand (2006) Screen actors, writers protest product placement, *Washington Post*, 6 February.

[38] Sharon Waxman (2005) Hollywood unions object to product placement on TV, *New York Times*, 14 November. See also Stuart Elliott (2006) In parody video, writers ridicule placing products, *New York Times*, 6 March.

in a regular series – and that the sums they were willing to pay gave them considerable negotiating clout.

The significant appearance of Toyota cars in the series *Six Feet Under* and *Three Wishes*, of the Ford brand in *24*[39] and *Desperate Housewives*, and the unavoidable presence of Coca-Cola in the programme *American Idol* are in no way fortuitous. In order to defend their point of view, the showbusiness professionals also emphasize the fact that if traditional advertising is constrained by certain ethical rules,[40] it does not seem right that the advertising message carried by means of a product placement can escape this rule. Some, such as the consumerist militant Gary Ruskin, of the Commercial Alert association, go so far as to claim, supported by a petition, that the placement of products equates to dishonest advertising.[41] The association's objective is to obtain a vote in the US Congress in favour of a 'Product Placement Disclosure Act' imposing an obligation to give a warning when products are placed on television in return for payment.

Although this approach might seem fundamentally praiseworthy, is it not somewhat exaggerated? Is this not to revive yet again the debate over the minimum intelligence of the (television) viewer? It is probable, even certain, that there are still people likely to believe that if characters in *CSI: Miami* travel in Hummer H2s, it is no doubt for security reasons; that if Bruce Wayne chose a Lamborghini Murciélago in *Batman Begins* (Christopher Nolan, 2005), it was because *murciélago* is the Spanish for bat, or even that the preference for a futuristic prototype Audi in *I, Robot* (Alex Proyas, 2004) was probably an aesthetic choice by the actor Will Smith (to mention but a few car placements). In all seriousness, though, how can we believe that the vast majority of the audience is unaware that these products and brands have simply paid their entrance fee? How can we believe that an unjustified or too ostentatious presence would not, in their eyes, merit rejection and condemnation? There should be an unreserved yes to consumer protection, but no to their ill-considered and systematic infantilization!

The limits of intolerable over-exposure

Some un-orchestrated placements may have little impact, because the impact of the brand's presence is hampered by that of many others. The film *Lonesome*

---

[39] T L Stanley (2005) Toyota vehicles to be integrated into Fox's *24*, *Advertising Age*, 5 December.

[40] Miguel Valenti, Les Brown and Laurie Trotta (eds) (2000) *More than a Movie: Ethical decision making in the entertainment industry*, Westview Press, Boulder, CO.

[41] Paul Siegel (2004) Product placement and the law, *Journal of Promotion Management*, 10(1/2), pp 89–100.

Jim (Steve Buscemi, 2006) contains a characteristic scene of this type, where the brands all enjoy a comparable placement space. During a wide tracking shot, actor Casey Affleck passes in front of a series of vending machines. In the same picture and in order, the brands RC Cola, 7Up, Diet Coke, Mello Yello, Pepsi and Mountain Dew all share the screen. There are also cases of too many placements. Nielsen Media Research calculated that for the first six months of 2005, the programme *The Contender*, hosted by Sylvester Stallone on NBC, totalled 7,500 appearances of deliberately placed products.[42]

Back in 1980, the Jerry Lewis film *Hardly Working*, was censured by some critics and by the public, for its too numerous and too obvious placements. In 1992, the Penelope Spheeris film *Wayne's World* made a mockery of this heightened commercial presence. The same is true of *Josie and the Pussycats* (Harry Elfont and Deborah Kaplan, 2001), which was set against the backdrop of the world of pop groups.[43] In the Renny Harlin film *Driven* (2001), Brandchannel managed to identify 102 different brand or product placements. This included placements of all types, paid and unpaid, authorized and unauthorized. The film was not, strictly speaking, the great success the studio had hoped,[44] but as the film was about a motor race, with its many sponsors, the over-exposure was not as blatant as it might have been in a different context.

The Angela Robinson film *Herbie: Fully Loaded* (2005) provoked a number of very negative reviews.[45] Essentially, the number of product and brand placements of all types, including of course Volkswagen, was deemed to be too great. As the film is set mainly in the world of motor racing, a meeting place for a great many sponsors, the phenomenon can be partly explained. It is true, however, that the density of logos in the same shot is sometimes startling.[46] In fact, Volkswagen, committed at the time to a contract with

---

[42] Dan Glaister (2005) US Networks cash in as advertisers turn to product placement, *Guardian*, 30 September.

[43] See also the round table hosted by Mary-Lou Galician about Product placement in the 21st century in the book she edited:(2004) *Handbook of Product Placement in the Mass Media*, Haworth Press/Best Business Books, Binghamton, NY.

[44] Grosses were US$54.744 million, with US$32.720 million in the US and US$22.024 million on the international market. The production budget was US$94 million (source Box Office Mojo LLC, November 2006).

[45] See also Ty Burr (2005) This bug isn't quite lovable, *Boston Globe*, 22 June. For similar critics regarding Michael Bay's *The Island* (2005), see Claudine Mulard (2005) Les marques commerciales en plein champ, *Le Monde*, 17 August.

[46] Other brands can also be identified: Tropicana, Goodyear, Pepsi, Dodge, Cheetos, Home Depot, Netzero, Popeye's, 3M, MBNA, Nextel, Mobil, Jesel, Auto Meter, McDonald's, Electronic Arts, Outback, Naked, ESPN, Ringers Gloves, Yamaha, Kodak, Cheetos, Dupont, Lay's, Bosch, Motorsports, Lowe's, Tyvek, Kobalt, Simpson, Target, Valvoline, GMac, StreetGlow, UPS, Clorox, Prestone, Wisk, HP, Viagra, Crystal Geyser, JVC, Jansport, Lo-Jack, Toyota, Firestone and so on. It is interesting to notice the prominence of Chevrolet: its logos also appear on the Peyton team's suits, while it participates in the NASCAR racing with a Volkswagen Love Bug!

Placements identified in the film Driven

AAA, Arai, Bayer, Bioptron, Bosch, Budweiser, Canada Life, Champion, Cheerios, Coca-Cola, Corona, Craftsman, DirecTV, Dodge, Dog Chow, elf, Energizer, ESPN, FedEx, Firehawk, Firestone, Fox, Freightliner, Fuji, Gillette, Hanes, Harley-Davidson, Havoline, Hawaiian Tropic, Herdez, Hilton, Hisamitsu, HMV, Honda, HP, Hugo Boss, Kirin, Kleenex, Kmart, Kool, Labatt, LifeSavers, Lincoln Electric, Lista, Magneti Marelli, Maker's Mark, Marlboro, Mazda, McDonald's, MCI, Mercedes, Miller, Molson, Monroe, Motorola, MTCl, Nextel, Nippo, NTN, PacWest, Pentax, People, Philip Zepter, Pioneer, Players, PlayStation, PPG, Puma, Quaker State, Safety-Kleen, Seibu, Shell, Snapple, Sonax, Sony, Sparco, Speed Stick, Speedo, Staff Service, STP, Suave, Target, Tecate, telegate, Telmex, Telstra, Tenneco, Texaco, Timken, Tire Club, Toyota, Troy Lee Designs, UOL, Via Magazine, Visa, Visteon, Volkswagen, Walker, Winfield, Worldcom, Xenadrine, Zepter.

Source: Brandchannel (Groupe Interbrand), 2001.

NBC Universal Pictures, only provided two cars, a Touareg and a New Beetle, without a specific placement contract for the brand. With total box office receipts of US$144,146 million worldwide,[47] the film was not a failure, but neither was it a huge success. Good reviews do not make a film successful, and neither can bad reviews take away a mediocre film's chances of success. On the other hand, repeated negative reviews can always damage the box-office career of a feature film.

Another possible limit on placements is created by the environment in which the product or brand can acceptably be integrated. In 2004, what seemed to be a product placement during the morning programme *American Morning,* from the round-the-clock news channel CNN, caused a furore in the United States. In part of the programme dedicated to dietary foods, a recipe using cereals offered two seconds of screen time to a packet of Total Corn Flakes, produced by General Mills.[48] The criticisms followed swiftly, on the principle that the clear division between editorial content and advertising no

---

[47] Source: Box Office Mojo LLC, November 2006.
[48] Stuart Elliott (2004) A sponsor's product appears on a CNN segment, and some see a weaker news-advertising division, *New York Times,* 11 February.

longer existed.[49] Although purely accidental, the placement had the power to seriously affect the credibility of the news channel, which apologized for the incident. This case, however, is revealing: it shows a threshold, this time an ethical one, that should not be crossed, since although it risks offering the product a very powerful recommendation at that moment, it also risks damaging the communication vector itself.

Taking into account the impossibility of putting planet-wide legislation in place, while the medium (film, series, programme) can be intended for world-wide consumption, it would be utopian to think that we can dictate strict laws relating to this communications technique. On the other hand, it is certain that self-regulation will quickly deal with the cases of excess or of poor brand integration.

Parasitic communication and undesired placements

Some brands like parody when it is justified. It enables them to exhibit their sense of humour and get closer to their consumers. For example, the Casio brand becomes Catsio in *The Cat in the Hat* (Bo Welch, 2003), and Tower Records became Tower of London Records for the purposes of *Shrek 2* (Andrew Adamson and Kelly Asbury, 2004). This is not a parasitic communication, however, since here the placement, even if it is altered slightly, remains under control.

In the majority of cases, permission to use a brand is requested from the holder of the rights, to avoid potential legal proceedings. This permission is not always granted, however, even if the placement is offered free. In 1994, 20th Century Fox decided to film a remake of George Seaton's classic film, *Miracle on 34th Street* (1947). In the original film, the New York department store Macy's is the setting for the story of Father Christmas. Macy's declined the offer made in 1998, not wishing to tamper with the magic of the 1947 classic, and the remake had to use a fictional brand name, in this case C F Cole. In 1998, for television this time, Warner Bros failed to obtain permission from the University of New York to mention the establishment in its new series

---

[49] In 1997, Jonathan Karl, reporter for CNN, agreed to be part of an ad campaign for the Visa credit card. He had even solicited and received approval from CNN, but his testimonial was contested on the same basis. After a request to Visa, the commercial was suspended. For an academic study on the subject, see in particular Dennis M Sandler and Eugene Secunda (1993) Point of view: blurred boundaries – where does editorial end and advertising begin? *Journal of Advertising Research*, 33(3), pp 73–80.

Felicity; the university feared that it could become a parasitic communication.[50] The First Savings & Loans bank that is robbed in *Waist Deep* (Vondie Curtis Hall, 2006) was created especially for the film, probably because real banks didn't rush to take part. Parasitic communication can take many forms: it can arise from an unfortunate, often unintentional placement, or the placement may be used as a 'weapon' against the brand.

Although it is rare, the parasite can appear even in the title, as is the case in the film *The Devil wears Prada* (David Frankel, 2006), taken from the novel of the same name by Lauren Weisberger.[51] Sometimes, however, it is only a tiny detail of the direction, and the placement can become extremely irritating to the brand or brands. This is the case for the film *Charlie's Angels* (McG, 2000). In one of the very first scenes of the film, while the actor Tim Curry is unconscious, Cameron Diaz goes through his briefcase with her two acolytes. She takes out a PDA that she describes by name as a Palm Pilot, before handing it to Lucy Liu. The attentive viewer will have noticed, however, in the following scene, that the PDA in question was in fact based on the Windows Pocket PC user system, a competitor to that sold by Palm Pilot. This means that the PDA in question cannot be a Palm Pilot. Even more 'amusing', some minutes later, the same Lucy Liu consults the said PDA, now branded as Handspring (at the time, also a competitor to Palm)!

Some of these undesired placements are not totally unfavourable to the brand. In 1980, the Atlanta giant had not been contacted by the director Jamie Uys when he had the idea of throwing an empty Coca-Cola bottle from an aeroplane in flight, in the South African comedy *The Gods Must Be Crazy*. The same is true for Khyentse Borbu, who provided the young Tibetan monks with a can of the same soft drink in *Phörpa*, in 1999, to be used as a football. In an even more direct case of supposed involvement, in 1985, the brand found itself central to the plot of Dusan Makavejev's *The Coca-Cola Kid*, although it was not a participant. The brand had no reason to take steps of any kind to prevent this, however, since it was not depicted in a negative manner.

In contrast, documentaries such as *Roger & Me* (1989), in which the director/actor Michael Moore pursues the managing director of General Motors to confront him with the social impact of his decisions on strategic restructuring, and *Super Size Me* (2004), directed by and starring Morgan Spurlock, which stigmatizes the possible problems of over-consumption of McDonald's fast food, are not exactly the type of placement that an advertiser dreams of. On the contrary, these last two examples illustrate undesired

---

[50] Anita Gates (1998) NYU says: 'No thanks' to star role in a sitcom, *New York Times*, 2 September.

[51] Lauren Weisberger (2003) *The Devil Wears Prada*, Doubleday/Random House, New York.

placements leading to a parasitic communication, often a powerful one for the brand. In these cases, legal proceedings for abusive and unauthorized use of a brand name may be undertaken. More often, however, brands are conscious that such proceedings give rise to even more damaging negative media coverage.

Harm to a brand can sometimes be unintentional. In 1934, the director Frank Capra finished filming *It Happened One Night* (marketed in France under the title *New York Miami*) in the middle of winter, with a limited budget and a schedule reduced to four weeks. As with many film projects, its genesis had been particularly difficult.

> I assure you I never anticipated – nor I was capable of – putting such esoteric 'meanings' in *It Happened One Night*. In fact, I was so dog-tired from all the road-work and shadow-boxing and suspense involved in putting this on-again, off-again project together, I felt like the overtrained fighter who left his fight in the gym. All I wanted to do was to get the bloody film over with …. So I shot scenes fast and unworried.
>
> (Frank Capra, *The Name Above the Title*)[52]

On 27 February 1935, the film picked up five Oscars.[53] This film, which recounts the relationship between two characters during a bus journey, contains a story within a story. In one of the film's scenes, Clark Gable, 'loaned' by MGM to Columbia, has to undress, and in particular, to remove his shirt. When he does so, the audience realizes that he is not wearing a vest. The detail might seem harmless; but it unleashed a storm from underwear makers, who quickly perceived that since this was Clark Gable, a trend had just been set! The plunging sales figures for vests very soon confirmed this.

Another unintentional but 'unavoidable' case occurred in 2006, with the Paul Greengrass film *United 93*. Logically enough, airlines normally refuse any placement in films showing hostage-taking on a plane or passenger casualties. *United 93*, however, was based on the events of 11 September 2001, so United Airlines had to relive, five years on, the real hostage-taking and the crash of its flight UA93, near Shanksville in Pennsylvania. In *The Marine* (John Bonito, 2006), the name of the gas station, destroyed by malefactors, is 'Manze'.

Attacks on a brand or its activities can be full-frontal. In 1999, the plot of Michael Mann's *The Insider* was based on the true story of a file sent anonymously from within Philip Morris to the TV magazine programme *60 Minutes* on CBS. The file described the manipulations undertaken by the cigarette manufacturer to generate addiction to smoking. Journalist Lowell

---

[52] Frank Capra (1971) *The Name Above the Title*, Macmillan, New York.
[53] The film won five Oscars: best picture, director, actor, actress and screenplay.

Bergman (Al Pacino) then contacted Jeffrey Wigand (Russell Crowe), in charge of research at another manufacturer, Brown and Williamson. The film tells the true story of Jeffrey Wigand and his revelations. It is easy to imagine the feeling that such a placement, plainly undesired, must have stirred up among the tobacco manufacturers involved, and among the sector as a whole.[54] The following year, Steven Soderbergh directed *Erin Brockovitch*, with Julia Roberts in the lead role, inspired by Erin's true story. She had entered into a struggle against the Pacific Gas & Electric Company, accusing it of poisoning the ground around a power station in southern California.[55] Of course, since the screenplays of these films dealt with actual facts, neither the producers nor the directors needed to request permission from the brands involved.

The final case is that of an undesired and disturbing placement, to which a brand must react, at the risk of being accused of hijacking and being pursued by the authorities. The Master Settlement Agreement (MSA) signed in November 1998 prohibits any remuneration for onscreen placements of a tobacco product. Consequently, in 2004, the tobacco producer Philip Morris felt constrained to intervene at Paramount Pictures, to request that a shot from Philip Kaufman's film *Twisted* be removed from the final cut and from all commercialized versions (cinema, television, video and so on). In the shot in question, the actor Samuel L Jackson lights a cigarette on which the Marlboro logo is clearly identifiable. Paramount Pictures refused, however, arguing that re-editing the film would require too much work. In 2003, under pressure from the attorney general of California, another cigarette maker, R J Reynolds, used the same approach with another studio, Sony Pictures Entertainment. The action of Mike Newell's film *Mona Lisa Smile* is set in the 1950s. One of the scenes shows a Camel advertisement and a packet of Winstons. Once again, the studio did not wish to make any changes to the film, alleging that *Mona Lisa Smile* was a precise representation of the 1950s, a period in which it was common for men and women to smoke.

---

[54] Parasitic communication can also be humorous, and still be corrosive, as was the case in 2005, with Jason Reitman's *Thank You for Smoking*. The movie showed insidious manoeuvres by a public relations agent for tobacco manufacturers.

[55] The legal action engaged by lawyer Ed Masry against PG&E ended with an arrangement in 1997, including a US$33 million settlement, representing the indemnities to the 648 concerned victims. See in particular the article by Michael Fumento (2000) Erin Brockovich exposed, *Wall Street Journal*, 28 March in which the writer raised doubts about the scientific basis of the case. And then the answer by Erin Brockovich (2000) Erin Brockovich affirmed, *Wall Street Journal*, 6 April, and finally the answer by a member of the Hudson Institute, Michael Fumento (2000) Michael Fumento responds, *Wall Street Journal*, 10 April. See also the essay by Professor Larry E Ribstein (2005) Wall Street and Vine: Hollywood's view of business, *Illinois Law & Economics, Working Paper LE05-010*, University of Illinois College of Law, Chicago, IL.

A study carried out by the University of California on 776 US films released between 1999 and 2003 shows that almost 80 per cent of them contain scenes where a character smokes.[56] In 2002, Lorrillard Tobacco censured Warner Bros studios for having placed the Newport brand of cigarettes, without permission, in Michael Caton-Jones's film *City by the Sea*. At the time, the studio hid behind the fact that it was only the distributor of a film co-produced by independents – Franchise Pictures, Epsilon Motion Pictures, Brad Grey Pictures and Sea Breeze Productions.[57]

---

[56] Vanessa O'Connell (2004) Tobacco makers want cigarettes cut from films, *Wall Street Journal*, 14 June.

[57] It is equally true that independent producers are sometimes less demanding with unwanted placements, because of their usually more troublesome financing requirements.

7 The expert opinion: Jean-Patrick Flandé

In France, Jean-Patrick Flandé is the undisputed professional expert in the matter of product and brand placements in the cinema. His experience and well-attested competence make Film Média Consultant today the leading player in the French market.

How do you personally define product or brand placements in cinema?
In order to be accepted by the audience, the fiction needs points of reference with reality, even in futuristic films. Among these links with reality, we count the objects and the brands that we come up against on a daily basis: food and drink, cars, modes of communication, choices of clothing and so on. The indirect medium of communication represented by product placement in cinema films and television films makes it possible to boast of (or sublimate) the qualities of a product or a brand, to impose a dynamic and attractive brand image by association with the hero. It is involved through various tricks: manipulation, citation, consumption and/or visualisation of the product.

In 1977, I founded Film Média Consultant (FMC) to be a specialist in product placements. To date, the agency has been involved in nearly 1,500 films, or around 60 films per year. FMC's goal is the exclusive search for advertising budgets for feature films. The producer mandates us, by means of a contract, to seek out exclusively advertising budgets for the film. Having read and 'dissected' the screenplay, we list the products that are useful in the film and we contact the various advertisers. Once the agreements (financial or based on the provision of merchandise) have been made, we make sure they are respected both during filming and in postproduction.

For the European Commission,

The definition of product placement introduced here covers any form of audio-visual commercial communication consisting of the inclusion of or reference to a product, a service or the trade mark thereof so that it is featured within a programme, normally in return for payment or for similar consideration. It is subject to the same qualitative rules and restrictions applying to advertising.

What do you think are the advantages that the brand can gain? Can you illustrate your answer with different cases that you have worked on?

Product placement is a playful and attractive communications technique based on a very popular medium: the cinema. Intended to strengthen the brand image on all the major markets by emphasizing notions relating to the usefulness, the dynamism and the quality of the product, the placement occurs in a natural and targeted context (consumers), is positively associated with film stars and reaches a massive and attentive audience. In order to turn this image quality into sales, FMC seeks to write the brand on to the consumer's 'shopping list', that is, to associate the product with the daily lives of as many people as possible.

Product placements offer the advertiser an average of 30 million contacts with its brand:

- National cinema release: 350,000 to 5,000,000 viewers.
- DVD release (six months later): 100,000 to 2,000,000 units sold.
- Multiple showings on Canal+ or TPS (12 months later): 3–6 million contacts.
- Showing on a co-producing channel (TF1, France 2, France 3, Arte, M6–24 months later): 5–12 million contacts.
- Multiple re-showings on different television channels: 4–12 million viewers per showing (minimum of four re-showings on TV over a five-year cycle).

Some product placements are particularly interesting to set up, when the screenplay offers a real performance and the director envisages an integration that is both convincing for the advertiser and fun for the viewer. For example:

- The *Taxi* series: the placement of Peugeot cars – memorable and yet difficult to carry out – considerably improved the brand's image with young people and internally.
- *La Vérité si je mens 2* (It's the truth even if I'm lying 2): the visual and the mention of Lenôtre in one of the film's flagship scenes are used again in the film's trailer.

- *3 Zéros* (3 zeros): a beautiful display of the Lion brand (Nestlé group), throughout the film, in particular with the filming of a fake Lion advert by Stomy Bugsy. Lion is also present in one of the trailers for the film.
- *Agents Secrets* (Secret agents): the creation of a prototype Motorola mobile phone with video function for Monica Bellucci.
- *Tout pour plaire* (Anything to please): insertion of the Clarins brand into the shopping bag carried by Anne Parillaud on the poster for the film.

Product placement is a springboard to communication for the brand. When a film is released, the film's distributor and the advertiser agree on tie-in promotional operations that ensure media visibility both for the film and for the brand. Some memorable examples:

- *Le Bonheur est dans le pré* (Happiness is found in the meadow): thanks to the echoing of the title in the slogan for its ad campaign, 'Le bonheur est dans le Gers' (Happiness is found in Gers), the Gers region saw tourism increase by 30 per cent for the 1996 season.
- *Les Couloirs du temps: Les Visiteurs 2* (The corridors of time: Just visiting 2): the introduction by Crunch of an on-pack promotion (8 million units) and the broadcasting of radio spots made possible an increase of 7–12 per cent in market share, compared with a similar period.
- *Tais-toi (Shut up)*: in all BMW sales locations in France, the showing of the trailer, the 'making of' and set photographs promoted the Series 7 placed in the Francis Veber film.
- *36, Quai des Orfèvres* (UK title: *36*): the introduction of a series of private premieres, POPAs and competitions for Alfa Romeo, Bell & Ross, Cutler & Gross and Redskins.

In your view, what is the biggest mistake to avoid when working on a placement project, from the brand's point of view? From the producer's or the director's point of view? From the agent's point of view?

For the French viewer, the film is first and foremost a work of art. Therefore, product placements risk becoming detrimental when economic issues outweigh artistic issues; here, we see an outright rejection of placements because they spoil the viewer's pleasure. Hollywood cinema is often condemned for the growing visibility of brands, but overall they are better accepted: the film is presented as a commercial product, in which product placement appears as a gimmick.

In France, the problem may arise that an over-abundance of placements lead to the film being classed an 'advertising object'. The director has to respect the presence of the brands, but not allow his film to be enslaved by them. The risk is creating a rejection by the viewer, who, identifying the brands too easily, will retain only a negative image of them.

The staging of the product or brand must be active: placing a brand in the decor, without a performance, is not effective. The product must be integrated into the film through its characters: it must play a role within the context of the story. This is why, in order to avoid over-saturating the film, only seven or eight active placements on average are carried out per film.

To what extent does a James Bond film represent a special case of placements? What lessons can you draw from your personal experience?
The films of the James Bond series represent a real war machine, produced for 40 years by the same company, Eon Productions. Since their creation, the James Bond films have been seen by approximately 3 billion viewers and have brought in more than US$3.3 billion over 20 films. A film costs US$200 million to produce (compared with US$6–7 million on average for a French film).

For the film's promotion, the production invests US$100 million in buying advertising space and in publishing fees worldwide, in order to target the 18–25-year-olds who represent the main target, that is, 70 per cent of the viewers. Secondary, much smaller targets are then defined using a few chosen brands to communicate to these targets. This is the principle of tie-in promotions.

First of all, there is the male target of 35–55 years. What attributes of James Bond will seduce this target? The car. Different types of partnerships have therefore been set up: a placement for car products in the film, but also a tie-in partnership with BMW for its cinema release, representing a total media investment of US$15 million for the advertiser, spread over the purchase of advertising space and intensive communication.

Then the film's promotion concentrates on women, an important target because they are often influential in choosing a film. Product placement and/or promotion operations are defined so that the chosen brand can communicate at its points of purchase (for perfumers, cosmetic products and so on) or set up promotional activities such as competitions. The film's heroine is often the ambassadress for a major brand, such as Halle Berry for Revlon in *Die Another Day*. Over 15 James Bond films, five agreements have been made with feminine brands to carry out this kind of tie-in promotion (Dior, Yves Saint-Laurent, L'Oréal, Maybelline and Revlon).

Another example: James Bond's watch is an Omega because it is one of the only brands that really fits the character's image. In order to permanently register the brand in the series, a partnership between Omega and Film Média Consultant was agreed, with a media investment by the advertiser of US$7–8 million per film. For its communications operations, Omega uses the image of the actor, here Pierce Brosnan, while he is remunerated for the brand's use of his image. Thanks to these operations, Omega has benefited from sales peaks of 35 per cent after the release of each of the films. Finally, another long-standing partner of the series is Bollinger champagne, which communicates on a global level about its integrations on the release of each film.

Statistically, 10 per cent of James Bond viewers are part of the secondary targets: 60 million people are therefore affected by the film's promotion. Finally, on each James Bond, there are three or four major partnerships – made up of both product placements and tie-in promotions (BMW, Omega or Bollinger, for example) – and four or five partners without placements in the film (such as Revlon), but who will engage in heavy-duty communication for the cinema release: this is tie-in promotion. All this investment in the film's promotion will generate US\$200–300 million in final box-office receipts.

We often criticize James Bond for this intensive advertising, to the point that the hero has sometimes been called a 'sandwich-board man'.[1] In reality, the viewer does not notice more brands here than in other Hollywood films, but it's always fashionable to criticize a commercial film that, year after year, is always so successful.

Placement and distribution practices differ from one country to another. For example, in France, where the idea of the auteur is still important, major brands say little about brand or product placements, so that the viewer is innocent of all this before discovering the film in the cinema. In the United States, in contrast, the 'hard sell' technique has the upper hand because the US viewer sees the film above all as a commercial medium.

The latest James Bond, *Casino Royale*, was filmed during the first half of 2006. In this film inspired by the first novel of the series, Bond is given his licence to kill, which causes him to consider some ethical and philosophical questions. The placement is involved in the key products of the film: vehicles, mobile phones (Sony is co-producing the film), watches, champagne and so on.

How would you describe the French product placement market in comparison with the US market from an economic, legal and technical point of view? Why does it differ?
Product placement in cinematic works is not subject to any restrictions. However, it is more developed in the United States: the advertisers grant big budgets to Hollywood films that will be exported abroad and will enable the brands to make contact with their clientele at a global level.

Nor is there any restriction in audiovisual works in the United States; however, France has very particular legislation. In fact, the Conseil Supérieur de l'Audiovisuel (Higher Audiovisual Council) (CSA) bans advertising, and therefore any product or brand placement on television (series and television films), except for cars (necessary props) and institutional products (a region, town or département can be partners). The CSA censors any brand recognizable onscreen using digital graphics.

---

[1] Pascal Galinier (1997) James Bond, homme-sandwich pour film publicitaire, *Le Monde*, 10 December. The term 'sandwich man' is also used by Guillaume Evin in his analysis of the franchise in the article Brand, James Brand, *Diffusion*, April 2004, Union européenne de radio-télévision (EBU-UER).

Since the 1981 law on decentralization, the regions have developed their axes of communication, particularly through audiovisual and film pieces. For example, the series *Dolmen* (TF1) enabled the region of Brittany to benefit from sizeable economic consequences (€5–6 million was spent for the production during six months of filming in 2004), from being promoted at a national level and from a cultural involvement in the French patrimony.

What is the main recommendation you would make to a brand interested in this communication technique at the first contact? Why?
The product placement agency is the interface between the producers and the advertisers, who are not in contact with each other. We therefore act as the pivot for the commercial relationship between the two parties, and our role is to satisfy both parties in order to maintain regular working relationships and develop our brand image. On the one hand, it is therefore a matter of selling door-to-door to as many advertisers as possible, to bring out original ideas and to 'sell' placements at a fair value, and on the other we work closely with the production so that the placements are positively coordinated.

FMC offers to set up a product placement strategy for the brand according to its marketing briefs:

● An in-depth study of the carrier films in which the brand has its legitimacy.
● The management of rejection of placement requests (because of negative characters, a failing, devalued or hijacked product, the presence of competing brands and so on).
● Supervision of the proper integration of the products throughout filming and during the film's post-production.
● Optimization of the number and type of products in order to affirm the brand's position as leader in the cinema.
● The opportunity to create specially adapted placements leading to ambitious tie-in promotional operations.

Product placement requires a budget to be set aside in accordance with the product marketing orientation. A real strategy bringing together the marketing department, the sales network, FMC and the brand's advertising agency is drawn up in order to exploit the results of a genuine product placements policy.

FMC gives priority to setting up long-term partnerships with brands, in order to commit to four or five, or as many as 10 films per year, and for the brand to have real visibility over time: the first year in cinemas; the second year in cinemas, on DVD, on Canal+ or TPS; the third in cinemas, on DVD, on Canal+ or TPS, on terrestrial channels, and so on.

How do you see the future of this communications technique? What are your reasons?
Product placements have a bright future since traditional advertising – seen
as invasive, boring and uninspired – is increasingly devalued. The consumer
expects something new from advertising in relation both to the product it is
promoting, and the advertising discourse itself. This is the strength of product
placement, which offers an alternative, non-aggressive communication,
associated with a make-believe world and with film stars. The effectiveness
of increasingly expensive television advertising spots is being challenged in
favour of public relations and direct marketing operations (samples, tie-in
promotions, competitions and so on). In this way, the cinema is a medium of
the future: the brand is involved in a context disconnected from the world of
advertising, and addresses a captive and positive audience.

We have entered an attention economy. Media planners are forced to seek
out new channels of communication by playing on the complementarities
between the different media, as Volvo did with *The Mystery of Dalaro*. Consumers are more and more sensitive to the price argument, but they also
need to be reassured. To recover the audience's goodwill, brands need to
think 'local' more than 'global'. Finally, let's recall the threat of TiVo, the tool
that allows you to record and draw up programmes while skipping through
the advertisements, which should be in 20 per cent of US homes in 2007, and
is set to shrink the advertising revenues of the major channels by the same
amount.

In the United States, professionals place a lot of hope in product placement
in programmes, in sponsored programmes, or even 'advertainment', a very
fashionable genre based on producing a fictional programme financed by
an advertiser and featuring its product or brand (for example the Ford films
broadcast around the series *24*). In France, this type of operation should also
become more generalized very soon (we have already seen its forerunner in
the M6 programme *Les Colocataires*).

In fact, the biggest change to come will be the authorization of product
placement in French audiovisual works. On 13 December 2005, the European
Commission adopted the legislative proposal for the revision of the Television
Without Borders directive, which advocates, among other things, an opening
for placements:

> Product placement is a reality in cinematographic works and with regard to
> audiovisual works made for television, Member States regulate this practice
> differently; to ensure a level playing field, and thus enhance the competitiveness
> of the European media industry, it is necessary to adopt rules with regard to
> product placement; the definition of product placement introduced covers any
> form of audiovisual commercial communication consisting of the inclusion of
> or reference to a product, a service or to the trade mark thereof so that it is
> featured within a programme, normally in return for payment or for similar con-
> sideration; it is submitted to the same qualitative rules and restrictions applying
> to advertising.

The text should be voted on before the end of 2006. The product placement market would see exponential growth, given the impact power of television: between 7 and 12 million viewers per showing.

Ultimately, the French cinema market represents about 700 communication opportunities per year for brands. Knowing that a product placement costs between €5,000 and €15,000, it immediately becomes plain that this market is tiny compared with the classic methods of communication. Concerning television, between 300 and 450 hours of fiction are produced per year, a figure that can be multiplied by six or seven active product placements to show the potential of the audiovisual works market.

What is the placement that you remember most fondly, and why?
About 30 years ago, as a viewer, I went to see *The Rescuers* with my son. We loved the film: we trembled, but we also laughed and cried. One scene in particular touched us: Bernard and Bianca, pursued by the villains, must cross an African river infested with scary crocodiles. A little dragonfly, perched on a leaf that he is using as a raft, offers to take them across. The dragonfly's name is Evinrude. Despite the waves and the crocodiles, he is determined, and he succeeds in transporting our two heroes across the perilous river.

I saw the film again 10 years later with my daughter: the image of Evinrude was as strong as ever. Our children in their turn will go and see the film or will buy the DVD, so that their children can watch it over and over again. For generations and generations, little Evinrude will be the brave and valiant motor that didn't let the heroes down![2]

My only regret is that I didn't 'set up' that agreement!

---

[2] Author's note: Evinrude was originally the patronymic of the Norwegian-born Ole Evinrude, who in 1903 participated in the conception and the making of the first Harley-Davidson carburettor. In 1907, he created the Evinrude Motor Company, specialized in building engines. Although numerous tests have been made by other inventors, he was the first to register the #1.001.260 patent, for the first marine propulsion system in 1919. In 1921, Ole Evinrude built the famous compact boat motor, a two-cylinder motor, called the Elto (Evinrude Light Twin Outboard). After being bought by several investors, Johnson-Evinrude's assets and brand have been the property of the Canadian Bombardier Produits Récréatifs Inc (BRP) group, since 2001.

PART III

Branded entertainment in all its forms

8 Using all available vectors

Flynn did not believe in anything but the beau geste. He once told me that when he bought perfume for a present, he always inquired for Chanel number 10. 'I don't like my women to be only half sure.'

(Raoul Walsh 'Regarding Errol Flynn', in Raoul Walsh (1974) *Each Man in His Time: The life story of a director*, Farrar, Straus and Giroux, New York)

In 2005, the German public channel ARD was propelled into the centre of a lively controversy, when product placements were identified in the television series *Marienhof*. Sometimes they were very indirect placements, such as a character's line indicating a preference for carpets because they absorb noise and reduce dust. A very innocent remark, on the face of things, if the studio Bavaria Film hadn't been paid by a floor covering corporation to include it!

German legislation is highly restrictive on the principle of placements. In hindsight, it was realized that such placements had been occurring for a long time in several other series such as *Schimanski* and *Tatort*. The 'scandal' reached such heights that the director of Bavaria Film, Thilo Kleine, and Frank Doehmann, former director of Colonia Media, were sacked.[1] Although recent, this 'affair' seems to hark back to a distant, bygone age! During that period, for the 2004–05 season in the United States, on the major television channels, Nielsen Media Research counted more than 100,000 appearances

---

[1] Scott Roxborough (2005) Scandal gives German TV pause, *Hollywood Reporter*, 26 July.

of placed products (a rise of 28 per cent over the previous season[2]), without anyone really finding fault. Brand and entertainment are allowed to pursue their commercial relations in any form possible, as long as these are tolerated, not by an often out-of-date legislator, but by the audience at which they are aimed, and which can prove swift to punish.

It would not be logical to leave by the wayside the various placement opportunities offered by the other vectors of culture and entertainment. The basic principle remains the same as for the cinema, and television viewers seem to share the same attitude as cinema goers regarding product and brand placements.[3] In practice, however, the methods of use always require adaptation.

Series and television programmes

In France, in television series, until the progressive relaxing of the rules, the 'non-prohibited' placements concerned props that were absolutely indispensable to the plot, cars and institutions such as towns or regions. In the United States, a much more permissive practice, particularly on cable channels, has for a long time permitted all types of placement. The detectives of *Hawaii Five-O* never drove anything but Ford cars. The Microsoft Xbox is played with exclusively in *Two and a Half Men*. People eat Oreo cookies and use their American Express cards in *Friends*. Nokia mobile phones are often present in the series *Alias*, as are Alienware computers in *Smallville*, the imposing Hummer vehicles in *CSI: Miami*, the newspaper *Los Angeles Times* in *Eyes*, M&M vending machines in *The West Wing*, iPods and Levi's jeans in *The Office*, Samsung flat screens in *Dark Angel* and *The District*. Mitel communications solutions are used in *Boston Legal* and *ER*. Burger King is integrated into *Arrested Development*, Philips and Sprint are partners of *24* and

---

[2] Caleb Stephens (2005) Marketing firm's deal could triple its staff, *Dayton Business Journal*, 23 October.

[3] Beng Soo Ong (2004) A comparison of product placements in movies and television programs: an online research study, *Journal of Promotion Management*, 10(1/2), pp 147–58. About game shows, very interesting resources can be found in a 2006 Gould and Gupta analysis, using two consumer studies. The authors point out the importance of the meanings consumers draw, and not only the usual effectiveness, especially because game shows naturally tie product promotion into their content. Stephen J Gould and Pola B Gupta (2006) Come on down, *Journal of Advertising*, 35(1), Spring, pp 65–81. See also Namita Bhatnagar, Lerzan Aksoy and Selin A Malkoc (2004) Embedding brands within media content: the impact of message, media and consumer characteristics on placement efficacy, in L J Schrum (ed), *The Psychology of Entertainment Media: Blurring the lines between entertainment and persuasion*, Lawrence Erlbaum Associates, Mahwah, NJ, pp 99–116.

While You Were Out, the *Financial Times* is must-have reading material in *Ally McBeal*, Tic-Tac sweets help the lawyers of the Donnell, Young, Dole & Frutt firm relax in *The Practice*, Campbell's Soup is cited in *7th Heaven*, the T-Mobile operator takes care of communications in *Veronica Mars*, and Buick cars are praised by Eva Longoria in *Desperate Housewives*.

Elsewhere, *Six Feet Under* prefers the Toyota Prius and *Prison Break* Yaris or Rav-4, while a Chrysler 300C was promoted in an episode of *ER*. The *NCIS* agents work on Dell computers, whereas Carrie Bradshaw (played by Sarah Jessica Parker) uses an Apple laptop in *Sex and the City*. Home Depot and American Express are placed in *Friends*, and Subway sandwiches were subtly integrated into the script of an episode of the series *Will & Grace* on NBC. This is not forgetting Tropicana, Nissan, Cadillac, Ford, Dunkin Donuts, Motorola, Hermès, FedEx, Toblerone, Coca-Cola, Pony, Philips and even Rémy Martin, Stolichnaya and Marlboro in *The Sopranos*. So far, everything seems to be – fine!

Television series are increasingly courted by advertisers. There are many reasons for this. In the United States, the series produced by the cable channels in recent years have been able to profoundly revive the genre, with their more liberal tone and their more original subjects. The result? They attract a large audience, all the more so since they have fewer commercial breaks than series on the major networks. Furthermore, an episode of a series lasts on average only 42 minutes, and this shorter format is suitable for the seduction of the modern consumer, who is always in a hurry and does not necessarily have the time to dedicate 90–120 minutes to a feature film. In addition, some of the series enjoy production budgets comparable to film budgets, and can therefore retain a high quality, so are likely to retain their audience from episode to episode, over several seasons. The use of recurring characters is the distinctive feature of a series in general. It is also, however, a certain advantage for product and brand placements. This not only acts as an aid to consumer memorization, it also enables brands to instil over time a certain proximity, even a certain familiarity between the character and the audience.[4] The brand discourse can thus enjoy a very positive implicit testimonial, either direct or indirect.

---

[4] See in particular very interesting research by Cristel Antonia Russell, Andrew T Norman and Susan E Heckler (2004) The consumption of television programming: development and validation of the connectedness scale, *Journal of Consumer Research*, 31(1), June, pp 150–61. See also Carrie La Ferle and Steven M Edwards (2006) Product placement – How brands appear on television, *Journal of Advertising*, 35(4), Winter, pp 65–86. The technique is not only used in occidental and US television series and television shows. India, for instance, is also practising the technique with the same professional approach and the same concern about the audience's potential rejection if the brands are overexposed. For example, with six sponsors in the *Indian Idol* show, the brand placement technique remains relevant. See Sulekha Nair (2006) Promos should jell with the story, *Financial Express*, 12 February.

The impact of the placement and the prescriptive effect of the characters of a series can be genuinely powerful. In 2004, an imaginary product was placed in the soap opera *All My Children*, shown on ABC since 1970. The brand in question was Fusion, a fictional perfume and clothing brand, used in the plot of several episodes and praised by the characters of the series: it was subsequently actually sold in shops and on the television channel's website.[5] Finally, unlike a film, a television series offers the considerable advantage of being able to identify its audience with some precision, and therefore to know what sector of the public it is managing to attract. For any advertiser, this is essential: this is how it knows whether the audience matches its target.

Placement in a television series is, however, not without its risks. Here, too, it is important to be vigilant over the details of the placement contract over time. The intensifying competition means that television channels are now particularly quick to shift a series to another time slot, or even to cancel it if the audience figures are not as expected.[6] What, therefore, are the implications for the advertiser, whose communication strategy may find itself somewhat

---

[5] Since the first licensing contracts proposed by Kay Kamen at Walt Disney's in the 1930s, licensed products have multiplied. See in particular Gérald Bigle (1987) *Droits dérivés: Licensing et character merchandising*, J Delmas et Cie, Paris, and also Jean-Claude Jouret (1991) *Tintin et le merchandising: une gestion stratégique des droits dérivés*, Academia-Erasme, Paris; and for a complete and updated legal framework, Gregory J Battersby and Charles W Grimes (1985–2005) *The Law of Merchandise and Character Licensing: Merchandising law and practice*, Thomson-West, Eagen, MN; Karen Raugust (2004) *The Licensing Business Handbook*, 5th edn, EPM Communications, New York. Furthermore, those product and/or brand placements, generating demand from consumers even if they are initially just accessories to a fictional identity, are revealing factors of the huge potential impact they might have on the public. In 1994, Paramount Pictures were surprised by the intensity of the *Forrest Gump* phenomenon after the release of the eponymous movie directed by Robert Zemeckis. A number of products – and especially the famous Bubba Gump Seafood Company – even though they had been fictional and created for the movie, were extracted from the movie fantasy world and translated to the real world. There are now Bubba Gump Seafood restaurants in New York, Maui, Miami, New Orleans, Chicago and San Francisco among others; and also in Tokyo, Cancún, and Bali (see www.bubbagump.com). This specific process is called 'reverse product placement'. In France, a similar phenomenon occurred, even if proportional to the smaller French market, with James Huth's *Brice de Nice* (2005) (see www.bricedenice.com).

[6] We may also mention the interesting case of the adventure and suspense mini-series *The Runner*: it was abruptly abandoned in 2000 by the ABC network which had invested several millions in producing it. Producer Mark Burnett and LivePlanet (Matt Damon and Ben Affleck's production company) got it back in 2004, with the purpose of reformatting the concept for an online diffusion on the Yahoo website in 2006. See in particular Kevin J Delaney and Brooks Barnes (2006) Yahoo hopes to make network flop a net hit, *Wall Street Journal*, 16 January.

altered by the decision? Placement should also be practised with caution by the television channels, particularly when they are also producers, so as not to accentuate the very thing – commercialism – the editorial content is supposed to enable viewers to avoid. In fact, the too-obvious presence of one advertiser in a given series can rapidly lead all other competing advertisers to shun the associated commercial breaks, and thereby accelerate the channel's loss of revenues.[7]

Television reality shows are also now a sought-after vector for product placement, given their target audience and the flexibility of integration possible for brands.[8] Levi's is present in the *Rock Star: INXS* programme on CBS. Coca-Cola was highly visible throughout an entire season of the successful programme *American Idol*, broadcast by Fox. Coors beers were present, and the American Express card was repeatedly mentioned, in several episodes of the reality TV show *The Restaurant*.[9] Pontiac appears in *Survivor* on CBS, and the Solstice model was at the centre of an episode of *The Apprentice* on NBC. In another episode of *The Apprentice* (on NBC), the participants were asked to work on a Home Depot case or to think about a new jingle for the restaurant chain Burger King. 24-Hour Fitness gyms are promoted in *The Biggest Loser*, still on NBC. 7Up is placed in the programme *Battle of the Network Stars* on Bravo, Jaguar in *Gilmore Girls* on the WB Channel, Hewlett-Packard in *That 70's House* on MTV, and Volkswagen New Beetles take part in *Shorties Watchin' Shorties* on Comedy Central. Each time, we find a placement contract.

Over the 2004–05 season alone in the United States, Nielsen Media Research estimated the number of products appearing on the six major American television networks to be over 100,000.[10] Naturally, not all of them

[7] Jeanne McDowell (2004) The sponsors move in, *Time Magazine*, 23 August. For an in-depth analysis of *The Sopranos* series, see Deborah L Jaramillo (2002) The family racket: AOL Time Warner, HBO, *The Sopranos*, and the construction of a quality brand, *Journal of Communication Inquiry*, 26(1), January, pp 59–75.

[8] For relevant research on this subject, see Alain d'Astous et Nathalie Séguin (1999) Consumer reactions to product placement strategies in television sponsorship, *European Journal of Marketing*, 33(9/10), pp 896–910. See also Rosellina Ferraro and Rosemary J Avery (2000) Brand appearances on prime time television, *Journal of Current Issues and Research in Advertising*, 22(2), Fall, pp 1–15. For original research that proposes a model based on the balance theory 'in which attitude alignment is the explanation for links between a triad composed of the consumer, the sitcom character, and the placed product' see Cristel Antonia Russell and Barbara B Stern (2006) Consumers, characters, and products, *Journal of Advertising*, 35(1), Spring, pp 7–21.

[9] Sharon Waxman (2005) Hollywood unions object to product placement on TV, *New York Times*, 14 November.

[10] Lorne Manly (2005) When the ad turns into the story line, *New York Times*, 2 October.

have the same importance. There are very few advertisers like Coca-Cola, that have large enough communications budgets to appear throughout the whole season on a popular programme such as *American Idol.* The figure is nevertheless revealing about the growth of the phenomenon. It is likely that some programmes such as *Survivor*, created by Mark Burnett, would never have seen the light of day without the financial support of product placements, and others would probably not have remained on television without it. This raises an additional question for certain programmes whose intention is to be controversial or critical. These programmes have as much need of finance nowadays as any other. The number of advertisers hurrying to associate their products and brands with them, however, is naturally fewer, conscious as they are of the risk that this type of programme represents.

In a television programme, testimonials in favour of a product or brand are of two types, both of which should be taken into consideration since the methods of placement, or simply of the appearance of the brand, differ according to type. Some programmes call on stars, others on unknowns invited or selected to participate in the programme. With the use of stars, the association gives the brand the advantage of being able to profit directly or indirectly from their celebrity.[11] Furthermore, as in most cases the stars are showbusiness professionals, their professionalism can be capitalized on, to promote the product in favourable conditions.

If an unknown is used, this professional approach is not always possible. Some training will often be necessary, if the production and the advertiser wish the brand's integration into the programme to appear as natural as possible. If the placement is successfully carried out, however, the fact that an anonymous consumer is used is not necessarily a drawback. The remuneration stars demand for their testimonial is well-known to everyone, which can in certain cases affect their credibility. When an average consumer is used, and rarely paid because participation in the programme is reward enough, the impact may be infinitely greater among another part of the marketing target audience, if the product or brand placement is well orchestrated, or by the fact of the consumer's natural credibility. Care should be taken, however, since the public are increasingly mature and it is not a question of duping them. Hence, clearly, the impulse for thinking 'integration' and not simply 'placement'.

Others still sometimes use the term 'stealth marketing' to describe these placements. They are committing two flagrant errors. The first is that if it were a matter of stealth marketing, the competent authorities would not be capable of decoding the placements, and this would not necessarily profit the

---

[11] Jean-Marc Lehu (1993) *Origines et modalités d'utilisation des stars dans la publicité*, PhD thesis directed by Professor Pierre Grégory, Paris 1 Panthéon Sorbonne University, Paris.

brands. The second is that the public itself would have to be incredibly naïve to see it as coincidence after coincidence that products turn up on certain programmes. In countries with more rigorous legislation on the subject of stealth marketing, such as France in comparison with the United States, authorities such as the CSA (Conseil Supérieur de l'Audiovisuel, Higher Audiovisual Council) are quick to act and to impose a punishment if the brand has not been 'blurred', or disguised by digital interference.[12]

In July 2002, the CSA issued a formal notice to the television channel M6 following an episode of *Honey, I Shrunk the Kids*, where the action was set in a McDonald's restaurant. In 1998, France 2 was criticized by the organization for what was perceived to be an 'unnecessary' showing of the daily newspaper *France Soir*, in an episode of the series *Nestor Burma*. As for the consumers, or in any case for the majority of them, they have long since ceased to be fooled by this. The essential question is how far we can go, and how we can do so without the development of a feeling of rejection, which would be disastrous for the brand and the programme.

Advertisers should take a further important precaution regarding programmes shown live. These generate larger audiences, but naturally, they always carry the risk of an uncontrollable incident. During the 38th Super Bowl in 2004, MTV was producing the show element of the broadcasting of the American football championship on CBS. During a song sung by Janet Jackson and Justin Timberlake, the latter tore off part of the singer's corset, revealing the whole of her right breast. Around 140 million viewers watched the broadcast.[13] The event sparked an instant controversy and led to severe condemnation from the FCC (Federal Communications Commission), which launched an enquiry. The NFL (National Football League), CBS and the singers offered their official apologies to anyone who might have been offended by this gesture.[14] However, the advertising sponsors such as AOL showed little appreciation for this live surprise.[15] Admittedly, the use of

---

[12] Pascale Paoli-Lebailly (2005) Fiction: les marques oui, le placement non, *CB News*, 843, 18 July. See also the report La présence de marques dans la fiction, *La Lettre du CSA*, 181, February 2005. In supplement for covert advertising: article 9 of the decree #92-280 March 27th of 1992, modified.

[13] See in particular Ann Oldenburg (2004) Jackson's halftime stunt fuels indecency debate, *USA Today*, 2 February, and Kenneth Li (2004) MTV blames Janet Jackson for Super Bowl incident, *Forbes*, 3 February.

[14] Incidents of this kind can also have consequences for celebrities. When the Superbowl's 'hold on tight' problem occurred, Justin Timberlake had a sponsorship contract with McDonald's. The restaurant chain, well-known for its family positioning, quickly officially stated that it was disappointed, regretting the 'inappropriate' behaviour, without however questioning its marketing relationship with the singer.

[15] Kenneth Li (2004) MTV blames Janet Jackson for Super Bowl incident, *Forbes*, 3 February.

digital technology means that transmission can be slightly delayed, making it possible to intervene if necessary before broadcasting, but the disadvantage is that the excuse of a live programme is no longer valid and the producers become possible targets for a formal rebuke.[16]

Novels and plays

In the novel *The Perfect Manhattan* (2005) by Leanne Shear and Tracey Toomey,[17] while the central character 'effortlessly lifted a case of Budweiser' (mentioned 15 times in the novel), a gentleman walks into a bar. He is described as wearing 'a Hermès tie' (p 40). Further on in the novel, one character is compared to Pierce Brosnan in an Armani suit (p 151), while another, female character takes a 'Chanel lip palette from her Louis Vuitton clutch' (p 294). The character of Rosalind doesn't merely look at her watch, but 'consults her platinum Cartier watch that hung delicately on her slender wrist' (p 175). Even when she lights a cigarette (p 332), it is with a 'signature Cartier lighter'. There are also numerous other brands mentioned in the novel.

Brand placement in a novel may seem logical, if it is perceived as an aid to description and to the development of a mental image to support the story. As we analysed in Part I, brands have an evocative power, which the author may make use of to fuel the reader's imagination. Placement can thus allow authors a certain economy, even as it enriches the scene, or renders it more precise in the reader's mind, if he or she knows the brand. Nowadays, many authors use this method of anchoring their descriptions in reality, both in novels and in plays – whether for financial recompense or not – when their story is set against a backdrop of everyday life.[18]

Even best-selling authors, who at first glance should not need the financial support, use brand placement. Dan Brown introduced the brands Citroën ZX, Mercedes, BMW, Audi, Rolls-Royce, Aston Martin, Porsche, Ferrari, Heckler and Koch, Smirnoff and the Ritz Hotel, among others, in *The Da Vinci Code* (2003).[19] Mary Higgins Clark mentioned, in particular, the Plaza Hotel, the *New York Globe*, the *New York Times*, MSNBC, Armani and Dodge in

---

[16] ABC uses this technique to broadcast the Oscars' ceremony to avoid live bad surprises. In 1974, a streaker (exhibitionist) appeared on stage during the live ceremony and there was no possibility of controlling the images.

[17] Leanne Shear and Tracey Toomey (2005) *The Perfect Manhattan*, Broadway Books, Random House, New York.

[18] Stuart Elliott (2005) On Broadway, ads now get to play cameo roles, *New York Times*, 22 April.

[19] Dan Brown (2003) *The Da Vinci Code*, Doubleday, New York.

The Christmas Thief (2004). John Grisham evoked the car brands Ford and Mercedes, the whisky Jack Daniel's and the fast food chain McDonald's in *The Last Juror* (2004),[20] and the brands Chivas, Montrachet, the *Wall Street Journal*, the *New York Times*, the *Washington Post*, *BusinessWeek*, CNN, Exxon, Honda Accord, Lamborghini, Ford, BMW, Porsche Carrera, Bentley, Toyota Celica, Mercedes, Gulfstream, Falcon, Challenger, Hawker and Lear, 'in particular', in *The King of Torts* (2003).[21]

Tom Clancy succeeded in placing Visa, American Express, AT&T, Airbus, Boeing, Viagra, Smith & Wesson, Beretta, Ingram, AK, Uzi, Glock, Mac, Remington, British Telecom, Lloyd's, Holiday Inn Express, Motel 6, McDonald's, Dunkin Donuts, Burger King, Sam Goody, Roy Rogers, K*B Toys, Tiffany, Sunglass Hut, LensCrafters, Kmart, Sears, 7-Eleven, Foot Locker, Toys'R'Us, JC Penney, Victoria's Secret, Gap, American Eagle, Nike, Belk's, San Pellegrino, Perrier, Miller Lite, Tetley Smooth, John Smith's, Coca-Cola, Kool, Marlboro, Gulfstream, FedEx, the *New York Times*, *The Lancet*, the *International Herald Tribune*, the *Wall Street Journal*, *Playboy*, the *Washington Post*, NBC, History Channel, Nick at Nite, ESPN, CNN, HBO, Fox, MSNBC, Sky News, AOL, Monopoly, Air France, Alitalia, British Airways, KLM, Hertz, and the cars Audi, Aston Martin, Lada, Porsche, Ford, Buick, Ferrari, Jaguar, McLaren, Hummer, Chevy, Volvo, and Mercedes, among others, in a single novel, *The Teeth of the Tiger* (2004)![22]

Placements in books are increasing, and more particularly in novels, of course. Thanks to a win–win product placement contract with Procter & Gamble, in 2006, *Cathy's Book* trained young girls to use Cover Girl make-up.[23] In the United States alone, the PQ Media firm estimates that investment in brand or product name placements in books is worth US$26.6 million. The most famous case to date remains that of the novel *The Bulgari Connection* (2001), by Fay Weldon, alluding to the products of the famous Italian jeweller.[24] It was by no means the first in historical terms, but it was undoubtedly the first to be so media-friendly, since it was the first in which the advertiser admitted to having paid the author to place its brand in the

---

[20] John Grisham (2004) *The Last Juror*, Doubleday/Random House, New York.

[21] John Grisham (2003) *The King of Torts*, Doubleday/Random House, New York.

[22] Tom Clancy (2004) *The Teeth of the Tiger*, Berkley/Penguin, New York.

[23] Sean Stewart (and) Jordan Weisman (2006) *Cathy's Book: If Found Call 650-266-8233*, Running Press Kids, Philadelphia, PA.

[24] See in particular Lance Morrow (2001) When novels become commercials, *Time*, 3 September; Capucine Cousin (2006) Le placement de produit s'attaque au roman, *Les Echos*, 8 September, p 10; Motoko Rich (2006) Product placement deals make leap from film to books, *New York Times*, 12 June; and the analysis by Richard Alan Nelson (2004) *The Bulgari Connection*: a novel form of product placement, *Journal of Promotion Management*, 10(1/2), pp 203–12.

novel.[25] In fact, one of the novel's first scenes takes place in a Bulgari jeweller's on Sloane Street, London, where the millionaire Barley Salt offers his second wife a brooch worth £18,000. The idea came from the managing director of Bulgari, Francesco Trapani, who believed that product placements, of whatever type, were an increasingly important form of communication.[26] While the author's contract stipulated that the name Bulgari should appear at least a dozen times, Fay Weldon proposed to make it a central element of the book and even to include it in the title. Although her publisher initially expressed some reservations on the merit of keeping the jeweller's name in the title, it was retained and the book was published for Christmas 2001.[27] HarperCollins printed 7,500 limited edition copies for a public relations operation organized by the jeweller.

As might have been expected, *The Bulgari Connection* gave rise to ferocious criticism from the literary community, particularly in the United States. However, the Bulgari 'case' was not the first example of brand placement in a novel, or even in a title. Some may recall the Truman Capote novel, *Breakfast at Tiffany's* (1958), which gave another form of shop window to another famous jeweller, in this case without it having paid for it. Whether imaginary or real, brands have entered into the writer's thoughts ever since they first appeared. Whether it is César Birotteau's indispensable Carminative Balm or the Double Paste of Sultans (1833), various brands illustrate Balzac's *Comédie humaine* (Human comedy). There are other, even more interesting cases. In his play *The Importance of Being Earnest* (1895), Oscar Wilde mentions the Grand Hôtel in Paris. None of his many biographies mention payment of any kind for this. The real brand even becomes an important element of precision when, in Act III, Scene 2, Jack explains to Lady Bracknell that her nephew Algernon lied his way into his house, pretending to be his brother, and drank a full bottle of Perrier-Jouet brut, vintage 1889. Not just champagne, Perrier-Jouet! Oscar Wilde! In 1895! The same Perrier-Jouet that would be drunk almost a century later in the film *Top Gun* (Tony Scott, 1986).

---

[25] Jeanny Lyn Bader (2001) Brand-name lit: call me Tiffany, *New York Times*, 9 September. Other sources considered that the first 'paid' author could have been Bill Fitzhugh, for his novel *Cross Dressing* (2000). The author may have signed a similar arrangement with Seagram to place the names of drinks from the beverages group in the text. See in particular Calvin Reid (2001) Weldon's Bulgari product placement raises eyebrows, *Publishers Weekly*, 10 September; Martin Arnold (2001) Making books: placed products and their cost, *New York Times*, 13 September; and Bridget Kinsella (2000) A novel idea: product placement, *Publishers Weekly*, 5 June, in which the author explains the arrangement was money-based but compensated for by a certain amount of scotch. Bill Fitzhugh (2002) *Cross Dressing*, William Morrow, New York.

[26] David D Kirkpatrick (2001) Now, many words from our sponsor, *New York Times*, 3 September.

[27] Fay Weldon (2001) *The Bulgari Connection*, Atlantic Press, London.

Once again, we find a classic showdown between two opposing camps. On one side, those who see a literary work as a sacred space that no brand should ever be permitted to desecrate (may this book never fall into their hands!), if only because they consider writing an art, and art and commercial notions are uneasy bedfellows. On the other, there are those who believe that brands are part of everyday life and that, as a result, their 'controlled' presence can do no damage to the intrinsic quality of the work. In the best cases, they can even contribute to the plot in one way or another, or in any case, root it in a very real world. It seems in fact that the battle against the invasion of brands into literature hails from a bygone era. On the one hand, free placements have existed almost as long as brands have, and in these conditions, the author and the editor might as well profit by charging for them. On the other, if these placements are badly orchestrated, too obvious or too numerous, the reading public will not hesitate to punish the authors by not reading their books. This is without question the most important and most legitimate form of censorship.

As with placement in a film, the insertion of a brand or a product can be repeated throughout the work. The book has the advantage of time, however, since readers can pause over the brand name when and how they please. In the same way as a film, it can also enable more precise targeting. In 2004, Ford signed a placement contract of this type with the British author Carole Matthews, for her next two books, with the aim of bringing its Fiesta model to the attention of active young women.[28] The development of this placement is original: the author had finished her last book, *With or Without You*, just before signing her contract with Ford.[29] This meant that her heroine would have to change cars in the following novel, *The Sweetest Taboo*, abandoning her New Beetle (Volkswagen) for a Fiesta. This agreement had an unexpected effect, inspiring numerous articles in the international press, which opened doors for the author into markets where her books were not or very little known, in Europe, the United States, Canada, New Zealand and Thailand, in particular.[30]

The examples of repeated placements are multiplying. In *Happiness Sold Separately*, by Libby Street,[31] the heroine Ryan Hadley, in the middle of a psychological crisis on reaching her first quarter-century, is presented as particularly liking Prada, admiring Ralph Lauren polo shirts and being thrilled at the possibility of being cared for in the Elizabeth Arden Red Door

[28] Danny Hakim (2004) The media business: advertising – would you base the purchase of a car on the prose of a chick-list novelist? Ford hopes so, *New York Times*, 23 March.

[29] Carole Matthews (2004) *The Sweetest Taboo*, Headline, London.

[30] For more information see Carole Matthews' personal website: www.carolematthews.com/carolefaqs.htm.

[31] Libby Street (2005) *Happiness Sold Separately*, Downtown Press, New York.

salon.[32] In the middle of the book (pp 100–1), she even draws up an itinerary to follow in Manhattan. Starting from Trump Tower, there are stops at Gucci, Ferragamo, Cartier, Versace, Harry Winston, Prada, Bergdorf Goodman and, of course, Tiffany's, which is like 'stepping into a dreamworld'.

In a book, placement can also be skilfully used as an element of character positioning. It can spare the author long pages of description that risk annoying readers or causing them to lose track. The positioning of known brands, meanwhile, can be subtly associated with that of the character to which they are attributed. In the case of a story integrating various characters, brands that are well known, but different for each character, can also enable the reader to categorize them more easily. In *Whiteout* (2004),[33] the novelist Ken Follett plays this game with the reader. To go unnoticed, the character of Kit Oxenford replaces 'his Armani wristwatch with a nondescript Swatch'. Cars are often the 'vehicles' used for this type of status transfer. Thus, again in *Whiteout*, the character of Michael Ross owns a Volkswagen Golf, whereas Stanley Oxenford travels in a Ferrari F50. While Miranda Oxenford drives a Toyota, Kit Oxenford owns a black Peugeot coupé, Nigel Buchanan travels in a Bentley Continental, Jim Kincaid uses a grey Volvo, Hugo owns a Mercedes, and Luke (the dogsbody) a 'dirty white' Ford Mondeo! The police, for their part, are limited to Range Rovers, without further identifying details.

Authors are not always *au fait* with the methods of setting up such placement contracts, and above all with the concrete advantages that they can ultimately gain from them. As a characteristic example, we can look at John E Mayer's noir novel *Shadow Warrior* (2005), set in the clandestine world of laundering drug money.[34] What might have been just another literary output was transformed into a veritable branded entertainment operation. Aiming to make the world of his novel more realistic, the author decided to integrate the names of brands such as the Grand Hyatt hotel in New York, Porta Bella clothing, Oakley, Jaguar, Nike, Louis Vuitton and Ketel One vodka. None of these placements had been subject to selling, much less to contracts with the brands in question. When the book was launched, the author somewhat modestly tried to contact the New York Grand Hyatt, to ask whether it would be willing to host a book-signing event, since the hotel was mentioned in the book. Highly familiar with publicity techniques, the public relations manager transformed the idea into a large charity cocktail party in aid of sporting associations, and invited several celebrities. The author then contacted Ketel One, which gave him a similar reception, and agreed to take responsibility

[32] Joe Piazza (2005) Prada placement, *New York Daily News*, 23 June.

[33] Ken Follett (2004) *Whiteout*, Dutton/Penguin, New York.

[34] John E Mayer (2005) *Shadow Warrior*, AuthorHouse, Bloomington, IN. For more information about this specific case, visit www.authorhouse.com/AuthorResources/CaseStudy/Mayer.asp

for sculpting an ice bar in which the book's cover would be presented, for the event planned at the Grand Hyatt. A veritable branded entertainment operation had just been born.

Song lyrics

It is not uncommon for brands to play a part in promoting a singer or musician. In 2006, Absolut vodka offered an exclusive download of the song *Breathe*, by Lenny Kravitz, on its internet site, in the context of a major promotional operation, 'Absolut Kravitz'. The previous year, the new album by the singer Alain Souchon, *La Vie Théodore* (The Theodore life), contained a song titled 'Putain ça penche'. Many press releases called it an 'acerbic criticism of the consumer society', or even a cynical vision of brands, since the singer 'listed 76 commercial brands' in it. The message is extremely subtle, as always with Alain Souchon's work, since he sings, after a stanza composed of brand names: '*Putain ça penche, on voit le vide à travers les planches...*' (Bloody hell! It's leaning. We can see emptiness through the boards ...). Nevertheless, it remains the case that from Nike to Le Temps de Cerises, via Hermès, Calvin Klein, Diesel, Chanel, Converse, Comme des Garçons, La Perla, Cartier, H&M, Puma, Dior, Mercedes, Reebok, Cartier, Weston, Gucci, Zara, Lacoste, Hugo Boss, Jean-Louis David, Zaza de Marseille, 501, Kookaï, Lancel, Cacharel, Porsche, Timberland, all these brands – essentially linked to clothing and luxury goods – received a free, almost four-minute-long, musical shop window.

It is not uncommon for brands to be 'borrowed' by certain singers, in particular today's rappers.[35] This approach is sometimes called 'brand-dropping'. Even if the media have only recently picked up on these placements, however, the phenomenon is not a recent one. Some may recall Janis Joplin asking God to buy her a Mercedes-Benz because her friends all drove Porsches, on the album *Pearl* (1971). Moreover, while searching the rap archives, we find the case of the song *Rapper's Delight* (1979), by the trio The Sugarhill Gang. An attentive listener will identify a Lincoln Continental and a sunroof Cadillac in the lyrics, and, above all, in the chorus, the fact that 'everybody go hotel motel Holiday Inn'! In 1976, the Eagles placed Tiffany and Mercedes in the now-classic *Hotel California*, without the fans seeming to notice.

Another forerunner, track three of the album *Raising Hell* (1986), by Run-DMC, was entitled without possibility of misunderstanding 'My Adidas'. The brand name is mentioned 22 times in the song. The majority of sources

---

[35] Michael Paoletta (2006) The name game, *Billboard*, 18 February. See also David Kiley (2005) Hip Hop two-step over product placement, *BusinessWeek*, 6 April.

found converge on the idea that the brand was not involved in the song's origins. Unlike certain undesired placements, however, this was a flattering one for the brand. The idea is thought to have come from Russell Simmons (brother of Joseph 'Run' Simmons) because the group wore Adidas trainers. At a concert during the *Raising Hell* tour, Run interrupted the music and asked the audience to take their shoes off and wave one shoe at the ceiling. Representatives of Adidas were in the auditorium: a contract with the group followed.[36] The same was true for Angie Stone. That Rémy Martin sponsored one of the singer's tours was not unrelated to the fact that on the album *Stone Love*, the track Remy Red is an ode to the brand's mixed drink.

In 1985, in the song 'Money for nothing', from the album *Brothers in Arms*, the group Dire Straits began and ended the track with a demand that has remained famous: 'I want my MTV. I want my ... I want my MTV.'[37] Another line from the song also takes up the refrain: 'You play the guitar on the MTV.' In 1999, on his album *18 Tracks*, Bruce Springsteen sings the track 'Pink Cadillac', in which the singer tells how his love for Cadillac is bigger than a Honda, and bigger than a Subaru! Militant Americanism? In any case, the commercial impact of such placements, especially if they are reinforced by the singer using/consuming the product, can be extremely rapid, since fans are generally very reactive.

The contamination effect in connected segments can become highly profitable to the brand. This was the case in the 1990s, when Grand Puba inserted the name of the clothing brand Tommy Hilfiger into their songs while wearing the clothes on stage. The brand is mentioned notably in '360 degrees (what goes around)' (1992), in 'That's how we move it' (1992), but also in 'What's the 411?' (1992) and in 'Leave a message' (1992), sung with Mary J Blige, and yet again in 'Watch the sound' (1993), sung with Fat Joe F and Diamond D. At the same time, however, the audience reached is highly volatile, and has loyalty to the brand at a moment t only because its singer seems to recommend it. It can completely abandon it at the moment $t + 1$, because the singer's tastes may themselves have changed, or simply because in order to follow the trend of the moment, it is fundamental to keep changing everything, including your favourite singer.

---

[36] Eric Parker (2002) Hip-Hop goes commercial, *Village Voice*, 11–17 September.

[37] 'Money for nothing' (written by Mark Knopfler and Sting) remains among the most aired songs on the MTV music channel. Strange? The album *Brothers in Arms* became number one in most of the countries where it was released, mainly thanks to 'Money for nothing', which was the first single released from the album. Nothing strange, on the other hand, that the video of the song was the very first one to be aired on MTV Europe when the channel was launched (six years after its US launch), on 1 August 1987.

Brand placement can also take place during filming of the song's video. General Motors thus paid US$300,000 for a Hummer to be placed in the video for 'Ching ching', sung by Ms Jade. Beware, however, of possible 'MTV censorship'. Conscious of its prescriptive power, the themed channel often eliminates these videos from its playlist, for fear that they will conflict with the commercials of its advertisers and the latter may look elsewhere.[38]

French songs have not escaped the phenomenon of brand intrusion into the lyrics of their authors. Whether for a rhyme or for a reference, many brands have benefited from placements over the years. The medication Charbon Belloc recommended by Marie Dubas in 1936 ('Le Tango stupéfiant') (The narcotic tango), the PMU bookmakers 'that closes by midday' in 'Ça sent si bon la France' ('France smells so good'), by Maurice Chevalier in 1941, Bourvil's Jeep® in 1947 ('Le bougie') (The boogie), the Casino de Paris and the Moulin Rouge to dispel Andrex's worries in 1952 ('À la Cabanne bambou') (At the Bamboo Cabin), the extracts from the *Reader's Digest* cited by Serge Gainsbourg in 1958 ('Le poinçonneur des lilas') (The ticket-stamper of the lilacs), Cardin, Carvil, Cartier, Fauchon, Ferrari and Harley-Davidson used by Jacques Dutronc to describe 'Les playboys' in 1967, the inevitable Harley-Davidson also ridden by Brigitte Bardot in 1967 ('Harley-Davidson') are examples. So are Françoise Hardy hidden behind a Kleenex in 1968 ('Comment te dire adieu') (How to say goodbye to you), the *New York Times* demanded by Yves Simon while vacillating between Ford, Buick, Chrysler and Cadillac in 1974 ('J'ai rêvé New York') (I dreamed of New York), the Mercedes in which Michel Delphech 'hides out' in 1975 ('Quand j'étais chanteur') (When I was a singer), Michel Sardou's Dom Pérignon in 1983 ('Bière et fraulein') (Beer and a girl), orgies of Minto, Car-en-sac and other Carambar 'candies' for Renaud in 1985 ('Mistral gagnant') (Winning mistral), Alain Bashung's Concorde in 1998 ('Aucun express') (No express), Alain Souchon's Audi in 1999 ('Le baiser') (The kiss), or Bénabar's Gore-Tex lining in 2001 ('Bénabar').

The most characteristic marketing case, however, is unquestionably that of US rappers. The insertion of brands into song lyrics anchors them in the real world of society and consumption. In the United States alone, the PQ Media firm estimated that US$30.4 million are invested in placement of product or brand names into songs, whether to praise or criticize them. In most cases they are high-end, even luxury product brands, and alcoholic drinks, cars and clothing are often emphasized. In 1999, in the song 'Daddy figure', Kool G Rap inserted notably Armani, Cristal, Martini, Jacuzzi, Bloomingdale's, Rolex and Moschino into his lyrics. In the original single 'Stylin' (2002), the rapper Foxy Brown mentions (sometimes with 'adapted' pronunciations) Burberry,

---

[38] Evelyn Nussenbaum (2005) Products slide into more TV shows with help from new middlemen, *New York Times*, 6 September.

Mark Jacob, Planet Hollywood, Frankie B and Bentley, among others. The remix also includes Mercedes-Benz, Lamborghini, Hummer and Gucci. KanYe West mentions Hennessy and Coca-Cola in the chorus of 'Addiction' (2005), and in the same year, in 'Diamonds from Sierra Leone', the singer wears Yves Saint Laurent sunglasses, reads the magazine *Vibe*, remembers that he could not afford a Ford Escort and mentions Porsche, Hennessy, Motown and Luis Vuitton.[39] In one song, explicitly titled 'Got me a bottle' (2003), 50 Cent and Lloyd Banks ask for bottles of Hennessy, Bacardi, Smirnoff, E&J, Absolut and Tanqueray, and also mention Crown Royal. And adept at brand-dropping, the singer Jay-Z mentions Versace and Guess in 'Coming of age' (1997), Cristal, Rolex, Cartier and Versace again in 'Imaginary player' (1997), Motorola, Bacardi and Nike in 'Reservoir dogs' (1998), and Belvedere, Reebok, Chanel, Prada and Gucci in 'Get your mind right Mami' (2000). As for the different remixes of 'The jump off' (2003), by Lil' Kim, Jaguar, Bulgari, Pac-Man, Ferrari, Sprite, Range Rover, Bentley, Hummer, Mercedes-Benz, Timberland, Porsche and, er, Barbie can be identified in them.

Such placements can also contribute to rejuvenating a brand, as was notably the case for Cadillac at the beginning of the 2000s, when the brand was mainly targeting a 'senior' population. In just a few months, the Escalade SUV model (purchase price: US$54,000 on average) proved especially popular with rappers, and the average age of the Cadillac owner fell by 12 years! The model quickly became a 'must-have' and also a 'must-mention', in order to avoid being 'out of it'. A study of the words of various tracks from this period shows that the model is explicitly named in 'Earl that's yo' life' (1999) sung by E-40, in 'I'll call before I come', sung by Outkast, in 'Pink lemonade' (2000) by Da Brat, in 'Put ya sings' (2000), sung by Three 6 Mafia, in 'Love don't cost a thing' (2001) by Jennifer Lopez, in 'The Inc' (2001), sung by Ja Rule, in 'Lick shots' (2001), sung by Missy Elliott, in 'Nasty girl' (2001), sung by Jadakiss and Carl Thomas, in 'Still fly' (2002) by Big Tymers, in 'Humble neighborhoods' (2003) by Pink and in 'Freaky' (2004), sung by Young Rome and Guerilla Black. Hardly surprising, therefore, that in the United States, if only 6.5 per cent of habitual Cadillac customers are black, the brand counted 19 per cent among purchasers of the Escalade model[40]

---

[39] As is usually the case with rap titles, lots of remixes are recorded. All of them do not include exactly the same lyrics, and as a result, they do not mention the same brand names. Those interested by song lyrics can find more information on various specialized websites, in particular azlyrics.com, songlyrics.com, lyrics-songs.com, musicsonglyrics.com, and paroles.net or chansons-paroles.com for French songs. For an analysis of the coded lyrics of rap songs and the link with drugs use, see Sarah Diamond, Rey Bermudez and Jean Schensul (2006) What's the rap about ecstasy? Popular music lyrics and drug trends among American youth, *Journal of Adolescent Research*, 21(3), May, pp 269–98.

[40] Earle Eldridge (2001) Escalade scores with athletes, rappers, *USA Today*, 23 October.

– purchasers whose average income was around US$150,000 (or US$30,000 higher than the average income of the classic Cadillac customer). In short, how to upset a marketing plan without even intending to? In 1992, Cadillac had already benefited from a musical ode from the group Mc Nas-D with the song 'It's my Cadillac' (on the album of the same name). One of the brand's cars even appeared on the album cover. The fashion phenomenon of the Escalade brand surprised the brand's managers by its breadth and above all by its rapidity.

Another case of market and target rejuvenation, and without doubt still one of the most significant today, was via the track 'Pass the Courvoisier' (2002). In this song, the rappers Busta Rhymes and Sean (P Diddy) Combs seized on different alcohol brands (see the extract on p 176) with such success that the lyrics are still circulating today around the four corners of the internet, as significant references for the genre. The New York agency Impact calculated that the following year, sales had seen an increase of 18.9 per cent.[41] Courvoisier then skilfully tried to capitalize on the event, in sponsoring events with P Diddy, Missy Elliott and Lil' Kim, in particular.

In reality, it is not uncommon for alcohol brands to be the subject of placements – without having been requested by the advertiser – in rap lyrics. The proactive approach is still however prudent for many brands, since the rap scene is often readily associated with violence, sex, alcohol and drugs. This may be a hasty and stereotyped association, but it is sustained by the brutality of certain lyrics and certain images,[42] and sadly by the tragic deaths

---

[41] Todd Wasserman (2005) Playing the hip-hop drop, *Brandweek*, 25 July. In 2006, in a very interesting study, Christian Schemer and his colleagues confirm the link between rappers and placed brand evaluation. The 'pairing' of a brand (conditioned stimulus) with positively evaluated rappers (unconditioned stimulus) produces positive attitudes towards the brand. In contrast, a negative conditioning procedure results in negative attitudes. See Christian Schemer, Jörg Matthes, J Samuel Textor and Werner Wirth (2006) Does 'Passing the Courvoisier' always pay off? Positive and negative evaluative conditioning effects of brand placements in rap videos, paper presented to the Association for Education in Journalism and Mass Communication Conference, Advertising Division, 2–5 August, San Francisco, CA.

[42] On the cover of G Unit's *50 Cent is the Future* album (2003), two of the three photo-graphed rappers prominently show a gun. One of them is directly pointed toward the photographer. The album was heavily criticized on its release. Some shopping websites (such as amazon.com) even suppressed it. See also the very explicit article by Sheila Rule (1994) Generation rap, *New York Times*, 3 April. We can also be preoccupied about specific placements, such as those for the AK-47 (Avtomat Kalashnikova, model 1947), the famous assault rifle conceived by the equally famous Mikhail Timofeyevich Kalashnikov. According to American Brands agency research, with 33 mentions in 2005 hits, AK-47 was the tenth most cited brand this year in song lyrics. Even more indicative, the brand stood at 14th place in 2004, with 'only' 23 appearances, and

of certain artists such as Biggie Smalls and Tupac Shakur, to name but two examples. In contrast, many brands do not hesitate to call on these artists to make advertising films, as did Reebok, which indicated that sales of its RBK brand increased with 50 Cent's placement in 2003. In this type of case, however, everything is controlled. In a song written and performed by the artist, it is another story altogether.

Chorus: Busta Rhymes and P Diddy

Busta: Give me the Henny, you can give me the Cris
             You can pass me the Remi, but pass the Courvoisier
Diddy: Give me the ass, you could give me the dough
             You can give me 'dro, but pass the Courvoisier
Busta: Give me some money, you can give me some cars
             But you can give me the bitch make sure you pass the Courvoisier
Diddy: Give me some shit, you can give me the cribs
             You can give me whaever, just pass the Courvoisier.

Extract from 'Pass the Courvoisier', 2002.

It is also noticeable that the brand names are often truncated or adapted to the particular style of rap: 'Cris' for the champagne Cristal, 'Remi' for the cognac Remy Martin, 'Hen', 'Hen Dog' or 'Henny' for Hennessy cognac, 'Burburry' for Burberry and 'Bently' for Bentley. Such modifications lend themselves to the development of a feeling of appropriation by the specific musical genre of rap and by the artists themselves. They remove part of the commercial character of the placement, and enable it to sound almost natural in the target audience's ears, which might make them more open to the implicit recommendation.

In addition, various research works have confirmed that even if comprehension of the song lyrics was poor, the simple schematic process used by listeners usually enabled them to orient their behaviour in the direction of

---

54th in 2003 with 'just' seven mentions. Should we blame marketing strength? Violence was often the main purpose of the lyrics concerned, but AK-47 was not the only gun brand chosen for mention. Beretta and Smith & Wesson among others were also regularly praised by many devotees. The AK-47 is probably to date the most extraordinary, international and institutional product placement. The assault rifle is clearly shown on the official Mozambique flag!

the lyrics.[43] Furthermore, in relation to all other musical genres, rap has a particular characteristic in the sense that the attention given to the lyrics is voluntarily heightened by phrasing, wordplay, hidden meanings and the rhythm itself.[44] In 2003, the research agency New Media Strategies published the results of a study indicating that 60 per cent of respondents considering themselves to be fans of hip-hop were interested in films by their favourite singers and in buying products mentioned in their songs, or for which they were spokespersons in an advertisement.[45] This information is important when we consider that not all placements are necessarily positive. In 2004, 'High all the time', from the album *Get Rich or Die Tryin'*, was telling the always image-conscious 50 Cent[46] that he didn't need Dom Pérignon, Cris(tal), Tanqueray or d'Alize, and that he hated being in a 'Benz', or in other words, a Mercedes.

Nowadays the palette of musical genres is so varied that placement in a song can be an excellent vehicle for reaching a specific target audience. Certain musical niches make it possible in particular to reach certain population segments, notably the youngest, who are sometimes cynical towards the content of traditional advertising messages, especially since many rappers criticize television in the lyrics of their songs. This is what led McDonald's to appoint the services of a specialist consulting agency (Maven) in order to research those rappers who might be interested, for a fee, in integrating one of its brands into a song.[47] It anticipated a placement contract that of course came with rights to control the methods of insertion of the brand name. This prudent approach seems logical for the brand manager, especially if we remember, for example, the lyrics of 'You knows I loves you baby' (2004),

---

[43] See in particular Christine H Hansen and Ranald D Hansen (1991) Schematic information processing of heavy metal lyrics, *Communication Research*, 18(3), pp 373–411.

[44] See in particular Christy Barongan and Gordon C Nagayama Hall (1995) The influence of misogynous rap music on sexual aggression against women, *Psychology of Women Quarterly*, 19, June, pp 195–207.

[45] Kenneth Hein (2003) Cognac is in the house, *Brandweek*, 22 September.

[46] In 2005, American Brandstand agency estimated that the 50 Cent group led the pack for brand name dropping among the chart's top 20. This year the most cited brands ranking put on top Mercedes-Benz, with 100 mentions, followed by Nike (63), Cadillac (62), Bentley (51), Rolls-Royce (46), Hennessy (44), Chevrolet (40), and finally Louis Vuitton and Cristal (dead level with 35 mentions each). See also Michael Paoletta (2006) The name game, *Billboard*, 18 February.

[47] Marc Graser (2005) McDonald's rap song product placement plan stalls, *Advertising Age*, 26 September. McDonald's proposed a US$5 compensation for each citation of its brand. See also Richard Jinman (2005) Big Mac rap may mean artists' payday, *Guardian*, 29 March.

from the always image-conscious Goldie Lookin' Chain. The retail grocers Tesco were mentioned therein, but it is primarily McDonald's that the group criticized for its chairs bolted to the floor.

As early as 1997, Will Smith was alluding to the fast food chain in 'Just cruisin', indicating that the 'Golden arches' had left him with some digestive problems. The brand's desire for control therefore seems at first glance to be justifiable. It is simultaneously associated with placing artistes' creative freedom under surveillance, however, leading to a potentially enormous reluctance by them to get involved, since they then risk being criticized by their audience for having 'sold out' to marketing.

To avoid such associations, many of these rappers have developed their own line of clothing or products, giving it their own name or recommending it. Hence, if Gwen Stefani mentions LAMB, if Sean 'Diddy' cites Sean John, if Beyoncé sings about House of Dereon, if Pharrell Williams evokes Ice Cream or if Jay-Z includes Armadale vodka or Rocawear in his songs, there is nothing surprising about that, just business logic, man! The marketing and music alliance is therefore only just beginning, and control of the marketing is shared.[48] Play it again, Sam!

Branded videogames

From the 1980s onwards, advertising banners began to appear in arcade game car races. Since then, however, the placements have multiplied and above all diversified. It is not difficult to identify the oil brand Castrol used in the game *Need For Speed Most Wanted* (Electronic Arts). The snowboards of *SSX* (Electronic Arts) surf between advertisements for Honda and 7Up. Sam Fisher would no doubt be less effective without his Sony Ericsson P900 and T637 phones in *Splinter Cell: Pandora tomorrow* (Ubisoft) and his Airwaves chewing-gum in *Splinter Cell: Chaos theory?* In *Enter the Matrix* (Shiny Entertainment), the player's avatar uses a Samsung mobile phone, of course. The energy drink Red Bull appears in *Dredd vs Death* (Vivendi Universal Games) and in *Worms 3D* (Sega). The Staples Center ring and Everlast equipment are provided to the boxers in *Fight Night* (Electronic Arts). Jeep® and Quiksilver accompany the professional skater Tony Hawk in the series of games that bear his name on Activision. Intel and McDonald's are present in the very popular *The Sims Online* (Electronic Arts). Puma trainers and outfits were specially designed for Nick Kang in *True Crime: Streets of L.A.* and in *True Crime: New York City* (Activision). The characters of *Ghost Recon II* wear Under Armour clothes, a brand that is also present in *Tiger Woods PGA Tour 2006.* An advertisement for

---

[48] See in particular Michael Paoletta (2006) Destiny's Child: a perfect fit for brands, *Billboard*, 14 January.

a Panasonic videocamera and another for the television channel Channel 4 are inserted into *Anarchy Online* (Massive Inc). And in *EverQuest II*, the player even has the opportunity to order a pizza from the Hut during the game! With what is commonly known as 'advergaming',[49] the console screen seems increasingly to rival the four other screens (cinema, television, computer, telephone) accessible to the modern consumer.

The primary motivation for a developer to insert a brand into a video game is the same as that found in the cinema: financial support.[50] Estimates vary too widely from one research agency to another to give a clear picture of the phenomenon, but from Forrester Research to Yankee Group via PQ Media, all estimate that the financial advantages can rapidly reach several tens of millions of dollars.[51] There is a genuine demand. On the one hand,

---

[49] The expression 'advergaming', 'in-game advertising' or 'advertainment' is used to described a product placement in a videogame, such as the McDonald's and Intel signs appearing in *The Sims*; an online videogame on a dedicated website specifically conceived for the brand, such as *BP Ultimate* (www.miniclip.com/games/bp-ultimate-rally-challenge/en/), a driving game using a Volkswagen vehicle consuming, guess what? BP petrol of course; or an offline video game focused on a brand or on a product of this brand, like *Adidas Power Soccer* or *Volvo Drive for Life*, for instance. It can appear on a cartridge, a CD, a DVD, a memory card, a download offer for a portable player or a cellphone. Some authors are still making a distinction between in-game advertising and advergaming, reserving the last expression for games specifically designed for a brand (See P P Gupta (2006) Emerging role of advergaming, *Advertising Express*, ICFAI University Press, June, pp 23–28), or for online games (see Susan B Kretchmer (2005) Changing views of commercialization in digital games: in-game advertising and advergames as worlds in play, paper presented during the Digital Games Research Conference, Changing Views: Worlds in Play, 16–20 June, Vancouver, British Columbia, Canada). See also Grant Burningham and Zubin Jelveh (2005) Virtual stars compete for real money, *New York Times*, 6 December.

[50] Karen J Bannan (2005) Companies try a new approach and a smaller screen for product placements: videogames, *New York Times*, 5 March. Paradoxically, the very first placement in a videogame might have been an unwanted one. On 20 November 1989, Philip Morris addressed an official protest to Sega asking it to withdraw the Marlboro signs from *Super Monaco GP* videogames, in which the brand appeared without Philip Morris's consent. In 1990, there were similar protests to Namco and Atari about the *Final Lap* videogame. See in particular Les Zuke and Sheila Banks (1991) Chronology of actions, official press release from Philip Morris USA, Corporate Affairs, New York, NY, Thursday 21 February.

[51] The value of the world videogame market exceeded US$24 billion in 2005. Estimates for 2008 place it around US$40 billion, without talking about the online videogame market, for which the growth is even more important. See in particular Gaëlle Macke and Claudine Mulard (2005) Microsoft, Sony et Nintendo relancent la guerre des consoles, *Le Monde*, 20 May. See also T L Stanley (2006) Advergames, content role juice up marketer's game, *Advertising Age*, 6 February; and Erika Brown (2006) In-game advertising: game on! *Forbes*, marketing section, 24 July, pp 84–86.

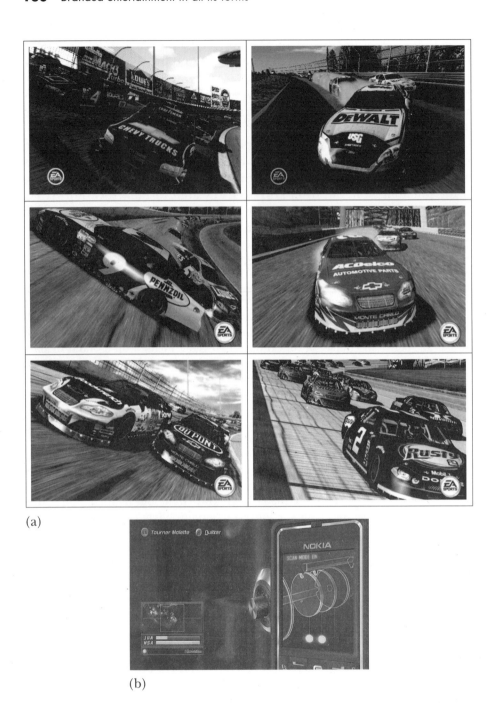

(a)

(b)

Figure 8.1 (a) Screen shots from *Nascar Chase for the Cup 2005* and from *Nascar 06: Total team control*, 2006. Reproduced by kind permission of Electronic Arts. (b) Screen shot from *Splinter Cell: Double agent*, 2006, where a Nokia telephone is used. Reproduced by kind permission of Ubisoft.

videogames are increasingly sophisticated, and the production costs are rising sharply – even if production is outsourced, partially or totally, to the Asian corner of the globe – so the cost of producing a single game can today exceed US$20 million.[52] On the other hand, successful titles that exceed the profitability threshold are rare. On the advertisers' side, the market for accessible platforms is highly concentrated, since to date only three console manufacturers (Sony, Microsoft and Nintendo) control almost the entire market. As for games publishers, the market comprises countless small actors and some major names such as Electronic Arts, Infogames-Atari, Ubisoft, Activision, Eidos, Konami and VU Games.

A placement in a videogame offers additional advantages over the same placement in a film. The player generally pays much closer attention than the viewer. The possibility of control and the concomitant feeling of mastering the environment are greater for players.[53] They must construct a mental map of the game space, as if it were a real space in three dimensions, each constitutive element of which is important.[54] Unlike film, the unfolding of events within the same world may be very different from one 'round' of a game to the next, thereby modifying the player's interactions with the environment.[55] Finally,

---

[52] Schelley Olhava (2003) *Marketing Through Games*, White Paper 3850B, August, IDC, Framingham, MA. See also Jean-Marc Lehu (2006) Il faut renouer le contact avec le consommateur, in the inquiry by Ava Eschwège (2006) Jeux vidéo, le nouveau terrain de jeu des marques, *Marketing*, Enquête, pp 32–6; and Matt Richtel (2005) A new reality in video games: advertisements, *New York Times*, 11 April.

[53] Torben Grodal (2000) Video games and the pleasure of control, in Dolf Zillmann and Peter Vorderer (eds) *Media Entertainment: The psychology and its appeal*, Lawrence Erlbaum Associates, Mahwah, NJ, pp 197–213. See also Dan M Grigorovici and Corina D Constantin (2004) Experiencing interactive advertising beyond rich media: impacts of ad type and presence on brand effectiveness in 3D gaming immersive virtual environments, *Journal of Interactive Advertising*, 5(1), September, pp 30–53, published at http://jiad.org/vo5/no1/grigorovici/ (accessed October 2006).

[54] Patricia M Greenfield, Craig Brannon and David Lohr (1994) Two-dimensional representation of movement through three-dimensional space: the role of video game expertise, *Journal of Applied Developmental Psychology*, 15, pp 87–103.

[55] William F Brewer (1996) The nature of narrative suspense and the problem of rereading, in Peter Vorderer, Hans J Wulff et Mike Friedrichsen (eds), *Suspense: Conceptualizations, theoretical analyses, and empirical explorations*, Lawrence Erlbaum Associates, Mahwah, NJ, pp 107–27. See also Dan M Grigorovici (2003) Persuasive effects of presence, in G Riva, F Davide and W A I Jsselsteijn (eds), *Immersive Virtual Environments, Being There: Concepts, effects and measurement of user presence in synthetic environments*, Ios Press, Amsterdam, ch 13, pp 191–207. About the mediating role of presence and the fact that the player's involvement affects his/her judgement of advertisements, and that the degree of experienced presence within the environment mediates this relationship, see Stefan G Nicovich (2005) The effect of involvement on

the duration of exposure is much longer. Admittedly, a film's life may be long and may give rise to repeat showings. A videogame, however, also allows this repetition to be concentrated in time. As with cinema, the cost of a placement falls within an extremely broad range, from a few thousand to several million dollars in the case of specific partnerships. Compared with the cinema, the flexibility of insertion methods in a wholly created graphic universe, and the possibilities for verification before the game is mass-produced, are also factors likely to seduce still-hesitant advertisers.

It would be difficult to miss the advertising signs for SoBe and Maxell in *Project Gotham Racing* (Microsoft), or those of MTV, among others, in *L.A. Rush* (Midway). As this car driving game comprises 337 miles of roads, Midway was able to sign contracts with 40 different brands. According to the PQ Media firm, the videogame sector is the one that will see the most rapid growth in the next few years. In 2005, for the United States, the firm estimated that investments in product placement in videogames totalled US$40.4 million (which was in the lower range of the different evaluations).

With each new generation of consoles, the graphics become closer to reality. The characters in games inspired by television series such as *CSI* or *24* resemble the actors of the series in every feature. The same is true for games inspired by films, such as *The Godfather* (Electronic Arts), *The Matrix* (Atari) and *007: From Russia with Love* (Electronic Arts), for example.

Sports games, for their part, no longer show players with anonymous features, but avatars, 'alter egos' of the real professionals, pixel for pixel, which enables them to benefit additionally from an indirect prescriptive effect from the famous sportsperson.[56] *Top Spin 2* (Power & Magic, 2K Sport) allows you to take up the racket of Amélie Mauresmo or Maria Sharapova, of Lleyton Hewitt or Andy Roddick, among others. It is possible to make the floor squeak and to score baskets in the skin of Tony Parker or Shaquille O'Neal in *NBA Live 06* (Electronic Arts). You are allowed to replace Richard Burns for a drive in *Richard Burns Rally* (Warthog/Eidos). Stepping on to Tony Hawk's skateboard in *Pro Skater* (Activision) is child's play, as is taking the wheel of a kart from Michael Schumacher in *World Tour Kart 2004* (10tacle Studios). You can take up the golf clubs of Tiger Woods or other famous golfers in *PGA Tour* (Electronic Arts), or choose from the 10,000 footballer avatars, from

---

ad judgment in a video game environment: the mediating role of presence, *Journal of Interactive Advertising*, 6(1), Fall, pp 38–51, published at http://jiad.org/vol6/no1/nicovich (accessed October 2006).

[56] Scott Jones, Colleen Bee, Rick Burton and Lynn R Kale (2004) Marketing through sports entertainment: a functional approach, in L J Schum (ed), *The Psychology of Entertainment Media: Blurring the lines between entertainment and persuasion*, Lawrence Erlbaum Associates, Mahwah, NJ, pp 309–22. See also David Kelley (2006) Rated M for Mad Ave, *Business Week*, 27 February.

Figure 8.2   Screen shots from *FIFA 06* and *PGA Tour 06* (2006).

Source: Electronic Arts.

Adu to Zidane via Rooney, Henry, Kaka, Beckham and so on, to dribble the ball in *FIFA 06* (Electronic Arts). (See Figure 8.2.)

From all these examples it is clear that the virtual universe of the game is becoming increasingly realistic. Consequently, if a game supposedly set in the real world and in our era shunned brands or inserted fictional logos, this could actually damage it; ultimately, it would distance it from the reality of the universe it attempts to reproduce. When a football player appears on the field, he wears a shirt with his sponsor's name on it. A sporting tournament of any kind always has one or more sponsors. Even the International Olympic Committee signs contracts for brands logos to appear up to the doors to the stadium. It is therefore no longer a question of wondering about the presence of brands in games, but rather one of deciding how to place them in a relevant manner, from both the advertiser's and the game's point of view.

For *London Taxi* (2005), Data Design Interactive (www.datadesign.uk. com) was innovative by showing the brands and products placed in three dimensions. Flash detergent (Procter & Gamble), in particular, was used to clean the taxi at the centre of the game (see Figure 8.3). The product therefore became a completely interactive icon for the player, and the game naturally turned into a medium for the demonstration of the product's advantages. A study carried out by AC Nielsen demonstrated the placement's effectiveness on the basis of an increased product awareness among players.

As with a placement in a film or television series, there are various different placement methods according to the advertiser's and the developer's object-ives. The most common consists of placing a banner or an advertising poster in the brand's colours. The positive role of the prominence of advertising banners on consumer memorization, particularly in expert players, has been

Figure 8.3 Screen shots from the videogame *London Taxi* (2005). Reproduced by kind permission of Data Design Interactive.

Figure 8.4 Screen shot from the videogame *London Taxi* (2005). Reproduced by kind permission of Data Design Interactive.

confirmed by academic research.[57] For example, in *Gran Turismo 4* (Sony-Polyphony Digital) there is a screen showing the Mercedes logo, a JVC advertising balloon, luminous signs for the brands Esprit, LG, Virgin and TGI Friday's, a UGC cinema in town, and banners for Michelin, Lexus, Bosch, Shell, Bridgestone, Chevrolet, Castrol, Peugeot, Magneti Marelli, Elf, Toyota, Dunlop and Motul.

The brand can also form an integral part of the scenery, such as a Starbucks café appearing on the corner of a street in *London Taxi* (Data Design Interactive), see Figure 8.4. The impact can be greater, however, if the player must interact with the brand or one of its products, such as choosing a Suzuki motorcycle in the racing game *Moto GP 2* (Climax), drinking Bawls in *Run Like Hell* (Virgin Interactive) and using a Nokia mobile telephone in *Kelly Slater Pro Surfer* (Treyarch). In *Test Drive Unlimited* (Atari), players can configure their car from an existing brand: a Dodge Viper, a McLaren Mercedes, a Pagani, a Lotus 240R and so on, all of which helps to anchor the game in reality (see Figure 8.5).

In extreme cases, the brand is placed at the centre of the game, as in the case of the Cheetos biscuits used to save Chester (the brand mascot) in *Chester Cheetah Too Cool to Fool* (Kaneko); likewise for M&M's confectionery in the Pearson educational game *The Lost Formulas*, for the motor racing game *Mercedes Benz World Racing* (Synetic), giving the German car maker exclusivity, or for the action game *Humvee Assault* (Atari), where the Hummer is indispensable to beating back the many enemies of the United States.

From the marketing point of view, placement may also allow the brand's positioning to be strengthened and its image nurtured. Thus, the Under

---

[57] See in particular Shlomo Ron and Michael F Weigold (1997) ADgames: integrating active brand messages into video games as a new medium for marketing, *Proceedings of the American Academy of Advertising Conference*, ed M Carole Macklin, American Academy of Advertising, Cincinnati, Ohio, pp 244–53. Lars-Peter Schneider and T. Bettina Cornwell (2005) Cashing in on crashes via brand placement in computer games, *International Journal of Advertising*, 24(3), pp 321–43; Michelle R Nelson (2001) Advertisers got game: examining effectiveness of product placements in new media, paper presented during the Association for Education in Journalism and Mass Communication Conference, 4–8 August, Washington, DC; David Deal (2005) The ability of branded online games to build brand equity: an exploratory study, paper presented during the Digital Games Research Conference, Changing Views: Worlds in Play, Vancouver, British Columbia, Canada, 16–20 June. And for an interesting and very relevant research about the role of the implicit memory on brand placement, see Federico De Gregorio (2006) Implicit memory as a complementary measure of brand placement effectiveness in video games, paper presented during the Association for Education in Journalism and Mass Communication Conference, Ad Division research, 2–5 August, San Francisco, CA.

Figure 8.5 Screen shot from Atari's *Test Drive Unlimited* (2006). Reproduced by kind permission of Daimler Chrysler.

Armour clothing brand arrived in the gaming world by choosing the games where the characters were placed in extreme physical conditions, corresponding perfectly to the brand's commercial promise.

> The virtual characters in these games truly represent men and women that require high-performance equipment. And this is a great opportunity to equip them with the same gear that their real-life counterparts demand, giving them a competitive performance advantage.
>
> (Steve Batista, marketing vice-president of Under Armour)[58]

Sport, action and shooting are the biggest segments of the market, with 30.1 per cent, 17.8 per cent and 9.6 per cent of sales in 2004 respectively.[59] As with placements in films, tie-in or promotional accompanying operations can be put in place. In parallel to the release of *Nascar 06: Total team control* (Electronic Arts), competitions were organized by Dodge, Fan Gear, Levi Strauss Signature and Old Spice (Procter & Gamble, see Figure 8.6), among others.

---

[58] Rebecca Logan (2005) Under Armour ventures into video game product placement, *Baltimore Business Journal*, 22 August.

[59] Source: ESA (Entertainment Software Association), quoted by Marion Rojinsky (2005) L'industrie des jeux vidéo veut conquérir les non-joueurs, *La Tribune*, 23 May. For a complete report about advergaming and the influence it can produce especially on a young target audience, see in particular Elizabeth S Moore (2006) *It's Child's Play: Advergaming and the online marketing of food to children*, Henry J Kaiser Family Foundation Report, Menlo Park, CA, July.

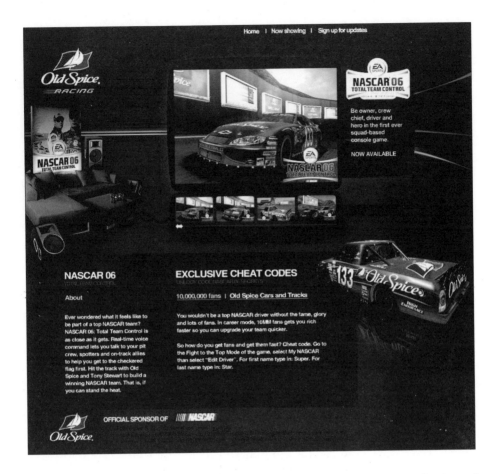

Figure 8.6 An example of a promotional association, between the brand Old Spice and the game *Nascar 06* (Electronic Arts). Reproduced by kind permission of Procter & Gamble France (2006).

The academic research carried out on this subject shows that placements in videogames can be effective,[60] particularly when they target adolescents

[60] Ashley Swartz (2004) *The Value of the Game*, Eiko Media, Detroit, MI. A study conducted by Activision and Nielsen in 2005 about the video game *Need for Speed Underground 2* (Electronic Arts), in which appeared a sign for Cingular, showed that 34 per cent of the respondents had a good opinion of the placement, 61 per cent were neutral and only 4 per cent had a bad opinion. Concerning the brand image, 51 per cent of all players answered positively, against 26 per cent of a control group (using a version of the videogame without the placement). See in particular Kenneth Hein (2005) Research: gaming product placement gets good scores in study, *Brandweek*,

and young men,[61] that they allow a relatively good memorization of brands placed,[62] and that they can contribute to improving preference for the brand.[63] This is particularly the case when the brand enjoys an intelligent integration, as in the case of the partnership between Activision and Puma,

---

5 December. See also the detailed and revealing 2006 report about advergaming by the Kaiser Family Foundation: Elizabeth S Moore (2006) *It's Child's Play: Advergaming and the online marketing of food to children*, Henry J. Kaiser Family Foundation Report, Menlo Park, CA, July.

[61] Michelle R Nelson (2002) Recall of brand placements in computer/video games, *Journal of Advertising Research*, 42(2), March–April, pp 80–92. For a specific study focusing on Hispanic players, see Monica Hernandez, Sindy Chapa, Michael S Minor, Cecilia Maldonado and Fernando Barranzuela (2004) Hispanic attitudes toward advergames: a proposed model of their antecedents, *Journal of Interactive Advertising*, 5(1), pp 116–31, September, published at http://jiad.org/vol5/no1/hernandez/ (accessed October 2006). Today the videogame target population remains mainly masculine, as boys and men represent the main part of the player population. See Justine Cassel and Henry Jenkins (1998) Chess for girls? Feminism and computer games, in J Cassel and H Jenkins (eds), *From Barbie to Mortal Kombat: Gender and computer games*, MIT Press, Cambridge, MA, ch 1, pp 1–45. But girls and women shouldn't be ignored, especially online: one never knows who is hiding behind an avatar. Stereotyped segmentation might be dangerous in the virtual worlds. See also James D Ivory and Hillary Wilkerson (2002) Video games are from Mars, not Venus: gender, electronic game play and attitudes toward the medium, paper presented during the Association for Education in Journalism and Mass Communication Conference, 7–10 August, Miami Beach, FL.

[62] Ashley J Swartz (2004), *The Value of the Game*, White Paper, Eiko Media, Detroit, MI. If advertisers have to be careful and respectful to the same integration principles as are valid for placements in movies, videogame publishers, for their part, should also manage their games the same way. Players are paying for the game, not for the ads. And as sequels can be a bonanza, those publishers have to choose the placed brands wisely, and integrate them carefully, or in other words, show proper respect to their players. If this is not the case, sequels might be rejected because of numerous prominent placements in the previous episodes. See Eric A Taub (2004) In video games, sequels are winners, *New York Times*, 20 September; and also Jean-Marc Lehu (2006) Le petit jeu vidéo des grandes marques, *La Revue des Marques*, April, pp 46–49.

[63] Susan Auty (2005) Toying with the mind: product placement in video games, paper for 34th conference of the European Marketing Academy (EMAC), Milan, Italy, 24–27 May. See also David Nichols, Tom Farrand, Tom Rowley and Matt Avery (2006) *Brands and Gaming: The computer gaming phenomenon and its impact on brands and business*, Palgrave Macmillan, Basingstoke; Seounmi Youn and Mira Lee (2004) Advergame playing motivations and effectiveness, in M R Stafford and R J Faber (eds), *Advertising, Promotion and New Media*, ME Sharpe, Armonk, NY, pp 320–47; and Isabella M Chaney, Ku-Ho Lin and James Chaney (2004) The effect of billboards within in the gaming environment, *Journal of Interactive Advertising*, 5(1), September, pp 54–69, published at http://jiad.org/vol5/no1/chaney/ (accessed October 2006).

Figure 8.7   Screen shot from *True Crime: New York City*. Reproduced by kind permission of Activision (2005).

which saw the perfect integration of the brand's products into the plot of the *True Crime* series of games (see Figure 8.7). In the same way as for the cinema, considering the attention that the player gives to the action, it is recommended that the placement be prominent.[64] The range of games is now very broad: from educational games for children to war games for adults, via sport, adventure, science fiction, role playing, simulation games, platform games and police thrillers. It has reached the point where the audience constitutes a mass market: on the one hand, because of its volume (hundreds of millions of players worldwide), and on the other, because the global turnover that it represents is now larger than that of the cinema.[65] In addition, it is also possible to segment the market and to target a particular, very precise player profile, according to the game in which the product is placed.[66]

Admittedly, as with placements in the cinema, criticism is heard from time to time regarding the possible commercial invasion of games. Too-obvious,

---

[64] Lars-Peter Schneider and T Bettina Cornwell (2005) Cashing in on crashes via brand placement in computer games, *International Journal of Advertising*, 24(3), pp 321–43. See also Peter Vorderer (2000) Interactive entertainment and beyond, in Dolf Zillmann and Peter Vorderer (eds), *Media Entertainment: The psychology of its appeal*, Lawrence Erlbaum Associates, Mahwah, NJ, pp 21–36.

[65] Martin Grove (2005) Video games could be new frontier for movie marketers, *Hollywood Reporter*, 15 April.

[66] Beth Snyder Bulik (2004) Interactive: games hot shot marketing, *Advertising Age*, 24 May. Johannes Schaaper (1999) Segmentation des produits enfants: le cas des jeux vidéo, *Décisions Marketing*, 18, September–December, pp 25–35.

and above all badly integrated, placements will quickly damage a game's chances of success. In contrast, those games that set their story in 'real' life would quickly lose their realism if they were free from brands. Nowadays, in an adventure game set in an urban environment in which the streets walked by the hero were innocent of all advertising, we would wonder exactly when and where the action was set. On what planet? A motor race where you could choose neither the exact brand nor the model would lose its charm and authenticity. A sporting encounter without advertising hoardings around the edges of the pitch would be unrealistic. Accessories of everyday life that did not show any brand logo, or only brands that it was impossible to identify, would appear almost bizarre. The characters are increasingly borrowing the appearance and voice of the actors from the feature films on which the games are based, as are the champions for games based on sports. Such realism should be rounded off, like it or not, by the commercial realism that the modern consumer society is acquainted with.

Marketing can benefit from a reasonably precise geographic targeting in the case of online videogames. In 2006, when placing their logo in the game *Counter-Strike*, Subway restaurants specified that only players logging on from the towns of San Francisco, Sacramento and Las Vegas should be exposed to the placement, since they only wished to promote their Subway Daily Special in this specific zone.[67]

The only two genuine limits relate to the nature of the game, on the one hand, and the tolerance of the players, on the other. Many games are set in imaginary or historical worlds where brands would never be found, except at the cost of a damaging incoherence.[68] In the same way, games 'for adults' are not particularly sought-after by advertisers, or at any rate by advertisers able to invest large sums, since they fear that their brand image will be altered.

When players pay for a videogame, they can be highly critical if the presence of advertising is too great. Massive Inc therefore allowed free access to MMO[69] *Anarchy Online* if the player accepted the advertisements. The market

---

[67] The project was abundantly discussed on specialized internet forums and the Valve company – which created the video game – legally contested it: the placement had to be withdrawn. See Kris Oser (2006) A subway in-game brand campaign goes awry, *Madison+Vine*, 8 February. See also Jason Chambers (2005) The sponsored avatar: examining the present reality and future possibilities of advertising in digital games, paper presented during the Digital Games Research Conference, Changing Views: Worlds in Play, Vancouver, British Columbia, Canada, 16–20 June.

[68] About this topic, see in particular the satirical essay by Michael Kinsley (1990) These foolish things remind me of Diet Coke, *Time Magazine*, 11 June.

[69] MMO is the acronym for massive (or massively) multiplayer online: that is, an online videogame allowing access to many players who can play simultaneously. MMORPG (massively multiplayer online role playing game) is the equivalent for an online role-playing game. For an interesting social analysis of the MMORPG see

for online multiplayer games is certainly the one with the greatest potential. Many of them, such as *EverQuest, Ultima Online* or the very famous *World of Warcraft* (WoW) already have several million players enrolled, particularly in Asia (more specifically Korea, China and Taiwan).[70] This context offers further advantages to the operator: on the one hand, a source of regular income (player subscriptions and advergaming); on the other, the possibility of a total or partial identification of the players with the brand interested in a placement, and therefore the possibility of a more targeted strategy of brand integration.

An academic study published in 2004 demonstrated that players remained fairly positive towards placements, if they added to the game's realism.[71] Thanks to the ever-increasing memory capacity of consoles and games, however, it is possible to avoid in part the potential annoyance of an advertising intrusion. In order to diminish the intrusion effect perceived in the game, placements may be associated with an interactivity algorithm that modifies their appearance, and even the shape of some of them, from one round to the next. This dynamic appearance (fleeting or not) contributes to renewing the game's environment. The developers of online games such as Massive Inc have also understood the profit that can be made from placement; in addition, they can afford the luxury of selling advertising spaces for limited periods. For the advertiser, the advantage is in seeing the return on investment (ROI) indicators as well as the CPM (cost per thousand) in order to evaluate the attractiveness of a placement. Certain advertisers such as GlaxoSmithKline, Volvo, PepsiCo, Siemens, Jeep®, Coast, Mitsubishi, Starbucks and Toyota are now prepared

Nicolas Ducheneaut and Robert J Moore (2004) The social side of gaming: a study of interaction patterns in a massively multiplayer online game, *Proceedings of the 2004 ACM Conference on Computer Supported Cooperative Work*, Chicago, IL, 6–10 November, pp 360–69.

[70] Roger Parloff (2005) From megs to riches, *Fortune*, 28 November. About the increasing role of communities in building a brand strategy, see Tomi Ahonen and Alan Moore's book (2005) *Communities Dominate Brands: Business and marketing challenges for the 21st century*, Futuretext, London.

[71] Michelle R Nelson, Heejo Keum and Ronald A Yaros (2004) Advertainment or adcreep: game players' attitudes toward advertising and product placements in computer games, *Journal of Interactive Advertising*, 5(1), Fall, published at www.jiad.org/vol5/no1/nelson (accessed October 2006). See also the very interesting research from Wonsun Shin, Yejin Hong and Yuening Jiang (2006) Effectiveness of product placements in video games: game players' perception and virtual reality experience, paper presented during the Association for Education in Journalism and Mass Communication Conference, 2–5 August, San Francisco, CA; and Michelle R Nelson, Ronald A Yaros and Heejo Keum (2006) Examining the influence of telepresence on spectator and player processing of real and fictious brands in a computer game, *Journal of Advertising*, 35(4), Winter, pp 87–99.

to develop their own videogames,[72] which are offered to their clients during promotional operations, downloaded to mobile phones or used to generate traffic on their internet site. Another solution proposed by WildTangent (www.wildgames.com) consists in linking the dynamic advertising insertions to free access to the game. With an *ad hoc* demographic segmentation of its many games, WildTangent also allows advertisers to distribute 'gaming chips' in the context of promotional operations. These chips can be used to play online. In contrast, if the game is purchased, the advertising broadcasting is stopped.[73] Game not over.

---

[72] Susan B Kretchmer (2004) Advertainment: the evolution of product placement as a mass media marketing strategy, *Journal of Promotion Management*, 10(1/2), pp 37–54. See also Beth Snyder Bulik (2006) EA places dynamic ads in video games, *Advertising Age*, 31 August; Erika Brown (2006) Game on!, *Forbes*, Marketing section, 24 July. In 2006, Toyota signed with Massive Inc (then part of the Microsoft group) to include real-time adapted ads for its Yaris 2007 in *Anarchy Online*. See Mike Shields (2006) Massive unveils Toyota ad units with *Anarchy*, *MediaWeek*, 19 July; and Jean-Marc Lehu (2007) Advergaming: Analyse comparative exploratoire de l'attitude des joueurs occasionnels et des hardcore gamers à l'égard du placement de marques dans le jeu vidéo, 6th Congress of Marketing Tendencies, Paris, 26–27 January.

[73] Oser Kris (2006) WildTangent introduces digital game ad currency, *Advertising Age*, 22 March. See also Paul Hyman (2006) Advertisers await game measurement, *Hollywood Reporter*, 25 January.

9 Controlling further opportunities

Product and brand placements are constantly diversifying and taking an interest in new vectors. The professional site LA Office (www.laoffice.com) regularly offers Virtual Sell Sheets, which inform potential advertisers about placement opportunities in cinema, television, musical, video and other projects. At the beginning of the year 2005, the journalist Adam Sauer found 497,000 occurrences of the phrase 'product placement' on the internet, using the Google search engine.[1] One year later, the same search returned more than 6,000,000 hits.

From credits to trailer

The film's (or the series') credits can also be subject to placement. Over 261 episodes, from 1993 to 2005, the successful series *NYPD Blue*, by Steven Bochco and David Milch, retained in its credits the placement of an advertising board for Coca-Cola, filmed in the streets of Manhattan. Although the appearance is brief, the brand's colour codes are sufficiently powerful to enable identification. In the cinema, two examples clearly illustrate the diversity of the modes of use. In 1994, in the David Carson film *Star Trek Generations*, the opening credits rolled while a bottle floating in space crossed the screen several

---

[1] Adam Sauer (2004) Brandchannel's 2004 product placement awards, *Brandchannel Newsletter*, 21 February.

times. The camera gradually closed in on the bottle, until the label revealed the identity of the beverage inside: 'Moët et Chandon, Cuvée Dom Perignon, Vintage 2265'. The credits ended on the image of the bottle of champagne smashing against the hull of a spaceship to christen it. In 2004, the plot of the David Ellis film *Cellular* centred on telephone communications between the two main actors. This time it was the end credits that were used to advantage: they rolled within the screen of a Nokia mobile phone, itself placed in the film.

The main motivation for an appearance in the opening credits of a film – such as the appearance of the face of an Audemars Piguet watch, Royal Oak model, in *Terminator 3* (Jonathan Mostow, 2003) – is to address an audience that is already captive, since they are within the cinema auditorium, before they are absorbed by the story or the action of the film. Moreover, some members of the audience watch the credits intently, in order to find the name of an actor or a member of the technical crew. Such a placement is therefore propitious for a good identification. Appearing in the end credits, in contrast, is much more risky. Few viewers wait for the end of the credits before leaving the cinema, or before switching off the film if they are watching at home or on a mobile terminal, and the end credits are often speeded up, shortened or eliminated altogether in a television showing. The credits are therefore an original medium, but cases of relevant placements are still somewhat rare. To make the placement stand out from the film itself, the poster, or better still the trailer, is a more adequate complementary medium.

In 2005, the best-selling novel by Ann Brashares, *The Sisterhood of the Traveling Pants* (2001), was adapted for the screen by Ken Kwapis. Central to both the book and the film are a pair of 'magical' jeans, which unite four adolescents. This case is a nice example of an opportunity skilfully exploited by the studios Warner Bros and Alcon Entertainment, for a brand and product placement, in this case Levi's. In return, the jeans brand mobilized its distributing partner Sears to promote the film. For a brand such as Levi's, not only was the placement – organized by Ketchum Entertainment Marketing – ideal in terms of the product, but the film's adolescent target audience made it a near-perfect medium.[2] The Levi's brand is not mentioned in the original book. In an interview given to the *Chicago Sun-Times*, however, Ann Brashares said of the film: 'There is a deal in place with Levi's. Which is good – I love Levi's, and I had always pictured these pants being Levi's. But in the book, the pants don't have a brand.'[3] The embodiment of an advertiser's dream! Not to mention the numerous press articles that mentioned the film, and the

---

[2] Matthew Creamer (2005) '*Sisterhood of the Traveling Pants*': a good fit for Levi's, *Madison+Vine*, 15 June.

[3] Paige Wiser (2005) Together in blue jeans, *Chicago Sun-Times*, 18 May. The movie was released in France under the title *4 Filles et un jean* (Four girls and a pair of jeans).

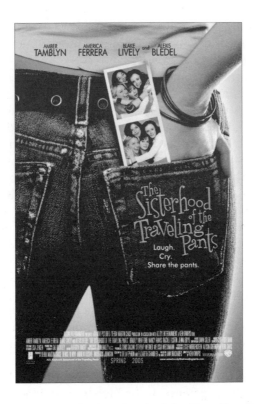

Figure 9.1 US poster for *The Sisterhood of the Traveling Pants* (Ken Kwapis, 2005). By kind permission of Alcon Entertainment.

brand. In addition, the placement was ideally amplified by the film's poster, on which it was impossible not to identify the brand, if only through the characteristic, small red Levi's label.

The poster is an interesting medium because it emerges from the purely cinematic universe. *Goal!* (Danny Cannon, 2005), is set in the world of football, and Adidas is unquestionably the most visible brand throughout the film. It is also present, however, by means of its characteristic three stripes, on the tracksuit worn by the actor Kuno Becker, photographed on the original film poster. During a film's promotional period, its poster may dovetail with the traditional networks of commercial displays and become an important communications medium for the inserted brand or product. The poster for the film *The Transporter* (Louis Leterrier, 2001) showed the BMW 735i car driven by the character played by Jason Statham. This integration was repeated in the poster for the second film, *Transporter 2*, released in 2005. The partnership had changed, however, and this time it was the Audi A8 used in the film that was inserted. In the latter two cases, the car had also been placed on the CDs of the film's soundtrack. Cars lend themselves relatively well to this type of insertion. Thus, various posters promoting *The Italian Job* (F Gary Gray, 2003) worldwide showed one or more of the Minis used in the film.[4] These cases remain rare, however.

The trailer, by contrast, is a medium that is not only more flexible, but also likely to have a greater impact. In the film *Hitch* (Andy Tennant, 2005) the viewer can easily spy the placement of the brands New York Knicks, Coca-Cola, San Pellegrino, Ford, Lacoste, Sony Connect and Polaris; and this trailer only lasted 2.20 minutes. In the trailer for the film *The Man* (Les Mayfield, 2005), the newspaper *USA Today* was afforded an unmissable placement. In the same way, the brands Planter's, Nike, Baskin-Robbins, Dean & Deluca, United Airlines, Baja Fresh, Star Alliance and La Perla all appeared in the trailer for *The Terminal* (Steven Spielberg, 2004).

The first trailer dates back to 1912, and the film being promoted was the first episode in a 13-part saga entitled *The Adventures of Kathlyn* (shown in 1913 and 1914), produced by Selig Polyscope Co. This shows that producers grasped the power of attraction of the trailer, and its capacity to develop audience loyalty, very early. It is at once an information medium and a promotional medium,[5] and it is crucial nowadays to introduce the film as early as possible. The viewers use it to guide their choice.[6] The number of cinemas is decreasing year on year, and more importantly, the biggest productions monopolize a large number of screens, so they sometimes stifle any chance of visibility, or even existence, for more modest films. The competition is therefore fierce, including between the bigger productions themselves.

The studios have almost all grasped – more or less quickly – the opportunities that the internet represents. Essentially since the boom in high-speed connection, film trailers are now accessible on different websites, with the aim of enlarging their communications spectrum. Cinema information sites

---

[4] Depending on the country where the film is released, the poster may differ tremendously and not contain all the original elements. Those modifications happen not only for marketing reasons linked to the positioning of the movie or to the perceived adequacy of the target audience, but also sometimes for legal reasons.

[5] See interesting research by Florence Euzéby and Carole Martinez (2004) La bande-annonce cinématographique: quel impact sur la décision d'aller voir le film? Une étude exploratoire, *Décisions Marketing*, 33, January–February, pp 39–50. In 2007, in the trailer announcing Les Mayfield's *Code Name: The cleaner* (2007), actor Cedric Kyles (*The Entertainer*) wore a black Lacoste polo. The famous green smiling crocodile on his chest is quickly identifiable and its communication easily helped by well-framed close-ups.

[6] Alain Kruger (1997) Les spectateurs et les films: les sources d'information utilisées lors du processus de choix d'un film, proceedings of the first research day of Marc Filser and Dominique Bourgeon-Renault (eds) *Recherche en Marketing de Bourgogne: Marketing des activités culturelles, touristiques et de loisirs*, Dijon, 27 November, pp 106–16.

(such as the indispensable www.allocine.fr in France and www.movies.com in the United States, for instance), specialized trailer sites and the production studio sites themselves, and those created specially for film promotion, are now the favoured places for the showing and downloading of trailers. This is not only because they are now accessible to the entire planet, 24 hours a day throughout the chosen promotion period, but also because they can be opened long in advance and can thus strategically orchestrate the teasing phase. In addition, they can also bring the film to life even before its cinema release. It is no longer uncommon to see a studio produce one or more teasers (mini-trailers preceding the trailer) and even several trailers (different editing, different languages) for a single film. The goal is to hold potential viewers captive until they can go to see the film in the cinema.[7]

More cases appear every day. In 2006, the Mercedes logo appeared clearly in the trailer for *X-Men 3* (Brett Ratner); Scrabble and Kellogg's Special K cropped up in the trailer for *The Shaggy Dog* (Brian Robbins); the Microsoft Windows logo was seen in *RV* (Barry Sonnenfeld); Pliko (Peg Pérego) and Old Navy in *Friends with Money* (Nicole Holofcener); and FedEx, Peta, New York Lottery and Casio in *16 Blocks*, (Richard Donner). A single viewer will generally have the chance to see the same trailer (or variants of it) several times before going to see the film in question, and the majority of spectators exposed to this trailer will not perhaps even go to see the film. As a result, for a product or brand placement, the trailer represents a shop window in which it may be wise to appear.

Furthermore, several studies carried out on product placement have shown that perception of the brand is made easier when viewers see the same film a second time. When they have been exposed to the placement in the trailer, viewers therefore have a greater chance of identifying it if they see the film. Hence in 2005, Coca-Cola, Dasani and Powerade could be identified in the trailer for *The Ringer* (Barry W Blaustein), and Marlboro, Titleist, MGM, Mercedes and McDonald's in that for *Two for the Money* (D J Caruso).

Beyond the credits and the trailer, some brands are even afforded the luxury of appearing in the film's title. Except for a few rare cases of official partnerships such as *Harold & Kumar go to the White Castle* (Danny Leiner, 2004), with its explicit mention of a fast-food restaurant, the majority of mentions take place without the brand's intent. Admittedly, it is easy to see

---

[7] Because the circulation cost on the internet is marginal, some movie studios also produce featurettes on the movie itself, for example on a main character, focusing on a member of the technical team, and/or about the special effects. Regarding the persuasiveness of weak advertising signals, see also Didier Courbet, Julien Intartaglia, Amélie Borde and Sylvain Denis (2004) L'influence non consciente des publicités vues furtivement et aussitôt oubliées: une méthode d'étude sociocognitive appliquée à Internet, *Questions de communication*, 5, pp 83–102.

the boost to awareness that it can represent, since every time the film is mentioned, the brand is also mentioned. This approach also brings potential risk for the brand, however: of the quality of the storyline, the script, the direction and so on, since it is associated with these elements throughout the film itself and the film's lifespan.[8] The risk is amplified if, in addition, the film is unsuccessful. In the case of the Danny Leiner film, Box Office Mojo LLC estimates that the marketing cost was US$20 million, whereas the production budget was US$9 million. Although the total investment remained small, the film's total receipts were only US$23.706 million (US$18.250 in the United States and US$5.456 worldwide).

The mention of brand names in titles is not a new phenomenon. In 1935, William C McGann filmed *A Night at the Ritz*, echoed by Harold D Schuster in 1937 when he directed *Dinner at the Ritz*. One of the most famous examples is still the adaptation of Truman Capote's novel by Blake Edwards in 1961, which kept the book's original title, *Breakfast at Tiffany's*, giving the famous New York jeweller added publicity (as if it needed it). In 1985, Dusan Makavejev directed a comedy entitled *The Coca-Cola Kid*, and in 1991, Simon Wincer filmed *Harley Davidson and the Marlboro Man*. Titles are sometimes modified for release outside the domestic territory, for reasons of meaning or simply pronunciation. Falling foul of the *'loi Evin',*[9] the title of the Simon Wincer film was adapted for its French release: *Harley-Davidson et l'homme aux santiags* (Harley-Davidson and the man in cowboy boots). As for *Breakfast at Tiffany's*, it was promoted under the French title *Diamants sur canapé* (Diamonds on toast).

Press relations transformed into intelligent lobbying

There are many who still perceive lobbying as a semi-confidential activity on the fringes of legality, the goal of which is to force an individual, a company

---

[8] See also Merissa Marr and Suzanne Vranica (2004) Burgers get star billing, *Wall Street Journal*, 28 July. Because the characters in *Harold & Kumar go to the White Castle* were a little bit eccentric, and more importantly, marijuana smokers, the movie and its poster are today referenced on many drug websites. That was probably not previously considered and planned by the White Castle restaurants chain, which has a family positioning. This example reveals the importance for the partner advertiser of checking upstream all the possible details of the placement contract.

[9] Law #91-32 about the fight against smoking and alcoholism, 10 January 1991, usually known as the 'loi Evin' (Evin law), named after Minister Claude Evin, who was then in charge of Social Affairs and Solidarity in France.

or an administration to act according to the wishes of an individual or corporation. In fact, in its most original form, lobbying consists above all of informing decision makers, admittedly in the direction desired by a given lobby client. Initially, however, it is an information process with the aim of enabling an informed decision to be taken. In an information-saturated, and therefore badly informed, environment, product placements cannot escape this rule. It is therefore not uncommon for companies to commission specialist agents to organize operations combining press relations, lobbying and direct marketing. The goal is to inform the right people of the existence of certain products and certain brands, while clearly presenting the advantages of these and the benefits of a placement. The goal here is not to lead to a paid placement contract, but to naturally prompt a placement, enhancing the brand or the product, even supplying it to the production for free. It is also a matter of ensuring that the placement is seen as useful and relevant to the medium (such as a film, series or individual programme). In 2005, the US agency 1st Approach thus sent a model of the AutoTape, the latest automatic tape measure from Black & Decker, to 1,000 contacts such as Hollywood screenwriters. Several months and several free samples later, the Black & Decker AutoTape appeared in episodes of the series *Still Standing* and *The King of Queens*.[10]

Editorial advertising is an age-old technique. As a reminder, it consists, for a brand or its agents, in designing an 'advertising' article in association with a magazine or newspaper, giving it a form as close as possible to the medium's usual editorial style. It may be an informative report on the product's characteristics, or, more subtly, on a broader subject in which the brand or product ideally appears. The approach can even take a more original form, as with this personality test: 'You're Cosmo ... are you Modus?' designed by *Cosmopolitan* and Renault for the Modus model,[11] which was additionally associated with a limited series named after the magazine (see Figure 9.2).

Products and brands can also be placed through custom publishing, where the advertiser controls all or part of the article. In this context, the so-called 'watertight bulkhead' between advertising and editorial content appears increasingly porous. In the United States alone, PQ Media calculate that product and brand placements in magazines had a total value of US$160.9 million in 2005 (up 17.5 per cent on the previous year, although the greater part of these investments concerned consumer magazines). Admittedly, this represents only a tiny fraction of the total amount of advertising investment (around US$16 billion that same year), but it is growing rapidly.

---

[10] Robert P P Laurence (2005) Product placement: the plot sickens, *San Diego Union-Tribune*, 4 November. See also Gail Schiller (2006) Brands take buzz to bank through free integration, *Hollywood Reporter*, 13 April.

[11] Catherine Gaudenz (2005) À la conquête des media tactiques, *CB News*, 855, 14 November.

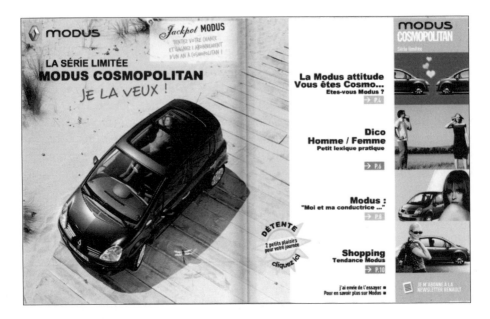

Figure 9.2 Screen capture of the Renault site for its promotion in association with *Cosmopolitan*. Reproduced by kind permission of Renault and Cosmopolitan (2006).

Brand placement in magazines can take two basic forms. The first is inspired by the editorial advertising technique: it consists of inserting the brand name into the text of an article, of using an example of the brand or a particular product by way of illustration, or, even more directly, of a case study dedicated to the brand or one of its products, when this or these have enjoyed an innovation, a new strategic orientation, a particular launch or a commercial success. Here, the line between editorial and flattering advertising language can be very fine. Naturally, not all the positive illustrations used by journalists are placements or even requested by an advertiser. Nevertheless, requests of this type are on the rise, and brands possess a weighty argument in the matter: the money of their advertising investments. In 2005, MediaPost revealed that Bayer Laboratories, wishing to promote the analgesic Aleve, had proposed this exchange (also called RFP, or 'request for proposal') to various magazines.[12] The majority of magazines are of course opposed to such

---

[12] Joe Mandese (2005) Good news is bad news for magazines, brand makes editorial demand, *MediaPost*, 10 October. See also Nat Ives and Jean Halliday (2005) Auto giants push harder for magazine product placement, *Advertising Age*, 16 August, and the report by Jon Fine (2004) Mags & Vine, *Advertising Age*, 12 April.

pressure, fearing that the mixture of advertising and editorial will ultimately harm them by driving their readers away.[13] Not all are resistant, however.

The second type of placement is subtler, and is aimed principally at mediums that favour pictures. Many magazines, particularly fashion magazines, use photographs set in a location or that use props. In this case, it is easy to imagine the integration of a brand or a product. The model will carry a bottle of soft drink, pose alongside a car, or adopt a pose allowing a close-up of the branded watch: all examples in which a brand is easily identifiable each time. Such practices are equally possible on television or radio, where, strangely enough, certain names can crop up on a regular basis.

Original advertising placements

In 2006, the French comic Jean-Marie Bigard excelled in his performance/adaptation of the *Bourgeois Gentilhomme*. The poster for this comedy showed the actor's legs dressed in period clothes, but he was wearing – a pair of red trainers with three highly recognizable stripes. Adidas could rest content. In 2005, the singer Michael Bublé launched his new album *It's Time*. He also appeared in an advertising spot promoting the brand-new Starbucks Frappucino, created by the Fallon agency, in which he sang *Come Fly with Me*. Moreover, his CD was on sale at Starbucks. Pure coincidence? No, an original tie-in placement operation: a boost to the singer's career and an original communication for Starbucks.[14]

The same year in France, in the new television advertising for tourism in the Dominican Republic, the camera passed over the names and logos of the Air France company. In a spot for the Pantene brand, the actress Christina Reali was leafing through the magazine *Biba*. In 2006, in the United States, it was a Motel6 sign (Accor group) that appeared in an advertisement for the soft drink Dr Pepper, whereas in France an advertising poster for Norauto vehicle centres featured a Sony CDXS11 car radio CD deck. In this latter case, there

---

[13] Jon Fine (2004) Marketers press for product placement in magazine text, *Advertising Age*, 12 April. Research conducted by WWP's research subsidiary Lightspeed Research in 2003 was already calling for carefulness. It confirmed that respondents had the feeling that the distinction between the editorial of programmes and advertising content was sometimes difficult to identify. Of the questioned sample, 72 per cent stated that branded entertainment could easily be pervasive. See in particular, Claire Atkinson (2003) Merger of advertising and content worries consumers, *Advertising Age*, 6 January.

[14] See also Melissa Allison (2006) Starbucks takes unique approach to marketing, *Seattle Times*, 12 October. The article explains the clever marketing communications move from Starbucks.

is nothing remarkable. When the close-up on the car radio clearly indicates the name of the radio station *Europe 2*, brand integration enters the scene. Confusion and genre mixing? No! Synergies born of effective partnerships.

Modern placements are innovators not only in their form, but also in the vectors they use. In 1991, Dennis Carter, in charge of marketing at Intel, launched the co-financed placement of the Intel brand. This was the beginning of the 'Intel Inside' campaign, which enabled it to appear in advertisements by computer makers and assemblers. Few end consumers then knew the name of the microprocessor manufacturer, although it had been the world leader for several years. This lag has been amply compensated for since: from a simple electronic component, the processor in question has become the indispensable heart of the computer.

In the cinema, it is not necessary for a placement to be ostentatious or for the camera to film it in close-up after close-up. In 2005, director Robert Schwentke made *Flightplan*, with Jodie Foster in the lead role. The plot is as follows: having dozed off in an aeroplane taking her to New York, Jodie Foster's character awakes to discover that her daughter has disappeared. Various classic or institutional placements are found in the film: Dodge, Palm Pilot, Canon, HP, Johnnie Walker, Mercedes, *Newsweek* and Hilton, for example. The airline is not emphasized; the placement could have been thought negative given the storyline. In contrast, the placement linked to the plane itself is exceptionally interesting. All the scenes shot inside it take place in a double-decker plane not yet available on the market at the time of the film's release. Officially, according to the production studio Buena Vista and Airbus Industries, there was no placement or cooperation agreement: the director simply needed the biggest plane possible, in order to make a person's disappearance in mid-flight credible.[15] For the new Airbus A380, however, due to begin its commercial career more than a year after the film's release, such a shop window constituted an original communication, and a global one at that. All the more so because, in the trailer, Jodie Foster's character explains that the plane is very new and that it is the biggest to date. In fact, the plane is by far the central character of the film.

Like other car brands, Cadillac has opened a merchandise website (www. cadillaccollection.com), enabling it to sell all kinds of accessories carrying the brand's logo. These are not car accessories but clothes, office equipment, watches, decorative objects, gift ideas, gadgets, golf accessories and so on. The boutique offers several dozen articles, of which some are part of seasonal collections. We are not on the threshold of human branding here, but by affixing its name and logo to quality products that consumers can use, wear or give as gifts, Cadillac has an exclusive placement that brings it closer to

---

[15] Marc Graser (2005) The non-product placement that boosts Airbus, *Advertising Age*, 4 May.

its clients and to consumers who, even if they do not drive Cadillacs, like to associate themselves with its quality connotations.

In the case of Mercedes, after studies showed that the car brand was not in contact with a younger clientele, it used the avenue of music from June 2004 to 'place' itself in the minds of young (potential future) clients. The Mixed Tape operation offered visitors to the brand's website the opportunity to download original songs and music for free.[16] If the traffic was initially from Germany, the United States, Great Britain, Japan and South Korea, the word-of-mouth effect allowed it to reach more distant countries, such as Yemen or the Faeroe Islands: in less than a year, over a million visitors from 88 countries had visited the Mercedes website and made over 10 million downloads. Some weeks after the idea was first raised, over 2,200 artists from 50 countries offered their works, allowing only the best to be selected, to the extent that the track 'Push it to the limit', offered by Urzula Amen (from Sweden) was used by Mercedes for the advertising film for its pan-European B-Class campaign in 2005.[17] For its part, in 2005, BMW supported the release of the film *Luther* (Eric Till, 2003), about the life of the monk Martin Luther. Given that he lived in the first half of the sixteenth century, opportunities for onscreen placement were limited: the car maker chose instead to supply an entire fleet of limousines for the film's premiere.

Placement after the event

The beer brand Stella Artois is linked to the world of cinema in particular by its position as official sponsor of the Sundance festival, but also by placements in films, as in *Diary of a Mad Black Woman*, (Darren Grant, 2005); not to mention the brand's advertising films, which often borrow from the seventh art. Even after films are released, Stella Artois continues to place its brand in the world of cinema, with the Stella Artois Screen Tour, which organizes the showing of films to the public at large, in particular and original places. It is even sometimes possible to turn back time, by placing the product or the brand in the film after it has been completed.

This is not a recent principle: several centuries ago, kings and nobles had paintings and sculptures altered to their advantage or to their design. When photography appeared, the specialists were not slow to manipulate the photographed elements, making them disappear or, on the contrary, inserting them after the fact. The archives of the USSR sometimes contain so many 'versions' of the same photograph that it is now impossible to tell who

---

[16] www.mercedes-benz.com/mixedtape/mixedtape.html
[17] Jean Halliday (2005) Mercedes-Benz reports millions of free songs downloads, *Madison+Vine*, 7 September

was actually there on the day that the photograph was taken! Since the advent of digital technology, the manipulation of images has become even easier, especially if the medium in question was also created digitally.[18]

Digital technology can easily change logos or packaging. In 2005, the CBS network digitally inserted the Chevrolet logo into five programmes of the season, among them the series *CSI*, of which it was the producer, since the placement contracts had been signed after these programmes had been filmed. A packet of Kellogg's Club Crackers was also digitally inserted into the series *Yes, Dear*. It is therefore possible to imagine product placements or brand integrations being modified between the moment when the film is shown in the cinema and the moment when it is sold on DVD or broadcast on television. This division of space is conducive to specialization and ensuring profitability.

Marathon Ventures is a company specializing in this practice of digital brand and product insertion in the United States. In 2005, CBS therefore requested it to insert a tin of Star-Kist Tuna, a NutriGrain bar and a packet of Club Crackers into the programme *Yes, Dear*.[19] This approach to product placements has several advantages. The technique is relatively flexible because the product or brand can be placed with perfect control of time and space. It can enable new placements to be inserted for a re-release of the film or for distribution on DVD, for example. In 1997, George Lucas invested US$10 million with Industrial Light and Magic (ILM) to restore and enhance *Star Wars* (1977). Various scenes were enhanced with digital insertions that had not been possible in 1976, when the film was shot. The same approach can be applied to brands and products. Digital placement also makes it easy to vary the placements according to different zones of distribution, so that they correspond as much as possible to the brands distributed in the film's zone of exploitation. Given that the lifespan of a film largely exceeds its showing in cinemas, digital placement will one day perhaps lead to the signature of placement contracts with a date limit.

---

[18] Rebecca J Brown (2003) Genetically enhanced arachnids and digitally altered advertisements: the making of *Spider-Man*, research paper, *Virginia Journal of Law and Technology*, 8(1), Spring. See in particular possibilities offered by Monet Systems, developed by British company Imagineer. www.imagineersystems.com. The very first digital ad inserts seem to be the ones for Coca-Cola and Blockbuster, in March, in an episode for UPN's *Seven Days* series. See also Kortney Stringer (2006) Pop-in products: images are inserted into popular television shows, *Detroit Free Press*, 16 February.

[19] Sam Lubell (2006) Advertising's *Twilight Zone*: that signpost up ahead may be virtual product, *New York Times*, 2 January. See also Terry Lefton (2001) Zapped out? Try virtual placement, *Newsweek*, 11 June and Lynn Smith (2006) Product placement drop names for profit, *Los Angeles Times*, 14 February.

Digital insertion after the fact nevertheless poses some problems. For films that were not shot in digital, the question of the higher cost of the necessary transfer still crops up. More and more directors, however, now shoot their films with digital cameras. Furthermore, digital placement offers fairly limited possibilities for integrating the product into the plot. In most cases, the placement is a passive one, in the background. Finally, digital insertion poses the problem of respect for the work and its author. Some may remember the clamour of indignation raised when, in 1970, the practice of industrially colouring black-and-white films began: those who opposed it argued that the results differed from the artist's original vision.

PART IV

Brand integration

10 Stage direction of brands in the twenty-first century

The essential thing is to move the public, and emotion comes from the way you tell the story, the way you juxtapose the sequences.

(Alfred Hitchcock, *Hitchcock, entretiens avec François Truffaut*, definitive edition, Ramsay, Paris, 1983)

It is to be hoped that the expression product or brand 'placement' survives in the language of the professional now only for historical and habitual reasons, and that, in reality, it does not represent the same approach that it did even a few years ago. The brand must be able to enjoy a genuine process of symbiotic integration: such a close relationship with the film's story, or more generally with the environment in which it is to appear, that its presence will seem natural. Branded entertainment should be, for the brand, an opportunity to write actual stories, integrating its identity and its personality, respecting its characteristics and promoting the stimulation of an emotional link between it and the individual. The strategic aspect of the process is now so clear that certain advertisers, such as PepsiCo, have embarked on the production of their own programmes as media for a perfectly controlled integration. The Pepsi Smash series of concerts is one example of this. Care must be taken, however, not to cross the line, as it did a century ago, imagining that it would be possible to go on creating programmes focused on one brand or product indefinitely. Once again, consumers have evolved a great deal since then.

A certain type of brand integration has long existed in the area of communication co-branding, or joint communication. In this precise case, it is not a matter of developing a common product or commercializing it together, but simply working together on publicity. One brand is therefore placed in the universe of another, hoping that both will profit from it. The car sector is well accustomed to this: for example, the outdoor clothing brand Columbia joined with Nissan in the context of a limited series. For Géraldine Michel, this 'symbolic co-branding seeks to construct a specific positioning based on symbolic attributes'.[1] Other approaches to brand integration, however, are equally possible.

The placement of products in the cinema also has its classics. Among them is Jack Daniel's and the Michael Curtiz film *Mildred Pierce* (1945), in which the lead actress Joan Crawford drinks the famous brand of whisky.[2] This example is often mentioned. However, although it is true that there are numerous scenes in the film where the actors drink bourbon, or Scotch, or rum, no brand ever appears or is mentioned onscreen! This is a typical case of unsubstantiated information, which is nonetheless reproduced without hesitation because it seems possible and probable. On the other hand, Jack Daniel's has never seemed in a hurry to deny the information. Why give up the consequences of such a free placement, even a nonexistent one? Furthermore, *Mildred Pierce* is rightly considered to be a masterpiece of *film noir*, therefore the association is also a flattering one. The brand is positively presented, and without any cost whatsoever.

Sixty years later, Ford used the entire spectrum of branded entertainment to present its Fusion brand in a markedly different way, producing 'webisodes' (short films shown on the internet), organising concerts in the form of flash mobs[3] and viral marketing campaigns, and integrating the car into series such as *24* (with Fox) and *Smallville* (with Warner Bros), as well as in successful

---

[1] Géraldine Michel (2004) *Au cœur de la Marque*, Dunod, Paris.
[2] See in particular J D Reed (1989) Plugging away in Hollywood, *Time Magazine*, 2 January; and Mary Cowlett (2000) Make it into the movies, *Marketing*, 17 August.
[3] Or flash mobilization (or lightning gathering): action which consists of gathering in a specific place (generally a public space) at a precise time the largest possible number of people, to lead a collective action for several minutes or seconds (lying down on the floor, shooting together, opening their umbrellas, showing a book, moving at the same pace in the same direction, or whatever). Most of the people gathering together do not know each other. They are informed via a network using mainly the internet or MMS/SMS messages to spread the 'assembly for action order'. Instructions concerning the action required are usually given a few minutes before the event. At the end of this short-lived action, people scatter spontaneously. The first brief and localized events of flash mobbing happened in 2003 in the United States. They can be used as event marketing communications (source: *L'Encyclopédie du Marketing*, Éditions d'Organisation Publishing, Paris, 2004, pp 350–51).

television programmes such as *American Idol,* in order to win the hearts of the female target audience, aged 18–34.[4]

Webisodes (for direct broadcasting and podcasting) have developed very quickly since the mid-2000s. In 2006, they proliferated on the net. Pirelli, in association with Leo Burnett Italy and Movie Magic International, entrusted the director Antoine Fuqua with creating the film *The Call* featuring John Malkovich and Naomi Campbell. Given its length (10 minutes), the film was not shown in traditional television commercial breaks, but on a dedicated website (www.pirellifilm.com). As for Unilever, it too provided its Calming Night (Dove) products with resources comparable to those of a feature film. The brand dedicated a new website to them (www.dovenight.com), and hired the services of the director Penny Marshall and the actress Felicity Huffmann (then one of the heroines of the series *Desperate Housewives*) to create high-quality mini-films that were eccentric in tone. It is also amusing that they were inspired by old successful television series.[5] Other advertisers such as Ford (for Mercury and Lincoln) and Procter & Gamble (for Febreze) also used these series to branch out from televised advertising communication.[6]

The bias of 'rejecting' advertising

In one scene of the famous film *Laura* (Otto Preminger, 1944), Lieutenant Mark McPherson, played by Dana Andrews, inquires about a bottle of Black Pony scotch that the central character may have bought. The brand Black Pony has never existed. It was invented to meet the plot requirements. At the time, placements were less common. Nowadays, to film such a scene without mentioning a known brand would be impossible without risking a loss of credibility. Sometimes the invented name means that over-exposure of a known brand name can be avoided, like in the film *Employee of the Month*

---

[4] See in particular T L Stanley (2006) Ford Fusion skews heavily toward non-traditional ads, *Madison+Vine*, 1 March. To valorize the car in the *Smallville* series, Ford signed a partnership contract for all season long, to benefit from a recurrent placement. Screenplay integration even allowed a nearly 'natural' flattering description of the car during a scene with the Lois Lane character, played by Erica Durance.

[5] Theresa Howard (2006) Marketers go fishing for female web surfers, *USA Today*, 19 March. See also Gail Shiller (2006) Dove web TV puts Huffman into the past, *Hollywood Reporter*, 24 February. Also in 2006, Procter & Gamble's Oral-B brand opened a website (http://brushwithromance.com) where visitors could compose their own romance, appearing as a semi-interactive book with actors A Martinez, Tia Carrere and Fabio.

[6] See in particular Stuart Elliott (2006) Pay attention to the story, but please also notice the goods, *New York Times*, 13 March.

(Greg Coolidge, 2006) in which the action takes place in a supermarket just called 'Super'. Nevertheless, some directors sometimes prefer to shun placements. In the Jon Amiel film *Entrapment* (1999), the final scene with Catherine Zeta-Jones and Sean Connery is set in the Pudu station of the LTR (Light Railway Transit) train in Kuala Lumpur, in Malaysia. Interesting fact: it is not Pudu station that was used, but, contrary to the signs, Bukit Jalil station, for logistical and aesthetic reasons. The alert viewer might however have noticed that all of the station's advertising boards have been emptied of their content, which gives the scene a sterile quality, more conducive to the tense atmosphere of the scene, and avoids any audience distraction.

Some advertisers attempt from time to time to play the suspensive integration card. This approach is similar to a sponsorship operation in the sense that the brand is generally integrated into the beginning and end of the programme, with an explanation that the programme in question is provided by the brand to the viewer free of commercial breaks. In 2003, for example, Ford used this approach in the United States to launch the new season of the series *24* on the Fox channel. In 2005, Grey Goose vodka produced a miniseries in six episodes entitled *Iconoclasts* for the Sundance Channel: the series contained no placements, none of the guests – such as actor Samuel L Jackson – talked up the vodka's merits, and there were no advertisements. The aim was clearly to position the brand against the tide of the growing tendency towards brand and product placement. At the same time, the brand sponsored launch evenings on 20 target markets, and fewer than three minutes of extracts from these events were shown at the beginning and end of the programme. An even more original operation: in 2006, Axe deodorant (Unilever) launched a reality show entitled *The Gamekillers* on MTV, inspired by its advertising communication created by the Bartle Bogle Hegarty agency. There was no brand integration into the series. Only the graphics chart and the visual environment echoed the brand and reflected onto the advertising campaign launched shortly after the reality show. The operation was further forwarded through www.mtv.com, in particular.[7]

Mini-films dedicated to the brand

In 2005, Toyota signed a placement partnership with the television series *24*, on the Fox network. This integration, which went beyond a simple placement,

---

[7] Always supporting its Axe male fragrance, in 2006 Unilever also co-produced with Fox Latin American an animated series targeting mainly adults, called *City Hunters*. Announced with the tagline '*City Hunters* powered by Axe', the series relies on stories that magnify seduction, the main claim Axe uses in its promotional material.

was particularly well negotiated. When Season 4 was released on DVD, a mini-film was created in partnership with the series production and included in the box set. This mini-film was in fact a passage from *24* Season 4 (finished) to *24* Season 5, which was due to be released by Fox some months later: in it, both a Toyota Avalon and a Toyota Prius were visible.[8] Kim Randall, vice-president of Visa – which participated in the production of the mini-film *The Ecology of Love* (with the hip-hop star Pharrell Williams) – explained that through these mini-films, branded entertainment offers advertisers the advantage of working in collaboration to benefit products and brands, without however seeking to systematically highlight them.[9] Let it be understood, this is no infomercial, in other words an advertising spot lasting several minutes.[10]

It was in 2001 that another car maker made a genuine innovation in branded entertainment. That year, BMW launched the first of a series of films dedicated to the brand, titled *The Hire*.[11] These were not ordinary advertising films, but genuine mini-films, with original plots, major production resources and well-known actors, and created by prestigious directors. John Woo,[12] Guy Ritchie, John Frankenheimer, Ang Lee, Wong Kar Wai, Tony Scott, Alejandro González and Joe Carnahan each directed a film. On the advice of David Fincher and the Fallon communications agency, BMW did not broadcast the films on television, but on a dedicated website.[13] Their length would have

[8] Eric Pfanner (2005) On advertising: dressing up commercials as short films, *International Herald Tribune*, 24 July.

[9] Nat Ives (2004) Commercials have expanded into short films with the story as the focus rather than the product, *New York Times*, 21 April. In 2006, Warner Bros Studios announced the creation of Studio 2.0, a new division designed to create short-form broadband and mobile content for potential advertisers. Craig Hunegs, exec VP-Warner Bros TV Group told *Ad Age* columnist T L Stanley, 'We've been hearing from advertisers that they want to closely align their messages with entertainment content. The goal is to create standalone content that speaks to the audience. It's not about creating something that looks like a commercial.' See T L Stanley (2006) Warner Bros creates short-form digital ad content division, *Advertising Age*, 4 September.

[10] Brett A S Martin, Andrew C Bhimy and Tom Agee (2002) Infomercials and advertising effectiveness: an empirical study, *Journal of Consumer Marketing*, 19(6), pp 468–80.

[11] Robert White, Adrian Ho and Lachlan Badenoch (2004) BMW Films, *The Hire*, Institute of Practitioners in Advertising, Bronze IPA Effectiveness Awards, London. See also Jean Halliday (2005) Car companies work to replicate buzz of *The Hire*, *Madison+Vine*, 3 August.

[12] *Hostage*, the short movie directed by John Woo received the 'Best Action' award at the short films festival taking place in Los Angeles.

[13] Jean-Marc Lehu (2005) Placement de produits dans les films et Internet: évolution et adaptation de la technique, 4th Research Seminar AFM, Nantes, 16 September. We can also note that the choice of the internet was relevant considering previous studies conducted by BMW, indicating that 85 per cent of the car brand's buyers went on the web before buying their car. See in particular John Jimenez (2001) Streaming films play key role in product placement, *Video Store Magazine*, 1 July.

Figure 10.1   Screen captures from the internet site www.bwmfilms.com, *The Hire* operation. Reproduced by kind permission of BMW North America, 2005.

proved a real obstacle not only in gaining acceptance from the channels, but also in terms of the high broadcasting costs. Naturally, the story in each case centred on a BMW car model, and in each film, the recurring character (the driver) was played by the actor Clive Owen (see Figure 10.1). Essentially promoted by word of mouth, this innovation generated a high volume of traffic on the site. More than 50 million downloads were registered over the site's lifetime (2001–05). The absolute advantage of the internet is that it allows global broadcasting of films at minimal cost. The operation was a huge success: in response to the requests it received, BMW offered web users the chance to buy a collector's DVD containing all eight films of the series.[14] At the end of the operation, BMW continued to exploit the idea by publishing, in partnership with Dark Horse publishing, a series of comic books also based on the principle of integrating one of the brand's cars into the story (see Figure 10.2).

---

[14] Scott Donaton (2004) *Madison+Vine*, Advertising Age/McGraw-Hill, New York. In the United States, companies like Film Movement are producing DVDs containing short movies distributed to their subscribers, with brand placements.

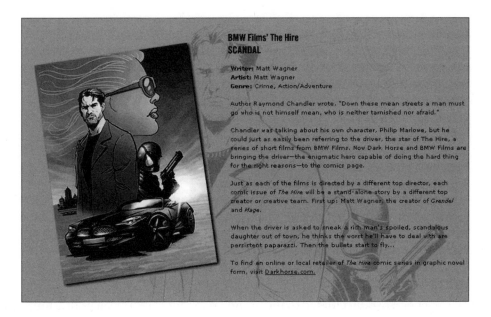

Figure 10.2 Screen shots from the internet site www.bwmfilms.com, *The Hire* operation. Reproduced by kind permission of BMW North America, 2005.

In 2002, Mercedes took a similar route to that of BMW. The German car maker hired the director Michael Mann to create the trailer for a film that, er, didn't exist.[15] The trailer for this new thriller, featuring the actor Benicio Del Toro, was shown in the UK, in cinemas and on television. Its essential focus was a chase through the streets of Los Angeles: pursued by a helicopter, the actor was driving the all-new Mercedes 500 SL convertible. Following the golden rule of subtle brand integration, however, the trailer contained no close-ups of the logo or the brand. In 2004, Ford did the same with the series of mini-films *Meet the Lucky Ones*.[16] The length of *The Hire* operation for BMW was exceptional. In general, these mini-films are only accessible for a few days, a few weeks or at most a few months. In fact, if they remain online for longer, incoherence with new brand communication might possibly ensue. Furthermore, the goal is to achieve a buzz effect as quickly as possible, generating traffic on the website. If the potential target audience knew that the film would remain available without any time limit, their perceived interest in visiting the site would be less.

---

[15] The film doesn't exist, but the director wished to take an option on the rights. See in particular Marc Graser (2002) Inside move: Mercedes' 'star' trailer, *Variety*, 14 July.

[16] David Kiley (2004) The new wave of Net films, *BusinessWeek*, 30 November.

In conclusion, the internet offers many advantages for the use of mini-films. It is universal and therefore makes it possible to reach everyone with access to an internet connection. It profits from permanent access, since it offers visitors the chance to connect when and where they like, unlike an advertising film, which only remains onscreen for a few moments. It is relatively cheap, compared with broadcasting on a television network. It is perfectly controllable, since the communication takes place on one of the brand's websites, which means that it is safe from possible parasite communication (such as a competitor's film inserted into the same screen). Once the communications operation is over, all that needs to be done is to disconnect the site from the web. More and more advertisers are using it: Dr Martens, in partnership with the director Doug Pray, Starbucks for the Red Cup operation, the SNCF with iDGTV, PepsiCo with Aquafina, and so on. Some advertisers even create a series of these mini-films to create loyalty among their target audience.

This brings us into the domain of the 'webisode', a type of digital modern soap opera serving the brand, inviting the public to follow the adventures of a character or a product linked to the brand on the internet (or via podcasting). General Mills took advantage of this branded entertainment approach for its cereals using Lucky, the Lucky Charms leprechaun (see the dedicated website www.luckycharms.millsberry.com). While advertising represented 4.8 per cent of General Mills' sales in 2002, it represented only 3.3 per cent in 2005, since it had reorientated its efforts to use 'non-traditional' media. In fact, the innovation of the series of webisodes entitled *The Quest* and all the promotional events surrounding it enabled the organization to generate a 12 per cent growth in sales between 2004 and 2005.[17] The series can sometimes also focus on less 'commercial' content, gambling on the fact that the

---

[17] From 2003 to 2005, media spending for cereals decreased 15 per cent in the United States. See in particular Stephanie Thompson (2006) General Mills turns cereal Leprechaun into movie star, *Madison+Vine*, 22 February. During the first 10 days following the launching of the Lucky Charms webisodes series, 400,000 visitors connected to the website. After four months, more than a million web surfers were involved, for a total budget lower than the cost of a 30-second commercial. In 2005, Lucky Charms also agreed a proposition from Saatchi & Saatchi, its advertising agency, to commission the viral marketing agency Asabailey to produce a short-film mocking F Gary Gray's *The Italian Job* movie (2003). In this spoof Lucky the leprechaun escapes from his pursuers using a Mini car, with a pack of Lucky Charms at his side. The movie was initially sent to a sample of 250,000 students. Since then, it has continued to spread all around the web world. Such a viral marketing action has to be managed with care. If not, the target audience will feel it as an ad intrusion and will be prompt to reject it.

Figure 10.3 Screen shot with a still from the film *Do Geese See God* (David Slade, 2004), with the actor Blair Underwood.

Source: amazon.com.

consumer will associate the provision of entertainment with the brand, and that this will benefit the brand image. It can also give rise to the production of 'mockumentaries',[18] if the brand wishes to adopt a more offbeat tone.

---

[18] 'Mockumentary' is a word formed from the verb 'to mock' and the word 'documentary'. It is used to designate a false documentary or a product documentary, which makes heavy use of humour while keeping the appearance of a real documentary. Using a parody technique, the mockumentary allows the brand to signal that it doesn't take itself seriously; this attitude can lure a greater attention from the target audience, as it perceives the entertainment before the advertising message. Although the mockumentary is part of the branded entertainment media portfolio, it is not new. On 30 October 1938, on the CBS network, H G Wells's famous Sci-fi novel *The War of the Worlds* was adapted, in a very realistic and pioneering way, by Orson Welles' Mercury Theatre. It gave the audience such a convincing impression of a live extraterrestrial invasion that it unleashed panic among thousands of listeners, starting an exodus from the big cities receiving the radio show. After the tremendous success of Mercury Theatre, Campbell's Soup became the sponsor of the show.

In 2004, the commercial site Amazon developed a highly original approach to product placement through mini-films. From 9 November 2004, web users visiting the amazon.com site had the opportunity to watch or download exclusive short films (see Figure 10.3). For five weeks, a new film was offered each week. The period and the rhythm of broadcasting were chosen to generate additional traffic and to capture the web users thus attracted for Christmas. The operation was carried out in collaboration with the Fallon agency (already originators of the operation *The Hire* for BMW, discussed earlier), and the RSA production company, which brought together experienced directors who were entrusted with the production. Contrary to the principle of the infomercial,[19] each film told a story that was not in any way linked to any product whatsoever. Each of the five films also told a very different story. The operation was sponsored by the financial establishment JPMorgan Chase & Co, already a partner of the internet site; in particular, it is the issuer of its Visa Amazon cards.

In reality, products had been perfectly integrated into the plot of each film. The only way to become aware of them was to pay close attention to the end credits, in which the products were mentioned (in order of appearance) in the same way as the actors. Following the film, the viewer was naturally directed to a screen presenting all the products featured in the film. Each product was coupled with a hyperlink enabling internet users to access its details, should they wish to purchase it. In terms of its storyline, décor and props, none of these films could be linked to Amazon[20] or to a specific brand. Nor were these mini-films dedicated to any particular product; but they presented different products that Amazon clients could buy directly through the site.

This is undoubtedly where the operation's great originality lies. In all ordinary cases of placement, there is a time lapse and a physical distance between exposure and the purchasing opportunity. In the case of Amazon, the whole of space-time folded in upon itself. Viewers could become buyers immediately following their exposure to the placement, and without needing even to move, since they were connected to an internet distance selling site. From a strategic point of view, this entertainment added value to Amazon's offer. It so happened that Amazon's prices were coming under mounting pressure, faced with the verdicts of price comparison websites and the direct or indirect competition of other marketplaces such as eBay.[21]

---

[19] Patricia S Chapman and Richard F Beltramini (2000) The impact of infomercials revisited: perspectives of advertising professionals, *Journal of Advertising Research*, 40(5), pp 24–31.

[20] Except maybe Jake Scott's *Tooth Fairy* with actor Chris Noth. Alert spectators may have noticed that the keeper who has a very small part is nevertheless played by Jeff Bezos himself, the CEO of Amazon.

[21] Nick Wingfield (2004) Amazon offers free short films in holiday push, *Wall Street Journal*, 9 November.

There was no brand placement, and no mention of brands during the film. The integration of products seemed perfectly natural in each of the stories. For Jordan Scott's film *Portrait*, since the beauty of the characters was central to the story, cosmetics products were naturally the most numerous in the credits (see Figure 10.4). In addition, on the Amazon website, each actress benefited from a special page, presenting all the products that had been used for her make-up and offering them for sale via the hyperlinks to the product pages (see Figure 10.5). Another advantage: by proposing that all the products be used side by side, Amazon subtly opened the door to possible tie-in purchases (skirt and blouse; telephone and Bluetooth headset; blusher and mascara and eye shadow, and so on). At the time, more than 41 million clients were likely to see these mini-films on the online shopping site. An e-mail campaign was also organized during the operation, to attract the attention of those clients who might not have visited the site recently. The films were offered for viewing on the three major readers on the market (Windows MediaPlayer, RealOnePlayer and QuickTime) and at different connection speeds, in order to allow all visitors easy access.

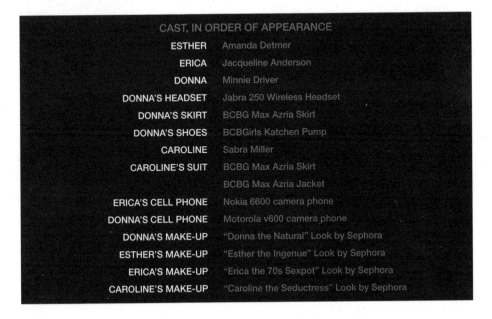

Figure 10.4 Extract from the end credits of the film *Portrait* (Jordan Scott, 2004).

Source: amazon.com.

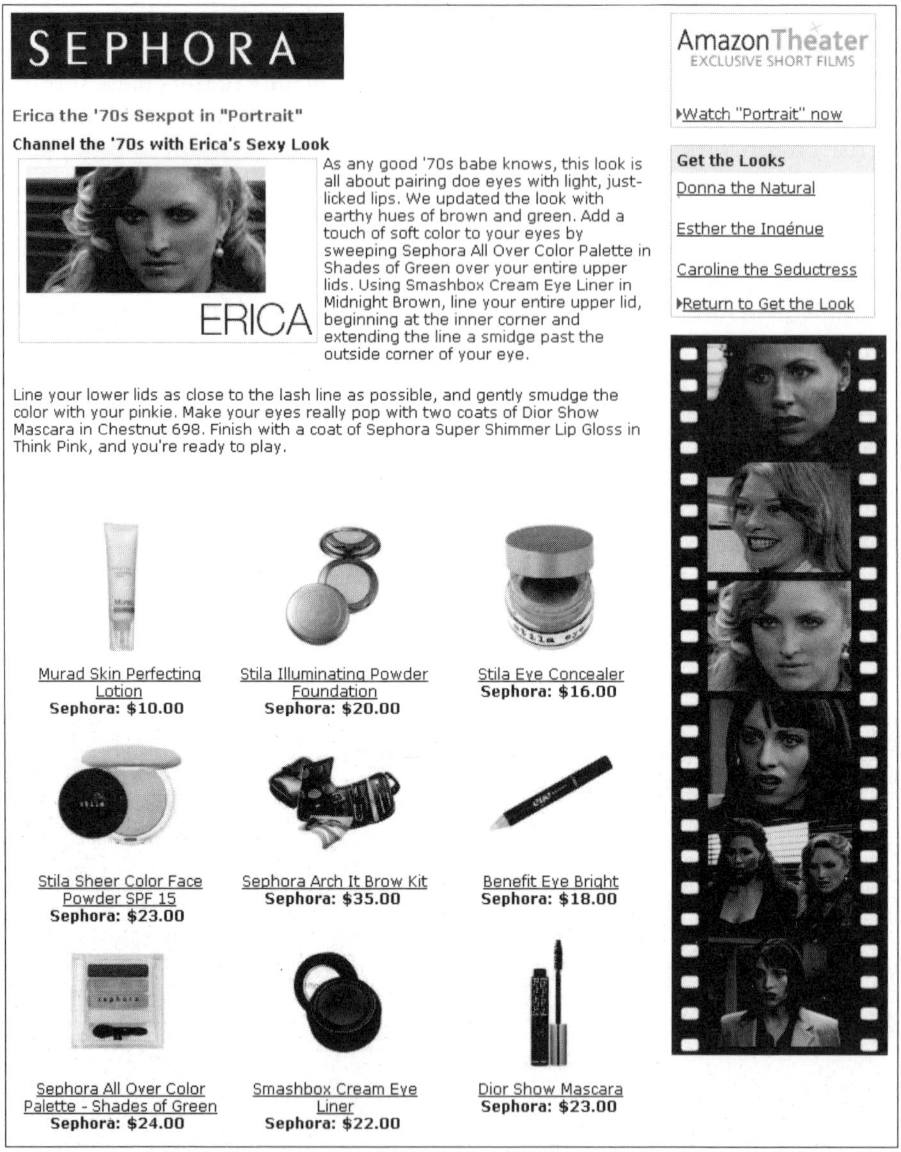

SEPHORA

Erica the '70s Sexpot in "Portrait"

Channel the '70s with Erica's Sexy Look

As any good '70s babe knows, this look is all about pairing doe eyes with light, just-licked lips. We updated the look with earthy hues of brown and green. Add a touch of soft color to your eyes by sweeping Sephora All Over Color Palette in Shades of Green over your entire upper lids. Using Smashbox Cream Eye Liner in Midnight Brown, line your entire upper lid, beginning at the inner corner and extending the line a smidge past the outside corner of your eye.

ERICA

Line your lower lids as close to the lash line as possible, and gently smudge the color with your pinkie. Make your eyes really pop with two coats of Dior Show Mascara in Chestnut 698. Finish with a coat of Sephora Super Shimmer Lip Gloss in Think Pink, and you're ready to play.

AmazonTheater
EXCLUSIVE SHORT FILMS

▶Watch "Portrait" now

Get the Looks

Donna the Natural

Esther the Ingénue

Caroline the Seductress

▶Return to Get the Look

Murad Skin Perfecting Lotion
Sephora: $10.00

Stila Illuminating Powder Foundation
Sephora: $20.00

Stila Eye Concealer
Sephora: $16.00

Stila Sheer Color Face Powder SPF 15
Sephora: $23.00

Sephora Arch It Brow Kit
Sephora: $35.00

Benefit Eye Bright
Sephora: $18.00

Sephora All Over Color Palette - Shades of Green
Sephora: $24.00

Smashbox Cream Eye Liner
Sephora: $22.00

Dior Show Mascara
Sephora: $23.00

Figure 10.5 Extract of the page dedicated to the actress Jacqueline Anderson, a character in the film *Portrait*.

Source: amazon.com (2004).

Given that famous actors and directors had participated in most of these mini-films, the placements also benefited from the implicit recommendation of the stars. In addition, each one also presented on its site a selection of Christmas presents, which enabled the synergies between the mini-films and Amazon's commercial offer to increase even further. According to the Fallon agency's calculations, traffic increased by 15 per cent on the Amazon site during the first week of broadcasting.[22] This innovative case clearly shows one of the major advantages of tomorrow's product placements, when television – by whatever means it is broadcast – will have become completely interactive. Viewers will then have the opportunity to immediately purchase the product or the service shown in the film they are watching.

Opportunities for digital mobility

The director Alfred Hitchcock once remarked, 'Television is like the invention of indoor plumbing. It didn't change people's habits. It just kept them inside the house.'[23] Indeed, half a century ago, how could we have imagined that television could become mobile? Another step was taken when mini-films began to be shown on mobile telephones. The advantage of mobile telephony is that it represents a vector that allows the advertiser to approach the consumer, rather than waiting for the opposite to happen. The mobile phone is now considered the third screen (after the television and the computer) on which it is imperative to appear. Brands such as Jeep®, McDonald's, Coca-Cola, Heineken, Masterfoods, Nestlé, Timex or Johnson & Johnson were quick to dedicate part of their communications budget to it. For their part, on film promotion websites, film production studios now offer connections to mobiles: to participate in prize draws, to download exclusive ringtones, or to participate in the testing of new campaigns, or even to gain exclusive access to the film's latest trailer.

Although this is not the place for discussing one-to-one marketing, we can note that the medium of the mobile phone is particularly well adapted to carrying out targeted operations. In 2005, Jeep® went even further. To begin with, the brand developed the 'We are the Mudds' operation, which offered a series of webisodes on a dedicated site (http://wearethemudds. com) about a family, the Mudds, who owned a Jeep® (see Figure 10.6). Mud,

[22] For a detailed analysis of the Amazon case, see Jean-Marc Lehu (2005) Placement de produits dans les films et sur Internet: évolution et adaptation de la technique – Le cas Amazon Theater 2004, 4th Research Seminar AFM, Nantes, 16 September.

[23] *AMA News*, 15 December 2005, American Marketing Association. About the specific case of mobile advergaming, see Ravi Shanker Bose (2004) Branding through mobile advergaming, *Advertising Express*, ICFAI University Press, April, pp 159–65.

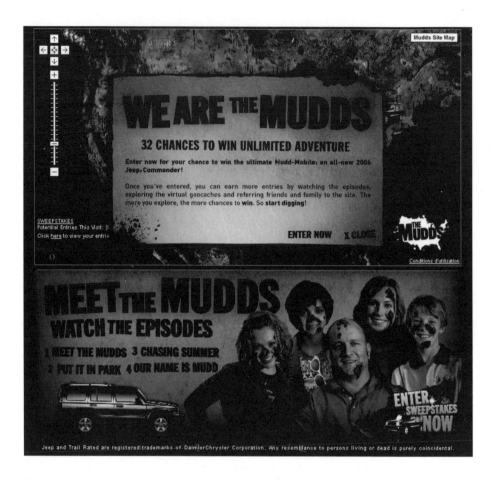

Figure 10.6 Screen shot of the internet site wearethemudds.com (Jeep®, 2005). Reproduced by kind permission of DaimlerChrysler.

intimately linked to the use of a 4×4 in its natural terrain, was presented in a humorous manner. The Google Maps service was used for the cartography. The operation was carried out via mobile phones. In partnership with MobiTV, every hour, the mini-films were relayed on several of the mobile radio and television operator's channels. This television broadcasting on mobile telephones constituted a kind of mobile television channel dedicated to the brand. It is easy therefore to imagine the many interactive applications that could be envisaged with subscribing 'mobile-viewers'.

Adapting continually to a constantly changing environment

If many of the functions and responsibilities labelled 'branded entertainment' have now been in existence for several years, both among advertisers and in communications consultancies, the exploitation of branded entertainment is not as simple as it appears to be. The world of entertainment is constantly metamorphosing to adapt itself to an audience that in turn changes without ceasing. If we add to this increasingly weighty economic imperatives, then flying by the seat of one's pants quickly becomes the norm. The basis of integration rests on strategic thinking. Strategy can only emerge if it is given the time for a coherent implementation. Time, however, is a luxury that actors can rarely afford. Many series and shows have been taken off the air or simply cancelled when they failed to find an audience after only one or two episodes! Moreover, as the demand grows, fees also evolve rapidly, in an upwards direction.

During the ANA survey in 2005, 79 per cent of advertisers surveyed felt that the price of branded entertainment operations was excessive.[24] This also contributes to destabilizing the environment, by reducing the number of potential advertisers capable of paying the asking price. The stated objective: constant INNOVATION. Innovation, to satisfy the marketers who are more likely to take a risk if the concept is genuinely new and therefore likely to attract a large audience, as the programme *The Apprentice* (by Mark Burnett), with Donald Trump, on NBC, was able to do in its early days. Innovation, to surprise an audience with hundreds of television channels at its disposal and many other media clamouring for its attention. Innovation, to keep the brand from growing old and falling into obscurity.

---

[24]John Consoli (2005) ANA Survey: 63 pct. use branded entertainment, *Brandweek*, 23 March. See also Stuart Elliott (2006) Pay attention to the story, but please also notice the goods, *New York Times*, 13 March.

11 Towards a new strategic brand management

Brands must constantly ensure their positive presence in the mind of consumers, if possible through recourse to media detached from purely commercial, and sometimes very damaging, connotations. As Andrea Semprini observes:

> The dissemination of the brand beyond the commercial sphere shows above all the capacity for the brand's logic to transform, to adapt, to transcend in order to take charge of a virtually infinite variety of content and discourse.[1]

If the brand chooses to have only a purely commercial discourse, it denies itself the opportunity to form a more affective relational link. The power of testimonial by a friend or family member in favour of a brand has nothing in common with the random aspect of an advertising argument presented over 30 seconds during a commercial break on television. To those who think that buzz is too uncertain and too difficult to master, Jonathan Ressler, founder of the Big Fat agency, replies: 'buzz doesn't happen by accident. This is just real life product placement.'[2]

---

[1] Andrea Semprini (2005) *La marque, une puissance fragile*, Vuibert, Paris.
[2] Daniel Eisenberg (2002) It's an ad, ad, ad, ad world, *Time*, 2 September. See also Mirko Ilic (2005) The revolution will be televised, *Entertainment Weekly*, 16 December; Marc

Accompanying the potential consumer

'We need to take our brand to them [the users], and not wait for them to come to us', said Hilary Dart, president of Calvin Klein Cosmetics, back in 2002.[3] Benoît Heilbrunn has analysed this brand entrism, even suggesting that the brand can thereby overcome the deficiencies of the social connection.[4] Yesterday no more than a fashion phenomenon illustrating a certain form of independence, mobility has rapidly become a general trend of our developed societies. The destructuring of the nuclear family, the disruption of times and working hours, and of course the transport facilities as well as the increasing length of journey times have all contributed to durably installing this characteristic in our lives.

Some were quick to see this as an added asset for product placement. From 2005, Apple, in partnership with Motorola, authorized access to iTunes and iTunes Music Store from mobile telephones. Some days later, Apple announced the launch of an iPod, its digital music player, with video function. At the same time, iTunes Music Stores offered the possibility of downloading video content (musical clips, US series, short films, video podcasts and so on, see Figure 11.1). Podcasting in all its forms has also rapidly contributed to disrupting still further the 'established' order of brand communication. Did you not have time to watch a news report on ABC, did you want to see the trailer for your favourite actor's latest film, did you arrive too late for the concert, did you miss the last episode of *Lost, Commander in Chief, Law & Order* or *Desperate Housewives*? You have only to download it before you leave for work, to watch at your leisure on your iPod or on a portable digital player, such as your mobile telephone or PDA.

The only disadvantage for advertisers who paid for the insertion of an advertising film in one of the programme's commercial breaks: you have disappeared from the original target audience, since downloading is carried out without commercial breaks. Of course, it is still possible to envisage lower downloading charges if the purchaser accepts some advertising content.[5] It

---

Gunther (2006) The Iger sanction, *Fortune*, 153(1), 23 January; and Daniele Dalli (2003) Il product placement cinematografico: oltre la pubblicità? paper presented to the 3rd Congress of Marketing Tendencies, Venice, Italy, 28–29 November.

[3] See note 2.

[4] Benoît Heilbrunn (2005) *La consommation et ses sociologies*, Armand Colin, Paris. See also some 'insidious aspects of branding' analysed by Howard Blumenthal (2006) in *Branded for Life: How Americans are brainwashed by the brands we love*, Emmis Books, Cincinnati, OH.

[5] A report from eMarketer published in 2006 estimated that podcasting advertising in the United States could represent a US$150 million market in 2008 and could double those figures in 2010. The numbers of podcasters (final users of podcasting)

Figure 11.1 Example of the downloading site Apple iTunes Music Store. *Source:* Apple iTunes Music Store, © 2006 Apple Computer, Inc. All rights reserved. Apple and iTunes are brands of Apple Computer, Inc, registered in the United States and other countries. iTunes Music Store is a service brand of Apple Computer, Inc, registered in the United States and other countries.

is much less risky, however, to make sure of a product or brand placement within the programme itself. This is all the more true since every day new programme producers, such as HBO with the operator Cingular for example, put in place downloading services for series, documentaries and other entertainment programmes via mobile telephones.

Consumers in developed countries spend more and more time on the internet. Many radio stations and television channels (bfmtv.fr, eonline.com, cnn.com, tv5.org, lci.fr, artevod.com, nationalgeographic.com, news.bbc.

---

is on a constant rise. This is only logical if we consider that most of the broadcasters now offer content formatted for podcasting. See Mike Shields (2006) Study: podcasting to grow ads, *MediaWeek*, 28 February. In April 2006, a press release from PQ Media stated that blog, podcast and RSS advertising were growing very fast among alternative media, surging 198 per cent from 2005. The study also forecasted that podcast advertising would be larger than the blog market by 2010.

co.uk, discovery.com, foxnews.com) have grasped this, by offering paid or free access, streamed or as podcasts, to all or part of their programmes by means of an internet connection. Some of them, such as bravotv.com, attempt to replicate the classic model by inserting advertising spots. Most of the time, however, the commercial content of these programmes is suppressed. Here also, the range is expanding. Sites such as the excellent youtube.com offer countless new windows created by web users themselves, watched by thousands of others. In addition to advertising films, it is not uncommon to find multiple brand placements in films created by individuals. Today the majority of them are involuntary, but tomorrow, who knows?

In 2005, Time Warner and its subsidiary AOL announced the launch of sitcoms broadcast exclusively online. The same year, the condom brand Durex used podcasting for a placement in a script of the audio 'series' *The Dawn and Drew Show* (Dawn Miceli and Drew Domkus), produced and broadcast direct from a Wisconsin farm. Using podcasting offers Durex 'a way to demonstrate the brand in a way that's very, very relevant. We could have the product actively being used. We're showing it exactly as we want to position the brand, as fun, as playful and sensual,' explained Liz Daney, senior vice-president and chief media officer for agency Interpublic Group of Cos. Fitzgerald & Co.[6] One important detail: in the matter of direct diffusion, legislative restrictions on advertising do not apply. Podcasting is now one of the new variables disturbing the traditional communications environment. Perfectly mastered by young web users in particular, and adapted to multiple mobile players (PDA, walkmans or mobile telephones), it is a crucial medium for branded entertainment.

Modern information can no longer do without images. News in brief with a crew of reporters, camera in hand, is worth more than a natural planetary disaster with just a soundtrack! In this sense, external advertising, particularly in strategic locations, remains a highly contested competitive stake for advertisers, since spaces with great potential are so rare. The case of Times Square is especially revelatory. As with all charismatic locations throughout the world, it is often used for shooting films, but also for news reports. It is then impossible to escape the gigantic advertisements found there. Each year, most of the world's televisions visit such 'typical' locations at New Year. Thanks to Times Square, AT&T, Coca-Cola, Panasonic, Discover, Budweiser, Yahoo, Samsung, Nissan and all the other advertisers present achieve an almost planet-wide placement.

What is being developed is an image of the brand placed where it can surprise, touch, sensitize. An example is Evian, which is participating in the repairing of an open-air swimming pool near Brixton in the United Kingdom,

---

[6] Jack Neff (2005) Durex buys condom product placements in podcast, *Advertising Age*, 12 May.

in return for its logo appearing at the bottom of the pool.[7] There is an image that reacts with RFID tags or new-generation barcodes (such as Shotcode, QRcode, PaperClick, mCode, Semacode, UpCodes and Color code for example) in Lancôme posters, tags and barcodes that allows information to be downloaded on to a mobile telephone or the product identified to be instantly ordered, even as consumers are enabled to assuage their ravenous hunger for information (a phenomenon now described by the expression 'infolust').[8] Another alternative is 'mobisodes',[9] found in the creation of the album *Meds*, by Placebo, and with acoustic versions downloadable by subscribers to the SFR telephone operator. And another is an interactive image, as when Nike invites passers-by in Times Square to call a telephone number that connects them to the interactive display and enables them to use their telephone keypad to directly design their own shoe, which can be downloaded for subsequent ordering via the brand's website.[10] Alternatively, an exclusive image can be shown in a new medium, as when Mark Burnett and Yahoo organize the first boxing match broadcast exclusively online, with Toyota and Intel as partners; an image that innovates, with advertisers as varied as Oral-B, Nike and Nokia who communicate via 'tryvertising', aiming to narrowly target the placement of their products in the context of everyday life.

New communication media appear every day in the street, in businesses, in shopping centres, in airports, in car parks, sometimes bringing together media that yesterday were competitors but now offer new brand placement opportunities, to bring offerings alongside the potential consumer. These examples naturally illustrate the need for coherence in the convergence of the communication media used by the brand. There is convergence between

---

[7] Tom Dyckhoff (2003) It's summer: take me to your lido, *The Times*, 5 August.

[8] See the April 2006 *Trendwatching* newsletter: www.trendwatching.com. For an interesting analysis about a constantly moving modern consumer, see Mark Andrejevic (2003) Monitored mobility in the era of mass customization, *Space & Culture*, 6(2), May, pp 132–150.

[9] A short video film, either an excerpt from another show or specifically produced. It is usually filmed with close-ups because it will be watched on a 3G cellular screen, which is usually tiny. In 2004 Vodafone used this medium to announce to its subscribers the first episode of Season 4 of *24* (the television show with actor Kiefer Sutherland). In 2005, Verizon and Vodafone speeded up the production of 26 one-minute mobisodes for *Love and Hate* and *The Sunset Hotel* (two television shows also produced by 20th Century Fox). Mobisodes may be also an opportunity to present movie trailers, with or without brand or product placements. But such placements can allow free downloads as they are already paid for by the placed advertisers.

[10] Abbey Klaassen (2005) Inside Times Square's Reuters sign, *Advertising Age*, 11 July. About an analysis concerning interactivity and advergaming, see E Kalyan Babu and K Padma (2002) Advergaming: the future of interactive advertising, *Advertising Express*, ICFAI Press, November, pp 89–98.

Madison and Vine, of course,[11] but also convergence on the same objective: the brand's communications strategy. Each communicative act must contribute to this communications strategy, whatever the channel used and the opportunity to communicate seized.

Prioritizing a multi-channel, multi-opportunity communication

1995 saw the highly media-friendly trial of the athlete-actor O J Simpson. For the trial, Sony did not hesitate to replace the monitor used by the judge, Lance Ito, with another model whose obvious logo would be more easily identifiable during televised broadcasting of the hearings.[12] The time when an original creative idea for brand strategy was enough is long past. The search for that differentiating idea goes on, of course, but it is also important to determine the most effective possibilities and methods possible for its implementation. The branding expert Georges Lewi pertinently emphasizes the fact that 'everyone wants to be, and calls themselves, different. But few companies are capable of taking this logic of differentiation to its extreme.'[13] Why shouldn't an alcohol brand pay bar staff in targeted establishments to sing the praises of its beverage to clients, using anecdotes and original stories provided, without pushing them directly to consume it? Peter Dang, vice-president in charge of marketing at the public relations agency Bragman Nyman Cafarelli, talks about the '360 package programme'.[14] The expression is symptomatic of the search for the most exhaustive vision possible of all communications opportunities.[15]

---

[11] In Hollywood, Vine Street symbolizes the showbusiness world, and in Manhattan, Madison Avenue symbolizes the advertising world. Scott Donaton (2004) *Madison+ Vine*, Advertising Age/McGraw-Hill, New York.

[12] Stuart Elliott (1995) Logo complaints at Simpson trial, *New York Times*, 7 February.

[13] Georges Lewi and Caroline Rogliano (2006) *Mémento pratique du branding*, Village Mondial-Pearson, Paris.

[14] Marc Graser (2005) A public relations firm into branded entertainment, *Madison+ Vine*, 9 November. Is the branded entertainment approach of modern marketing giving the top signal for a total brand cultural entrism? Maybe not, but it probably leads us to mediatization of consumption pulling as never before all the strings of the society's culture. See also André Jansson (2002) The mediatization of consumption: towards an analytical framework of image culture, *Journal of Consumer Culture*, 2(1), pp 5–31.

[15] A convergence that must be confirmed by relevant technology that offers the consumer the freedom of choice without any technological constraint. See on this subject Allison Enright (2006) The urge to merge: marketers explore implications

In the preceding pages, numerous films were mentioned to illustrate the argument. The vast majority of these films were commercially successful. The advantage of choosing these films was twofold. First, there was a greater chance that the majority of readers would recognize them. Second, the brand or product placements contained within them involved brands known to everyone. The desired illustration could therefore be relayed through the reader's personal experience.

If a multi-channel and multi-opportunity communication can be the road to salvation for the brand's publicity strategy, however, more humble projects should not be neglected, in either the cinema or other potential placement media. Of course, the audience is generally smaller, but often more homogeneous; the placement contracts are generally more elementary, but often much more affordable; they do not generally have the media reach of a cinema superproduction or a multicast show, but they often offer the perfect time and space for raising the profile of the brand's identity with a highly targeted audience. It is not a matter of choosing between one and the other. It is simply a case of perceiving that the opportunities for brand integration in an entertainment environment are many and varied.

A revealing example of the possibility of a powerful original communication is that of the Oxbow sports products brand (Lafuma group). Its resources were limited compared with those of the major players such as Quiksilver, Rip Curl and Billabong. The only creative solution possible: differentiation marketing and integration of the brand into communications media that were original and coherent with its positioning, all of which must be accessible, while the marketing budget could not exceed 5 per cent of turnover. On the other hand, when you claim to be the brand for freeriding and soul surfing, you need to respect the 'community' of ambassadors you are addressing. With a balanced distribution of its resources – 50 per cent assigned to above-the-line and 50 per cent to below-the-line – Oxbow therefore launched into the creation of quality multi-sports audiovisual content.

This approach led to the production of short programmes, 30 seconds to 52 minutes in length, in which the brand is intelligently integrated (logo on accessories, labels on clothing, boards placed in the background of sporting events, and so on). Each film was inserted into a series: LFX (for Last Frontiers Explorers), Legends (for the legends of the brand), Escape Special (on board sports subjects), and Quest (for reality television programmes, and simultaneously intended for 3G mobile telephones). There was no showy presence, but a presentation of the brand values of escape, quality,

---

of technology's convergence, *Marketing News*, 40(5), 15 March, pp 9–12. See also William Misloski (2005) An opportunity for tomorrow's multi-channel integrated marketer, *Journal of Integrated Marketing Communications*, Northwestern University, Department of Integrated Marketing Communications, pp 17–25.

authenticity, conscience, community and 'smart attitude'. As a result, the programmes can be widely shown, because the content is not perceived to be an advertising message. In several countries, some hundred channels, such as Ushuaia or Eurosport, welcomed its programmes: short films that profited from 15 years of image production, and that could also be broadcast on the site www.oxboworld.com and at points of purchase referencing the brand.

In 2005, Oxbow also produced a musical compilation aimed at rejuvenating the target audience, to sensitize tomorrow's customers. As Vincent Stuhlen, director of marketing, explains:

> Our position as an outsider on the market forces us to imagine innovative communications strategies, based on the power of the content, on the creation of true stories, which perfectly illustrate our identity, our values, our territory. This transversal audiovisual strategy offers exceptional visibility to our brand, with a cost/expense ratio of 1 to 10. Additionally, the stories told in the editorial slots are always more credible than the ones told in advertising. Especially when they are authentic and shared by as many people as possible.

It is important that the brand be as well referenced as possible, everywhere that it has a chance to come into contact with its stakeholders. Since the internet is a governing point, referencing professionals thought up SEM (search engine marketing), in order to ensure that the brand in question is associated with the most powerful key words, in the fastest and most precise manner possible. Since internet users can also be particularly frank in giving their opinions on the brand, it is equally important to observe discussion forums, as well as the blogs that seem to be most active. Different brands and groups have taken the next step, by creating their own blogs.[16] The approach is technically very simple. It does, however, require a few ethical precautions. Care must be taken not to fall into the trap of attempting to manipulate. Some bloggers are hardened internet users who are rarely deceived, and it is very dangerous for brand image if they realize they have been fooled. In 2005, Vichy turned a product manager into a false consumer on its blog: the brand had to apologize when she was unmasked.[17]

In 2006, the HBO network also used the internet for the (re)launch of its series *The Sopranos*, transmission of which had ended in 2004. In a highly original manner, HBO used the cartographic technique offered by Google to place extracts from different episodes of the series on the map of New York and New Jersey (see Figure 11.2). The stated objective was to enable potential viewers to make the link between Season 4 (2004) and Season 5 (2006). In

---

[16] Sophie Péters (2005) Comment les marques infiltrent les blogs, *Les Echos*, 27 June.
[17] Sandrine L'Herminier (2005) La publicité s'invite dans les jeux vidéo et dans les blogs, *La Tribune*, 22 June.

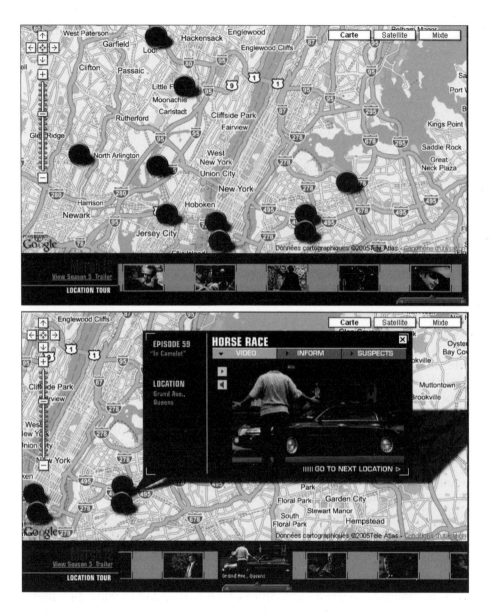

Figure 11.2 Promotional operation for the launch of Season 5 of the series *The Sopranos* on HBO: www.hbo.com. © Google Maps (2006). Reproduced by kind permission of Google Corp, Mountain View, California, United States.

fact, the goal was to put in place an original communications operation likely to construct a potential audience between 27 February (opening of access to the map) and 12 March (showing of the first episode of Season 5). All the functions of Google Maps were operational, and the programme allowed visitors to choose the locations they wished to visit, or to be taken from place to place. At each place, information on the characters, the story and a video extract were available.

Integrating the limits of globalization

In 2002, Finlandia vodka replaced Smirnoff in the composition of James Bond's vodka martini, in *Die Another Day* (Lee Tamahori, 2002). The brand saw the opportunity for global communications, since at that time over 80 per cent of its sales were outside the United States. The cinema has not escaped the globalization of markets. Having said this, although it is possible to refer to the cases of successful international films such as the *Star Wars* or *Lord of the Rings* sagas,[18] care must be taken not to generalize. Cinema is an art and, like any art, it is naturally subject to tastes that may vary considerably from one culture to another, or simply from one country to another.

A glance at the weekly box-office totals published by the benchmark professional magazine *Variety* for the different countries analysed (the United States, Japan, Great Britain, Spain, Australia, Germany, France, Italy and Mexico) is enough to demonstrate this: although comparable for the most part in terms of economic development, these countries differ in their film preferences. In terms of product placement, those works of academic research that provide comparative analysis of countries are particularly instructive. They confirm the differences in tastes, perceptions and impacts.[19] Moreover, US (and French) films were not the only ones deemed worthy of advertising interest. Motorola, for example, benefited greatly from its highly visible

---

[18] In addition it is interesting to notice that, because of their genre and because of the worlds in which their story takes place, those two sagas do not include brand nor product placements.

[19] See in particular research by James A Karrh, Katherine T Frith and Coy Callison (2001) Audiences attitudes towards brand (product), placement: Singapore and the United States, *International Journal of Advertising*, 20, pp 3–24; Sally A McKechnie and Jia Zhou (2003) Product placement in movies: a comparison of Chinese and American consumers' attitudes, *International Journal of Advertising*, 22, pp 349–74; N Devathan, M Nelson, J McCarty, S Deshpande, H J Paek, R Punnahitanond, S E Stein, A M Vilela and R Yaros (2003) Product placement go global: an examination of contacts across five countries, in *Advances in Consumer Research*, 30, ed Punam Anand Keller and Dennis W Rook, AAA, Atlanta, GA, October 16–20, pp 170–1; In-Myoung You (2004) *Product placement belief and product usage behaviour in South Korea and the United States*, Master's thesis, Advertising Department, University of Florida, Gainsville, FL; Antonio C La Pastina and Joseph D Straubhaar (2005) Multiple proximities between television genres and audiences, *International Journal for Communication Studies*, 67(3), pp 271–88.

integration into the plot of the Chinese film by Xiaogang Feng, *Shou Ji* (Cell phone, 2003). In the same way, Hyundai automobiles were very present in the Indian film *Josh* (Mansoor Khan, 2000) and placements for Tata tea, ICICI Bank, Ford, Pepsi-Cola and Nokia can be clearly identified in *Baghban* (Ravi Chopra, 2000).[20]

It is also possible to envisage an 'adaptation'. The favourable coverage of the Peugeot 406 in the *Taxi* trilogy (1998–2003), produced by Luc Besson, was highly positive for the brand's image and undoubtedly had a knock-on effect on sales of the model. As the central 'character', the car even appeared on the film posters and on the covers of CDs and DVDs; this had previously been the case for the *Back to the Future* trilogy (Robert Zemeckis, 1985–1990), where a DeLorean DMC-12 played an important role. The 406 was not, however, on sale in all the countries where the film was shown. Some might say that this is a lesser evil, compared with the explosion and conflagration suffered by the same model in the first few seconds of the trailer for *Syriana* (Stephen Gaghan, 2005)! This was particularly significant since the still of this scene was published in the press and was used on the front page of *Le Monde* (on 22 February 2006), to accompany an article on the film's release. Regarding the *Taxi* trilogy, its adaptation in 2004, by Tim Story, relocated the story to the heart of New York City, without a 406 but with a (modified) Ford Crown Victoria.

In 1993, to avoid an uneven global implantation, PepsiCo had no hesitation in insisting that the same scene of the Marco Brambilla film, *Demolition Man*, be filmed twice. This scene featured a placement for the Taco Bell fast-food brand, then a priority for PepsiCo. Taco Bell, however, was not widely known outside the United States, and the scene was filmed a second time in a Pizza Hut restaurant, a brand much more widely recognized internationally. To this day, two versions of the film are in circulation. It is easy to imagine the production costs of such a placement.[21]

In contrast, digital technology has made things considerably easier, at an increasingly affordable cost. It can be exploited to mask a too-obvious or un-desired placement, as was the case, under pressure from critics, for the Apple

---

[20] In 2007, Dr Prateek Kanchan edited a book exploring in-film advertising and including the Indian perspective: *In-film Advertising: Brand positioning strategy*, Icfai University Press, Hyderabad, Andhra Pradesh.

[21] Jean-Marc Lehu (2005) Le placement de marques au cinéma, proposition de la localisation du placement à l'écran comme nouveau facteur d'efficacité potentielle, *Décisions Marketing*, 37, January–March, pp 17–31. We may also point out Andy Wachowski and Larry Wachowski's *The Matrix Reloaded* (2003), in which a fighting scene takes place in front of a television screen wall. The used television screens were LG, but those same screens bore the Zenith brand logo when the same scene was shot for the second time for the version of the movie planned for the US domestic market.

logo on a computer used in the UK series *Spooks*, shown on the BBC.[22] For certain placements, it is entirely possible, during post-production, to modify the elements that appear onscreen by simply erasing them, modifying them or replacing them. This technique, borrowed from special effects, opens the way for placements that are partially adapted to the film's geographical target.

It is not uncommon for the international market to be as important as, if not more important than, the domestic market. Therefore US viewers at a showing of *Spider-Man 2* (Sam Raimi, 2004) might have noticed the logo of the soft drink Dr Pepper in the pizzeria where the film's hero works. In the majority of countries other than the United States, however, the same scene bore the logo of the soft drink Mirinda, also distributed by PepsiCo outside its domestic market. The cost of a digital swap of this kind varies from several thousand dollars to more than US$100,000, depending on the nature of the placement and the difficulty of insertion.[23] When the film is shot directly with a digital camera, however, modifications after the fact are simpler and therefore less expensive. In *Charlie's Angels: Full Throttle* (McG, 2003), the majority of viewers will have noticed the logo of the telephone operator T-Mobile (Deutsche Telekom AG) on several occasions. In contrast, those who saw the film during a transatlantic flight or during a visit to the United States will have had the possibility of identifying another operator, Cingular Wireless, which had only paid for its logo to be placed on US territory.

The other advantage of these 'a la carte' placements is that they enable some advertisers to reduce their costs if they are only interested in a given area. Simultaneously, the production studio will have the opportunity to multiply the contracts from one geographical zone or one country to another. In fact, the adaptation that technology offers to placements is a natural consequence, since it already existed for tie-in promotional operations associated with the film. The only possible disadvantage is parallel contractual incompatibility. Such a case might occur if one of the lead actors appears in a scene where the placement is located. It is possible that his/her contract specifies other marketing links with certain advertisers who might justifiably refuse any association, of any kind, with competitor brands. In such a situation the management of major sports stars and their multiple contracts, for example, can quickly become impossible.

---

[22] Eric Pfanner (2005) Product placements cause stir in Europe, *International Herald Tribune*, 2 October.

[23] Charles Goldsmith (2004) Dubbing product plugs, *Wall Street Journal*, 6 December. See also the research by Josef Sivic and Andrew Zisserman (2004) Efficient visual content retrieval and mining videos, *Proceedings of the 5th Pacific-Rim Conference on Multimedia*, Tokyo, Japan, 30 November–3 December, pp 471–78.

Designing targeted placements

In 2002, in the version of Puccini's opera *La Bohême* directed by Baz Luhrmann, they served Piper-Heidsieck: in Act II, when the curtain rose, advertising boards for the champagne brand, and others for the pen brand Mont Blanc,[24] could also be seen. For marketers whose product or service is not aimed at the undistinguished mass of consumers, targeting is a primary function of marketing. There is no interest in wasting money and time communicating with individuals who, marketers are convinced, are not interested in the product or service in question. Product and brand placement make it possible to partially target the audience they desire to reach. The more refined the target, the more the audience's involvement can be hoped for. The more involved the audience becomes, the greater its receptivity.[25] In contrast, those integrating a brand into a children's comedy or a thriller rated 18 are not pursuing the same objective. When companies seek to have their logo present on a golf course, around a boxing ring, on the stage of a burlesque reality television show, in the context of a scientific programme, and so on, the goal is not the same.

Having invested in programmes with extremely broad audiences such as *The Apprentice, Survivor* and *The Contender*, Home Depot, the world leader in DIY, started developing a targeted programme of brand integration in the United States in 2006, in order to make minorities more aware of its products, with vector programmes such as *Girlfriends* (UPN), complemented by *ad hoc* media planning in the adjacent commercial breaks.

Unlike what can already be done in direct marketing, however, this targeting is not yet very accurate in terms of placements. The population segments reached are estimated in advance and surveyed afterwards, and it is not (yet) conceivable to push personalization to the individual. Nevertheless, the placement of products and brands one-to-one is only a matter of time and technology. Some advertising films already benefit from it as a result of grouped broadcast by cable or satellite. United Airlines has already used it in the United States, in partnership with the cable operator Comcast and the IT services of Visible World, to launch Ted, its low-cost subsidiary. Different messages were sent to subscribers to the cable network according to their geographic location, with different offers and conditions. This represents a fundamental complementary advantage for marketing: the possibility of measuring the comparative effectiveness of different messages after the fact.

---

[24] Vanessa O'Connell (2002) It's product placement, per Puccini, *Wall Street Journal*, 18 October.

[25] Steffen Hormuth (1993) *Placement: Eine innovative Kommunikationsstrategie*, Franz Vahlen, Munich. About audience involvement, see also the research by David Morley (1993) Active audience theory: pendulums and pitfalls, *Journal of Communication*, 43(4), pp 13–19.

An original case of targeting, supported in this case by a tie-in operation accompanying the placement, is the videogame *FIFA Street 2* (Electronic Arts). As its name indicates, it is a street football game. More than 320 avatars of professional footballers are at the player's disposal, in a cityscaped world. From Rio to Marseilles via eight other pitches, it is played in a world where the rules of football are somewhat lacking, but that too is part of street football. The soundtrack was also adapted to the preferred target, using DJ Cut Killer and Leeroy (from the group Saïan Supa Crew). Like other brands, Adidas had a significant placement in the videogame. On its release in France in 2006, the brand participated, with Electronic Arts, in organizing a street football competition, with the aim of reaching the fans of the real game, who were likely to be or to become fans of the videogame. The participants were supposed to leave a video clip of themselves with the ball at their feet on the specially created internet site.

Even today, the same sporting event (even shown live) can feature different placements according to the broadcasting zone, as a result of technological digital substitution solutions. Certain channels, such as those broadcasting on digital satellite or on DVD, enable viewers to choose their language, subtitled or otherwise, and, in some cases, the version of the film (theatrical cut, integral, long, coloured, director's cut, widescreen format or 16:9) that they wish to watch. With the help of technology, it is possible to imagine, in the near future, the opportunity of integrating into a film certain placements that will differ according to the viewers at whom they are aimed: these placements would then be 'adapted' to the spectator's identified characteristics (demographic, social, economic, geographic and so on).

This is similar to the targeted offers that internet shopping sites already offer to web users, when users have given them prior authorization to identify and recognize them automatically using cookies. It is probable that some will be quick to protest against this artistic and commercial manipulation of the individual. How long will this possible reluctance on the viewers part last, however, when they have the possibility of watching such and such a broadcasting channel free, in return for accepting this identification? In particular if the goal is not to place products without warning, but to proceed – in the shared interest of the broadcaster and the advertiser – with the intelligent integration of brands, respecting the viewer, the brand and the programme.

It should be remembered that if there has been a progressive development in the feeling of advertiphobia, it is not only because of what is seen to be an excessive volume of advertising, but also because many viewers feel that they are not interested in the advertising to which they are involuntarily exposed. An identification method would easily make it possible to find a match between the commercial range on the one hand, and the needs and desires of consumers on the other. Is this to say that the 30-second spot of yesterday will turn into 90 or 120 minutes of advertising film tomorrow? Absolutely not! It would do so only at the risk of losing its audience, and above all because such an individualized approach can only validly function in a 100 per cent opt-in environment: in other words, with the full and complete agreement of the consumer. Without this prerequisite, there can be no success. Let us bear in mind the 1990s and the promises of interactivity: we were sure that consumers would embrace it without a moment's hesitation, because they would therefore become master of their programmes by interacting fully with them. The result? Consumers were clearly not all that interested in interactivity, or not actively, in any case.

Recreating an emotional link with the consumer

Even if communication is everything, not everything is 'good' communication. Branded entertainment should not 'simply' be perceived as the emergence of a new vector of communication, as 'just another'! Through the show and entertainment dimension of its communication, it should be seen as the opportunity to recreate an emotional link with a consumer, for whom the brand has often lost its legitimacy over recent years. Let us stop blaming all the misfortunes of the brand on the economic downturn and hard discounters, in one of the most hypocritical, artificial complaints! Many brand managers have toyed dangerously with their brand, forgetting its profound identity, flouting its intimate personality and neglecting, consciously or not, its precious capital. It shows! It is high time that we courageously accepted the consequences. It is in fact possible to perceive the brand as a simple designation given to a good or service to identify it, in the same way that numbers might be given to individual group members to tell them apart.

It is also possible to see that a living brand may not be the exclusive property of its legal owners alone, and that it is necessarily, in part, the property of its consumers. In order for it to live, it must share emotions with these same consumers: create wishes and desires, and, more simply, identify needs and expectations. The task is admittedly more difficult, since, as Marie-Claude Sicard has written, with her usual shrewdness:

> Wishes come and go; you must catch them in mid-air. It's a degraded form of desire, but it is nonetheless a good lever for marketing. The expert in brand strategy analyses that desire is a 'phoenix that is continually rising from its ashes'. This is the reason why it is so important for marketing to observe more closely how it works, while leaving all prejudices at the door, if possible.[26]

---

[26] Marie-Claude Sicard (2005) *Les ressorts cachés du désir: Trois issues à la crise des marques*, Village Mondial-Pearson, Paris. See also Chris Hackley and Rungpaka Tiwsakul (2006) Entertainment marketing and experiential consumption, *Journal of Marketing Communications*, 12(1), March, pp 63–75.

Among the 63 per cent of US advertisers already using branded entertainment in 2005, 72 per cent justified it by explaining that it enabled them to create a stronger emotional link with the consumer, and with generations X and Y in particular. These 72 per cent seek a different relationship with advertisers,[27] a more original, closer and more entertaining relationship. They have the ability to master technology and therefore to better control their choices. Between 2001 and 2005, more than 50 million people would not have rushed to the BMW website to see just another advertising film. Their numbers are just an illustration of a successful operation, during which BMW offered an entertaining show and not just a commercial message.

The Bulgari brand is attached to the world of luxury jewellery. For several years now, however, it has also appeared on perfumes, accessories (handbags, ties, sunglasses and so on) and watches.[28] It is, moreover, a futuristic watch bearing the brand name that the character played by Tom Cruise concentrates on throughout the film *Minority Report* (Steven Spielberg, 2002). The brand has also participated in many other films. For example, Kate Hudson also wears a Bulgari watch in *How to Lose a Guy in 10 Days* (Donald Petrie, 2003), Elizabeth Hurley wears a Bulgari necklace in *Serving Sara* (Reginald Hudlin, 2002), Cameron Diaz wears a double Bulgari ring in *Vanilla Sky* (Cameron Crowe, 2001), and jewels by the brand are also present in *The Thomas Crown Affair* (John McTiernan, 1999). In *City of Angels* (Brad Silberling, 1998) the aftershave used by Nicolas Cage onscreen is none other than Eau Parfumée by Bulgari.

Some might say that from jewellery to perfume, indeed to watches and accessories, the different compartments of luxury are regularly breached. Nevertheless, although stepping out of its jeweller pigeonhole, the brand, entirely in control and respectful of its capital, both financial and emotional, has always been able to maintain its identity and protect its own image. Moreover, it remains independent to this day, in contrast to Cartier (within the Richemont group), Gucci (within the PPR group), or Dior (within the LVMH group), to mention but a few. It is when the brand ventures into the hotel business, however, that its controlled extension becomes more original. In 2004, in association with Marriott International,[29] Bulgari opened its first luxury hotel with 52 rooms, in via Montenapoleone, Milan, close to the famous La Scala. The second, located in Bali, on the south of the Jimbaran

---

[27] Hank Kim (2002) The changing world of content & commerce, *Advertising Age*, 7 October.

[28] John Tagliabue (2003) Bulgari builds on brands in many ways, *New York Times*, 5 August.

[29] Gail Edmonson (2001) Bulgari: from *Lord of the Rings* to hotelier, *BusinessWeek*, European edition, 17 September. Jane L Levere (2004) Shop until you drop, but don't sleep in the store, *New York Times*, 15 February.

peninsula, was opened in 2006. On each occasion, the standard of comfort and the service offered were in perfect accord with the positioning and status of the brand. The Bulgari emotion remains intact, while the brand name treats itself to a new and luxurious placement.

'The consumer derives as many immaterial benefits as tangible satisfactions from brands and products', explains Georges Lewi.[30] This emotional link appears wholly indispensable nowadays in order to cross the threshold of commercial squabbling, which is often close and is above all thickly populated by the competition. The creation of this emotional link that the brand needs so badly is not simple, since the brand discourse can no longer be content with the cognitive elements habitually found in its argumentation. The goal is not to disown them, but to understand that they are no longer sufficient. The creation of this link can be orchestrated by the brand itself, and in a sometimes very original manner. When questioned, at the fourth conference on branded entertainment in 2006, Steve Heyer insisted on the importance of integration in the common interest of the programme and the brand. He emphasized the limits of technical innovation, which can ultimately be quickly copied, and the importance of prioritizing the development of an emotional space in favour of the brand's positioning. The CEO of Starwood Hotels & Resorts Worldwide explained: 'We don't sell rooms and hotels, we sell experiences, we deliver memories, we provide opportunities for people to create memories. What would you be willing to pay for a room, and what would you pay for a memory?'[31]

At Christmas 2005, the New York department store Saks put a new illustrated book by Christopher Corr exclusively on sale. The intended audience was 9–12-year-olds. Its name was a play on words: *Cashmere if you can*. It is the story of Wawa Hohhot and his family of Mongolian cashmere goats, who live on the roof of the Saks stores. In collaboration with the publisher HarperCollins, Saks had the idea for this project, which, although it also mentioned the Elizabeth Arden Red Door salon, was not there to sing the brand's praises and was not a blatant example of brand placement. It was not the first time that a brand had invested in the world of children's books.[32] Admittedly, the book did mention

[30] Georges Lewi (2005) *Branding management: La marque, de l'idée à l'action*, Pearson Education, Paris.

[31] Steve Heyer and Scott Donaton (2006) *4th Conference Madison+Vine*, 15 February, Beverly Hills, CA.

[32] These kind of deals could easily (and probably legitimately) frighten some consumers associations. In 1998, Kellogg's Cheerios cereals brand was the main character in Will McGraph and Barbara McGraph's *Cheerios Counting Book*, Cartwheel, Scholastic, New York. The same brand was also a partner the same year in Les Wade's book *The Cheerios Play Book*, Little Simon, Simon & Schuster, New York. And the next year, *The Cheerios Animal Play Book* was published by Les Wade. If similar known cases are rarer in continental Europe or in Asia, the approach is often used in the United

a Mr Saks, but the story did not fall into the trap of a commercial discourse, bouncing from product placements to brand placements. The objective of the group was simply to place its brand in a positive imaginary story. 'If you can get into the lexicon of the public, I think we'll have accomplished something', Terron Schaefer, vice-president in charge of marketing at Saks, the originator of the idea, told the *New York Times*.[33] The book constituted a communications operation to help the brand's emotional capital. Besides, in communicating with 9–12-year-olds, the group can hardly be seriously accused of aiming at its core target audience. The book was offered on other distribution circuits from 2006.

States. Amongst the most relevant cases, we may point out the illustrations in Barbara Barbieri McGrath and Roger Glass (2001) *Skittles Riddles Math*, Charlesbridge, Watertown, MA. Also Jerry Pallotta and Robert C Bolster's books, *Reese's Pieces Peanut Butter: Counting Board Book* (1998), *The Hershey's Milk Chocolate Fractions Book* (1999), *Reese's Pieces Count By Fives* (2000), *Hershey's Fraction Book and Game Pack* (2000), *The Hershey's Kisses Addition Book* (2001), *Twizzlers Percentages Book* (2001), *The Hershey's Kisses Subtraction Book* (2002), *Twizzlers: Shapes and Patterns* (2002), *Hershey's Milk Chocolate Weights and Measures* (2003), *Hershey's Kisses Multiplication and Division* (2003), and *From Addition to Multiplication* (*Hershey's Chocolate Math*) (2004), from Cartwheel. All those books were dedicated to mathematics and learning calculus, with the help of Hershey's sweets. Its competitor and market leader, Mars, was also involved in the game with *The M&M's Brand Chocolate Candies Counting Board Book* (1997), *More M&M's Brand Chocolate Candies Math* (1998), *The M&M's Christmas Gift Book* (2000), *The M&M's Brand Valentine Book* (2000), *The M&M's Halloween Treat Book* (2000), *The M&M's Brand Birthday Book* (2001), *The M&M's Brand Easter Egg Hunt* (2001), *The M&M's Thanksgiving Feast* (2002) and *The M&M'S All-American Parade Book* (2002), all of theme written by Barbara Barbieri McGrath, and published by Charlesbridge, Watertown. There are also do-it-yourself learning books such as *The Home Depot Big Book of Tools* (2001), by Kimberly Weinberger, valorizing the home improvement and construction retailer The Home Depot; and, for the same chain, books dedicated to specific tools like *My Drill, My Hammer, My Saw, My Screwdriver*, all by Kimberly Weinberger and Billy Davis, and all published in 2001 by Cartwheel. Finally, examples can also be found using Necco sweets, Pepperidge Farm biscuits, Kellogg's Froot Loops cereals, Sun-Maid raisins, Oreo cookies and so on.

[33] Lorne Manly (2005) The goat at Saks and other marketing tales, *New York Times*, 14 November.

Conclusion

All directors must ponder and meditate in their own way. For they all have this common problem: keeping each day's work in correct relationship to the story as a whole. Scenes shot out of time and context must fit into their exact spot in the mosaic of the finished film, with their exact shadings in mood, suspense and growing relationships of love and conflict. This is, as one can imagine, the most important and most difficult part of directing, and the main reason why films, perforce, are the director's 'business'.

(Frank Capra, *The Name Above the Title*,
Macmillan, New York, 1971)

Some advertisers are still doubtful as to the power and the real advantages of staging the brand, and therefore of branded entertainment. Directing is a very difficult job. However, like it or not, brand managers have become the daily administrators of the brand's life, shrewd managers who direct the stages of the brand's life cycle one day at a time, permanent visionaries of the architecture of that brand, guarantors of its identity, protectors of its positioning, and orchestra conductors attentive to the sum of the individual publicity actions to which it may lend itself, in order to achieve perfect coordination.

If it may seem to some that there is only a single step between product placement and brand integration, nevertheless the whole philosophy of the process must be revised, so that the brand can be inserted into a world of entertainment as naturally as possible, arousing emotions and desires on its own account. Strategic thinking about the brand is therefore even more crucial since the goal, the role and the attraction of a brand integration will also vary widely, according to the communications medium under consideration and the characteristics of the environment in which the operation is envisaged.[1]

More than a hundred years of 'traditional' above-the-line and below-the-line communication have inevitably left traces of a natural resistance. Even if the elements set out in the previous pages might be thought to provide an objective legitimacy to the argument, however, the economic and social conjunction must also be taken into account. The roles, and even the justifications, of brands are being reappraised by consumers who we know to be more mature, more sophisticated and therefore more demanding. The choice that marketers are presented with seems incredibly simple. Either we leave brands, or in any case the majority of them, to complete their metamorphosis into a simple element for designating one good in relation to another, whereupon hundreds, if not thousands of them will disappear; or we decide to curb the impoverishment, to struggle against the suicidal erosion of brand capital and to give the brand back a genuine legitimacy.

A note of caution: it is of course not a matter of assimilating branded entertainment into a miracle solution able to cure all marketing's ills, or the even more numerous ills of the brand in particular. It is a matter of envisaging it as the relevant saving complement of a powerful marketing strategy serving consumers, and bringing them the *ad hoc* solution to their problems every day;[2] a complement to original discourse, suitable for presenting another face of the brand to them, beyond its habitual models of communication, and beyond their own certainties, which seem a little more fragile every day.

As Marie-Claude Sicard put it so well, brands 'don't need certainties, although they waste much valuable time in continuing to purse them. They

---

[1] Fantasy sports (games where fantasy owners build a team that competes against other fantasy owners based on the statistics generated by individual players or teams of a professional sport) are today available in many disciplines (baseball, hockey, soccer, auto racing, golf, football), offering the possibility for potential advertisers to take advantage of segmentation and positioning. See Abbey Klassen (2006) Fantasy sports generate booming new online ad market, *Advertising Age*, 8 August. For a more general point of view, see also the analysis by Namita Bhatnagar, Lerzan Aksoy and Selin A Malkoc (2004), Embedding brands within media content: the impact of message, media and consumer characteristics on placement efficacy, in L J Schrum (ed), *The Psychology of Entertainment Media: Blurring the lines between entertainment and persuasion*, Lawrence Erlbaum Associates, Mahwah, NJ, pp 99–116.

[2] In his Master's thesis, Craig Welsh insists on the fact that if considered alone, product placement may not generate a greater value for the advertiser; therefore it may represent a high potential complement. Craig Welsh (2004) *Tethering the Viewer: Product placement in television and film*, Master's thesis, Graduate School of Syracuse University, Syracuse, NY.

need openness, methodological regeneration, exploratory hypotheses.'[3] A brand that rushes too hastily into a branded entertainment strategy, however, without its managers having questioned beforehand what it really is, what its objectives are, what could and should be its message and to whom that message should be delivered, will be wasting its money. In this context, we often in a symptomatic manner refer to a brand's DNA. The analogy is a relevant one, and taking it into consideration is fundamental. Branded entertainment should make it possible to *reveal* the brand's DNA, confirming its legitimacy and offering it an emotional dimension. Those who think that it will help them to *replace* it, quickly and easily, are making a grave mistake. A brand's DNA cannot simply be changed with a publicity operation.

Care should be taken not to repeat the errors of the past, through urgency and because the promises of brand integration into many and varied programmes of entertainment seem to be within easy reach. The advantages of branded entertainment can only serve the brand if it forms an integral part of its communications strategy. If it is only envisaged as a supplementary 'tactic', disconnected from any logic of identity, then it risks rapidly becoming the involuntary instrument of the persistent degradation of the brand's capital.

The effects of a branded entertainment action go far beyond the only direct benefit of the integration of the brand into a programme of any kind. It contributes to short-term awareness of the brand, but also to its image and all its constitutive elements in the medium to long term. Yesterday considered a distraction by advertisers in love with cinema, branded entertainment is now a communications medium that is increasingly better defined, more rigorous, and genuinely strategically orchestrated. Paradoxically, at first glance, this professionalization of the process contributes to blurring the lines a little more between what is entertainment, and what flows from brand strategy. This is merely the expression of the success of an accomplished integration. It is difficult then to know whether the advertiser is the brand or in fact the programme that is its medium. Scott Donaton defined it perfectly:

> Madison+Vine is no longer an intersection; it's a destination. The two have become one, in a true integration branded entertainment is emerging as a discipline in its own right.[4]

---

[3] Marie-Claude Sicard (1998) *La métamorphose des marques: Le roc, l'étoile et le nuage*, Éditions d'Organisation, Paris. In 2001, Morris Holbrook wrote a very interesting essay about entertainment and commercialism, brand discourse and possible hegemony feelings. Morris B Holbrook (2001) Times Square, Disneyphobia, HegeMickey, the Ricky principle, and the downside of the entertainment economy, *Marketing Theory*, 1(2), pp 139–63.

[4] Scott Donaton (2006) The dramatic difference at the year, M+V Conference, *Madison+Vine*, 15 February.

You might have the best product in the world, but familiarity breeds contempt, and it will one day see your consumers seduced by another offer. You can renew and renew that offer again to attempt to keep their loyalty. If it is only based on rational marketing, however, no matter how polished, it will not be enough. If, on the other hand, you add to all these necessary efforts sincere and legitimate emotion, then you are opening the door to another relationship with the consumer: an intuitive, personal, privileged relationship, which only a brand is able to ensure. Not a price. Not a product or a service. Not a distribution network. A brand, a name, an identity, a positioning, a status, a recommendation, a trust relationship, an emotion.

The mercantile prophets of the dark forces of tactics over strategy will certainly be quick to criticize the proposition, arguing that when the brand is called Bulgari, Dior, Maserati, Vertu, Chanel or Dom Pérignon, it is 'easy' to play the emotional card, without even having recourse to branded entertainment; but that in contrast, when you are selling nappies, tins of pâté, soft drinks, tyres or packets of washing powder, the natural 'emotional' thread is much harder to find, branded entertainment or not. *Gone with the Wind, Love Story, Kramer vs. Kramer* and even *E.T.* are not cinema's only examples generating strong emotions. The emotional spectrum is a broad one, and this is why it constitutes an extraordinary opportunity for the brand, no matter what its business sector. As long as each one finds the correct wavelength linking it to its consumers, no potential participants are automatically excluded by this approach.

The great classic among the classics of placement is Steven Spielberg's *E.T. the Extraterrestrial* (1982). This case is often mentioned as the first case, or if not, as an exemplary case of product placement for a then little-known confectionery brand: Reese's Pieces, the famous sweets used to attract the creature and already mentioned earlier. Less well known, however, is the fact that it was not a product placement. In reality, the director had initially made contact with the brand leader in the confectionery market, Mars, to ask permission to use M&M's. But Mars declined the offer![5]

How can we explain such a refusal? The risk associated with an unknown director? At that time, Steven Spielberg had already directed several films that were very successful, such as *Raiders of the Lost Ark* (1981), *Close Encounters of the Third Kind* (1977) and *Jaws* (1975). Commercial risk? Mars was already the leader in its segment and there was nothing dangerous about the context of the proposition. Costs too high? Product placement contracts of this type were still rare at the time, and therefore inexpensive. The too-conservative vision of a family company faced with an innovative commercial

---

[5] Phil Dougherty (1985) Diener builds ties to movies, *New York Times,* 29 October; Paul Farhi (1998) AOL gets its message out in mail, *Washington Post,* 17 December; Monica Soto Ouchi (2005) Bit roles, big business, *Seattle Times,* 30 November.

communication opportunity? Possibly. A failure to perceive the real potential of a medium of communication that was still little exploited, and whose usage methodologies were as yet unmastered? Most certainly. Result: the scene was filmed with Reese's Pieces from Mars' competitor Hershey, and once the film was finished, Steven Spielberg proposed a tie-in promotion to Hershey, which it accepted. The brand participated in the film's launch campaign, investing US$1 million;[6] in return, it was allowed to use the film in its own advertising communications. At Mars, if managers acknowledge that this case of placement was successful, they are quick to add that Mars is still the leader today.

What lessons can we draw from this? Branded entertainment offers exceptional advantages for creating a link with consumers, but it will not do everything. Although a brand leader has the luxury of hesitation, missing such an opportunity could cost a smaller brand dearly. Bearing in mind the explosive success of branded entertainment, it is probable that Mars would respond differently today. M&M's have been seen recently in *Hostel* (Eli Roth, 2005) and *The Wedding Planner* (Adam Shankman, 2001). We are no longer in 1982; the fragmented world of communications and the intensity of the competition encourage us to be vigilant for opportunities for differentiating communications. Propositions for product or brand placements can prove an extraordinary springboard. Brands must be quick to analyse these opportunities, so as not to offer them to the competition on a plate.

In the United States, certain rappers, who do not wish to lose part of their potential target audience and above all opportunities for broadcasting on large networks, have been recording different versions of their songs for several years now. Certain versions are classed as 'explicit', indicating that some of the lyrics might be thought violent and vulgar. Other versions are labelled 'clean', since their text has been bowdlerized. If product and brand placement is developing uncontrollably, perhaps it will one day be possible to see a film in its 'explicit' version, or in other words full of all kinds of placements, or in its 'clean' version, that is, stripped of any reference to a product or brand. The strategic opportunities of branded entertainment would then be reduced to nothing. Consumers, and particularly the youngest among them, are today able to identify the faintest marketing approach and the smallest sign of advertising. If it seems to them that there is no technical, artistic or simply practical justification for a placement, it is immediately rejected, or in any case sufficiently well identified that it has none of the impact expected by the advertiser. It is quite simply a case of respecting the target audience and consequently potential consumers.

---

[6] L M Sixel (1999) Chocolate empires: journalist probes the secret world of America's candy kings, *Houston Chronicle*, 14 March, p 22.

By entering into a film, a brand can contribute to its entertainment. By hijacking the film or even a simple scene to turn it into an advertising spot, it breaks the possible emotional link that a natural integration might have offered it. Whether it is a programme, a novel, a song, a videogame or any other vector, every medium must be the opportunity for a fusional relationship, benefiting both the brand and the medium. It seems a simple rule. It is often still neglected, however, by brands in search of common-sense publicity tactics to cure all their ills, in the very short term. Branded entertainment is not a miracle solution. Respectfully and strategically orchestrated, however, miracles cannot be ruled out.

Cut! Print! That's a wrap!

Appendix 1

Original press release from Universal Studios for the promotional campaign accompanying the release of the film *King Kong* (2005), by Peter Jackson

News Release

Tuesday 6 September 2005, 13:00 GMT

Universal Studios Announces Promotional Partnerships For Worldwide Theatrical Release of Universal Pictures' King Kong

LOS ANGELES, September 6/PRNewswire/– Universal Studios has made agreements with a select group of brand partners to promote the worldwide December 14, 2005 theatrical release of director Peter Jackson's highly-anticipated action-adventure film "King Kong", it was announced today by Stephanie Sperber, Executive Vice President, Universal Studios Partnerships.

The marketing alliances, which include such globally recognized brands as Volkswagen, Kellogg's, Toshiba, Chase, the City of New York, Nestle and Burger King, represent the first full-scale implementation of the studio's new partnerships strategy under the year-old Universal Studios Partnerships (USP) division. USP was formed in June 2004 by combining Universal's theatrical and home entertainment promotions and corporate partnership groups into a single unit.

"We've listened carefully to what our partners have told us, and we have responded by creating innovative alliances that we believe will be extremely effective both for our partners and for our entertainment properties," said Sperber. "For instance, one of the things we heard from our partners was that they want a less cluttered field. So we've taken a 'quality over quantity' approach, limiting alliances to only those that provide a clear strategic fit. We also heard a desire for exclusive access to unique content and a more collaborative approach to creative campaigns, and we're thrilled to have been able to deliver both with "King Kong"."

Highlights of the "King Kong" partnerships include:

Beginning in October, Kellogg's will offer "King Kong" packaging on 18 million units of breakfast cereal available in 24,000 retail locations nationwide. The packages will include 18 oz. "Collector's Packs" of Kellogg's Corn Flakes as well as Kong-emblazoned 15 oz. boxes of Apple Jacks and Corn Pops. All of the special packages will contain an offer for a free "King Kong" t-shirt. Kellogg's will be executing additional promotions in international territories.

The Nestle campaign, which also kicks off in October, will include "King Kong" packaging graphics featured on more than 10 million units of the company's top-selling candy bars including Nestle® Crunch®, Butterfinger® and Baby Ruth®. Nestle's King bars will feature an instant-win sweepstakes, while the company's Beast bars will be promoted as "King Kong" Limited Edition Bars during the campaign.

As part of its previously announced global strategic alliance with NBC Universal, Volkswagen continues its "King Kong" campaign in September at the auto industry's premiere event, the upcoming IAA International Motor Show in Frankfurt. During the exhibition, which runs September 15–25, Volkswagen plans an impressive "King Kong" presence, including presentations of the trailer and behind-the-scenes production footage for the expected one million show visitors.

Volkswagen's worldwide "King Kong" promotions will expand in November with television, print, outdoor and online campaigns as well as in-store displays at Volkswagen dealerships, sweepstakes and giveaways. The company also will have a significant presence at "King Kong"'s U.S. and international premieres.

"The worldwide excitement surrounding the release of "King Kong" makes it the ideal property with which to launch our new marketing partnership with Universal Studios," said Joern Hinrichs, Head of Volkswagen Global Marketing. "And we think that this highly anticipated film fits well to the promotion of the Touareg, with its off-road capabilities and ability to move confidently from rugged jungle outposts to city streets."

Volkswagen's "King Kong" promotions started June 27, 2005, when it hosted the exclusive online debut of the film's trailer for 48 hours. Viewers of the NBC networks' "King Kong" "roadblock" were directed to http://www.volkswagen.com if they wanted to see the trailer again. The result was a 100-fold traffic increase to the VW site.

Chase will offer a Limited Edition King Kong Universal Entertainment MasterCard that gives cardmembers the opportunity to earn points towards Universal products including DVDs, movie tickets and gift cards. Chase will support the launch of the limited edition credit card roll-out with branded direct mail packages as well as online and event marketing. Consumers can pre-register for the Kong Card at http://www.kingkongmovie.com.

"With the "King Kong" credit card, Chase is able to demonstrate a unique approach to leveraging what promises to be Universal's biggest movie release of 2005," said Joe Venuti, Senior Vice President for JPMorgan Chase & Co.'s Card Services Division. "The launch of the card extends our promotional presence beyond the theatrical window and into an everyday interaction with our customers. It gives movie enthusiasts a chance to easily earn rewards and experience "King Kong" in a whole new way."

Chase will also have a presence at "King Kong"'s New York premiere and participate in cross-promotional efforts with the City of New York that will populate the city with significant outdoor media and other grass-roots marketing tactics.

Starting in December, approximately 7,500 U.S. Burger King locations will begin serving limited-run "King Kong"-themed menu items. The company will support the products, which are targeted at adult consumers, with television and online campaigns as well as point-of-sale displays. Burger King is also promoting "King Kong" in a number of its international territories.

"Movie fans with king-sized appetites can expect big things at Burger King locations worldwide when we bring the larger-than-life world of "King Kong" off-screen and into our restaurants," said Brian Gies, Vice President, Marketing Impact, Burger King Corporation. "Many of our adult customers are familiar with the legendary original film and are eagerly awaiting celebrated director Peter Jackson's film."

"King Kong" is the first film to enjoy a marketing alliance with the City of New York. The city's role will including hosting the U.S. premiere of the film. Details will be announced at a later date.

Toshiba will provide a significant global media campaign in support for "King Kong", including television, print and online campaigns tied to its new home and personal entertainment products in major territories including the U.S. and Japan.

Several of the corporate partners announced today, including Volkswagen, Kellogg's, Toshiba, Chase, Nestle and New York City, will also be involved in cross-promotional efforts for "King Kong"'s home entertainment release. Universal has been an industry leader in alliances across multiple entertainment distribution platforms. DVD-exclusive partnerships will be announced in the future.

"King Kong" director Peter Jackson and his colleagues have taken an active role in the partnership process, participating in a global summit on the film's New Zealand locations, where key executives from partner corporations experienced an immersive tour of all facets of the production. In an unprecedented move, select partner TV commercials for "King Kong" are being developed in conjunction with the "King Kong" production company, with digital effects produced by Weta Digital, Jackson's award-winning effects company. This was done to ensure seamless presentation of the "Kong" assets tied to brand images. "This lends our partners' spots a level of authenticity that only the filmmakers could bring," said Sperber. "It also allows for unique product integration with a film in which there is no modern-day product placement."

Universal Pictures' "King Kong", a new version of the classic adventure story first brought to the screen in the 1933 RKO motion picture, is directed by triple-Academy Award® winner Peter Jackson ("The Lord of the Rings" trilogy) and stars Oscar® nominee Naomi Watts ("21 Grams", "The Ring"), Jack Black ("School of Rock") and Oscar® winner Adrien Brody ("The Pianist"). It is co-written by Jackson's three-time Oscar®-winning partner Fran Walsh, their "Lord of the Rings" co-writer Philippa Boyens and Jackson. "King Kong" is produced by Jan Blenkin, Carolynne Cunningham, Walsh and Jackson under their WingNut Films banner. The film will be released worldwide on December 14, 2005.

Universal Pictures is a division of Universal Studios (http://www.universal studios.com). Universal Studios is part of NBC Universal, one of the world's leading media and entertainment companies in the development, production, and marketing of entertainment, news, and information to a global audience. Formed in May 2004 through the combining of NBC and Vivendi Universal Entertainment, NBC Universal owns and operates a valuable portfolio of news and entertainment networks, a premier motion picture company, significant television production operations, a leading television stations group, and world-renowned theme parks. NBC Universal is 80%-owned by General Electric, with 20 % controlled by Vivendi Universal.

Web sites:
http://www.kingkongmovie.com
http://www.volkswagen.com
http://www.universalstudios.com
Distributed by PR Newswire on behalf of Universal Studios

PR Newswire Europe Ltd.
209 - 215 Blackfriars Road, London, SE1 8NL
Tel : +4 (0)20 7490 8111
Fax : +44 (0)20 7490 1255
E-mail: info@prnewswire.co.uk

Appendix 2

Recent examples of alcoholic drinks brands benefiting from a placement

Brand	Original film title (and release date)
Absolut	*Maid in Manhattan* (2002), *Bridget Jones's Diary* (2001), *Ocean's Eleven* (2001), *The Mexican* (2001)
Amstel	*Madea's Family Reunion* (2006), *Fahrenheit 9/11* (2004), *Ocean's Twelve* (2004), *The Recruit* (2003)
Asahi	*Austin Powers in Goldmember* (2002)
Bacardi	*Miami Vice* (2006), *Batman Begins* (2005), *Collateral* (2004), *The Forgotten* (2004), *The Recruit* (2003), *Underworld* (2003), *Exit Wounds* (2001)
Bass	*Jackass: The Movie* (2002)
Beck's	*The Departed* (2006), *Mr & Mrs Smith* (2005), *S.W.A.T.* (2003), *Save The Last Dance* (2001)
Beefeater Gin	*The Dukes of Hazzard* (2005), *Hardball* (2001)
Belvedere vodka	*Guess Who* (2005)
Blatz	*Save The Last Dance* (2001)
Bollinger	*Casino Royale* (2006), *Die Another Day* (2002), *The World Is Not Enough* (1999)
Bombay Sapphire	*Invincible* (2006), *Mr & Mrs Smith* (2005), *The Dukes of Hazzard* (2005), *Ocean's Twelve* (2004)
Brahma Beer	*The Rundown* (2003)
Brooklyn Brewery	*Click* (2006)
Budweiser	*Talladega Nights: The Ballad of Ricky Bobby* (2006), *Mission: Impossible III* (2006), *Click* (2006), *Superman Returns* (2006), *The Departed* (2006), *Madea's Family Reunion* (2006), *Failure to Launch* (2006), *The Break-up* (2006),

The Pursuit of Happyness (2006), *Batman Begins* (2005), *Four Brothers* (2005), *Sahara* (2005), *The 40 Year Old Virgin* (2005), *The Dukes of Hazzard* (2005), *Wedding Crashers* (2005), *Dodgeball* (2004), *Hellboy* (2004), *Ocean's Twelve* (2004), *American Wedding* (2003), *Anger Management* (2003), *Charlie's Angels: Full Throttle* (2003), *Cradle 2 the Grave* (2003), *Darkness Falls* (2003), *Head of State* (2003), *How to Lose a Guy in 10 Days* (2003), *Just Married* (2003), *Phone Booth* (2003), *S.W.A.T.* (2003), *Terminator 3: Rise of the Machines* (2003), *8 Mile* (2002), *Mr Deeds* (2002), *Panic Room* (2002), *Analyze That* (2002), *Queen of the Damned* (2002), *Spider-Man* (2002), *Sweet Home Alabama* (2002), *The Sum of All Fears* (2002), *Bridget Jones's Diary* (2001), *Driven* (2001), *Hardball* (2001), *Ocean's Eleven* (2001), *Rush Hour 2* (2001), *The Fast and the Furious* (2001), *Vanilla Sky* (2001), *The Perfect Storm* (2000)

Busch	*The Dukes of Hazzard* (2005)
Canadian Club	*Hardball* (2001)
Carlsberg	*The Hitchhiker's Guide to the Galaxy* (2005), *The Interpreter* (2005), *Blade II* (2002), *Spider-Man* (2002)
Château Margaux	*Something's Gotta Give* (2003), *Intolerable Cruelty* (2003)
Chivas Regal	*The Exorcism of Emily Rose* (2005)
Clos du Val	*The Terminal* (2004), *21 Grams* (2003)
Colt 45	*Kill Bill Vol 1* (2003)
Coors	*Talladega Nights: The Ballad of Ricky Bobby* (2006), *The Departed* (2006), *Collateral* (2004), *Scary Movie 3* (2003)
Corona	*Fantastic 4* (2005), *Hitch* (2005), *Mr & Mrs Smith* (2005), *Man on Fire* (2004), *Charlie's Angels: Full Throttle* (2003), *S.W.A.T.* (2003), *Driven* (2001), *Jurassic Park III* (2001), *The Fast and the Furious* (2001), *The Mexican* (2001), *America's Sweethearts* (2001)
Cristal	*The Rundown* (2003), *Austin Powers in Goldmember* (2002), *Barbershop* (2002), *The Wedding Planner* (2001)
Cuervo	*Wedding Crashers* (2005)
Dewar's	*Four Brothers* (2005)
Dom Pérignon	*How to Lose a Guy in 10 Days* (2003), *Just Married* (2003), *Mr Deeds* (2002), *The Wedding Planner* (2001)
Dos Equis	*Fantastic 4* (2005), *Four Brothers* (2005), *The Dukes of Hazzard* (2005), *I, Robot* (2004), *Hardball* (2001)
Finlandia	*Die Another Day* (2002), *Ocean's Eleven* (2001)
Foster's	*Kangaroo Jack* (2003), *X2: X-Men United* (2003), *Jackass: The Movie* (2002)
Guinness	*Mr & Mrs Smith* (2005), *The 40-Year-Old Virgin* (2005), *S.W.A.T.* (2003), *Minority Report* (2002), *The Mummy Returns* (2001)

Grand Marnier	*Bad Boys 2* (2003), *School of Rock* (2003), *Hardball* (2001)
Grant's	*The Recruit* (2003)
Grey Goose	*Superman Returns* (2006), *Hitch* (2005), *Monster-in-Law* (2005), *Mr & Mr Smith* (2005), *The Interpreter* (2005), *Sweet Home Alabama* (2002), *Ocean's Eleven* (2001)
Heineken	*The Departed* (2006), *V for Vendetta* (2006), *Madea's Family Reunion* (2006), *Eight Below* (2006), *Phat Girlz* (2006), *Just Like Heaven* (2005), *Be Cool* (2005), *Transporter 2* (2005), *Anger Management* (2003), *Daredevil* (2003), *S.W.A.T.* (2003), *The Matrix Reloaded* (2003), *The Recruit* (2003), *Austin Powers in Goldmember* (2002), *Mr Deeds* (2002), *Hardball* (2001), *Swordfish* (2001), *The World is not Enough* (1999)
Heisler	*Training Day* (2001)
Hennessy	*Austin Powers in Goldmember* (2002), *Barbershop* (2002), *Exit Wounds* (2001)
Highlander beer	*Don't Come Knocking* (2006)
Ice House	*Exit Wounds* (2001)
Jameson	*The Hitchhiker's Guide to the Galaxy* (2005)
J&B	*The Break-Up* (2006), *Ocean's Twelve* (2004), *Cradle 2 the Grave* (2003), *XXX* (2002), *Hardball* (2001), *Training Day* (2001)
Jack Daniel's	*Miami Vice* (2006), *Mr & Mrs Smith* (2005), *The Interpreter* (2005), *Man on Fire* (2004), *S.W.A.T.* (2003), *Monster's Ball* (2002), *Pearl Harbor* (2001), *Vanilla Sky* (2001), *Driven* (2001), *Rock Star* (2001), *Almost Famous* (2000), *Coyote Ugly* (2000), *Gone in 60 Seconds* (2000), *Ring of Fire* (2000), *Pitch Black* (2000), *Nice Guys Sleep Alone* (1999), *The Minus Man* (1999)
Jägermeister	*Scary Movie 3* (2003), *The Rundown* (2003)
Jewel of Russia Vodka	*Inside Man* (2006)
Jim Beam	*Talladega Nights: The Ballad of Ricky Bobby* (2006)
Johnnie Walker	*Flightplan* (2005), *Four Brothers* (2005), *Just Like Heaven* (2005), *King Kong* (2005), *Mr & Mrs Smith* (2005), *The Exorcism of Emily Rose* (2005), *Wedding Crashers* (2005), *Black Hawk Down* (2002), *Swordfish* (2001)
Kahlua	*Hardball* (2001)
Kaiser	*The Rundown* (2003)
Ketel One Vodka	*Just Like Heaven* (2005), *Something's Gotta Give* (2003), *Ocean's Eleven* (2001)

Kirin	*Driven* (2001)
Labatt	*Invincible* (2006), *Driven* (2001)
Löwenbräu	*The Dukes of Hazzard* (2005)
Malibu	*Swordfish* (2001)
Martini & Rossi	*Mr & Mrs Smith* (2005)
Michelob	*Invincible* (2006), *Talladega Nights: The Ballad of Ricky Bobby* (2006), *The Break-Up* (2006), *Four Brothers* (2005), *Collateral* (2004), *How to Lose a Guy in 10 Days* (2003), *Sweet Home Alabama* (2002), *Heartbreakers* (2001), *Ocean's Eleven* (2001)
Miller	*Mission: Impossible III* (2006), *Just Like Heaven* (2005), *The Dukes of Hazzard* (2005), *Collateral* (2004), *Bad Boys 2* (2003), *Bringing Down the House* (2003), *Darkness Falls* (2003), *S.W.A.T.* (2003), *X2: X-Men United* (2003), *Jackass: The Movie* (2002), *Driven* (2001), *Exit Wounds* (2001)
Moët & Chandon	*Failure to Launch* (2006), *V for Vendetta* (2006), *Hitch* (2005), *Meet the Fockers* (2005), *Wedding Crashers* (2005), *American Wedding* (2003), *Bringing Down the House* (2003), *Just Married* (2003), *Heartbreakers* (2001)
Molson	*Driven* (2001)
Mount Gay	*Meet the Fockers* (2004)
Mug	*Dickie Roberts: Former Child Star* (2003), *Barbershop* (2002), *Black Hawk Down* (2002)
Mumm	*Pearl Harbor* (2001)
Negra Modelo	*Hitch* (2005), *The Mexican* (2001)
Old Style	*Hardball* (2001)
Pabst	*Invincible* (2006), *Fantastic 4* (2005), *The Dukes of Hazzard* (2005), *8 Mile* (2002)
Pacifico	*Monster-in-Law* (2005), *Hardball* (2001)
Pastis	*Hitch* (2005)
Patron	*Vanilla Sky* (2001)
Pernod	*Johnny English* (2003)
Perrier-Jouet	*The Break-Up* (2006)
Red Bull	*Snakes on a Plane* (2006), *Hostel* (2006), *Boogeyman* (2005), *Hellboy* (2004), *Mean Girls* (2004), *Ocean's Twelve* (2004), *Dickie Roberts: Former Child Star* (2003), *Just Married* (2003), *American Pie 2* (2001), *Legally Blonde* (2001), *Save the Last Dance* (2001), *The Fast and the Furious* (2001)
Rheingold Beer	*Invincible* (2006)
Ricard	*Swordfish* (2001)
Rolling Rock	*Vanilla Sky* (2001)
Royal Crown	*Miami Vice* (2006)
Sauza Tequila	*Sahara* (2005)
Samuel Adams	*Hardball* (2001), *Ocean's Eleven* (2001)

Schlitz	*The Dukes of Hazzard* (2005)
Seagram's	*Bringing Down the House* (2003)
Skyy Vodka	*American Wedding* (2003), *Bad Boys 2* (2003), *How to Lose a Guy in 10 Days* (2003)
Smirnoff	*Casino Royale* (2006), *The Banger Sisters* (2002), *Swordfish* (2001)
Southern Comfort	*Miami Vice* (2006)
Steinlager	*Eight Below* (2006)
Stella Artois	*Diary of a Mad Black Woman* (2005)
Stolichnaya	*Ocean's Eleven* (2001)
Suntory	*Phone Booth* (2003)
Taittinger	*Dickie Roberts: Former Child Star* (2003), *The Wedding Planner* (2001)
Tanqueray	*Big Momma's House* (2006), *The Exorcism of Emily Rose* (2005), *Meet the Fockers* (2004), *How to Lose a Guy in 10 Days* (2003), *The Wedding Planner* (2001)
Tecate	*Driven* (2001)
Tingstao	*The Ring* (2002)
Veuve Cliquot	*Intolerable Cruelty* (2003)
Yuengling	*Invincible* (2006)

(Main sources: author's direct identification, *Variety*, *Hollywood Reporter*, *Time Magazine*, Brandchannel (Interbrand), iTVX)

Index

NB: page numbers in *italic* indicate illustrations